ADVENTURES OF A LAWYER

Best wishes

Allan A.

ALLAN AINSWORTH

ADVENTURES OF A LAWYER

by

ALLAN AINSWORTH

Published by Magic Flute Publishing Ltd. 2022

ISBN 978-1-915166-10-4

Magic Flute Publishing Limited

231 Swanwick Lane

Southampton SO31 7GT

www.magicflutepublishing.com

A catalogue description of this book is available from the British Library

MAGIC FLUTE
PUBLISHING

CONTENTS

Introduction

I would like to thank Isabel Barnbrook for her enthusiastic and constant support over the past four years while I have been writing this book and for the hard work and long hours she has put in to proof reading and spell checking. Her work has been invaluable.

It shouldn't
happen to a
lawyer

recollections by

Allan Ainsworth

Allan Ainsworth is also the author of
It Shouldn't Happen to a Lawyer
published in 2014
ISBN: 978-1-909054-25-7

INTRODUCTION

I was never very good at school with languages; in fact my French teacher suggested I leave her class when I was in the second year of the senior school. I did enjoy my German lessons in my last year at school, but, unfortunately an academic year was not really long enough to say I could speak the language fluently. What I have been able to do is to pick up many words from my actual travels. My Italian is probably my leading language, and I can, once brushed up hold a sensible conversation. My French, my German and a very small amount of Arabic have also been picked up from conversations which have helped when added to those already learnt. My German teacher had, for me, the best system of learning. He would have a projector and, on the wall would show a drawing. First of a boy, then of a girl, then of a dog, then of a mother and father. Each picture you would add the word from the one before. Soon the pictures brought in were the house, the rooms, the car, the school and the fathers occupation. By then selecting one of the words from one of the pictures short sentences could be made. This system also worked in my Italian course that I learnt on the train each morning for the three years I travelled into London. A conversation could then be made from those various situations in the marketplace, or the café, or the shop or other location that had been highlighted. My travels over the years have also been a huge lesson to me that we are all equal, and in most cases share the same dreams and desires. Also, that we from Britain are in fact the foreigners when visiting a foreign country and not to expect everyone to have learnt English or English culture. My travels have taught me that Acceptance, Tolerance, and Understanding are the three secret words that will help towards breaking down barriers. In addition, I was taught long ago that to have the humility of trying to eat the food in the country being visited, drink their drink and try to speak a few words of their language go down very well in showing that I have respect for the people and nation I am visiting. Throughout my travels I have met many wonderful people with various cultures religions and ways of life, many became friends. By maintaining these values, I believe they help to break down barriers and make us all more approachable.

Being born in the early nineteen-fifties and less than a decade after the second world war, life was still very difficult. Our parents still had food rationing and shortages. Unemployment was still high, and everyone was struggling and juggling the best they could with limited resources and money. Most meals were simple, conjured up mostly from knowledge learnt from the first and second world wars. As children we thought the suet puddings, the potato pies, meat pies, shepherd's pies and cheap end cuts of meat were all wonderful. Little did we know that these were all to help save precious money. A lot of food was grown on allotments or in peoples back gardens. There were no such things as fridges. Most homes had some form of larder or cold room which kept perishables preserved a little longer. Bread was baked and home preparation of food was a must. Re-cycling as they call it today, was leaving the empty milk bottles on the doorstep to be replaced by the milkman and reused. Empty Lucozade bottles, bought mostly when we were sick, were taken back to the shop for the few pennies return. Brown bags and shopping bags were used again and again. Any newspapers or wastepaper were used to light the fires as was any old wood chopped for kindling. We had very few material pleasures but measured happiness from the food on the table and clothes on our backs. Anything else was a bonus. Toys and little pleasures such as sweets were saved mostly for Christmas and birthdays. To entertain ourselves we spent most of our time outdoors with neighbouring children. We would make up games and pass the time climbing trees. making dens and generally using our imaginations. Old prams were turned into carts. Old broom handles would become pretend swords, spears, guns etc., lumps of wood became cars, lorries, aeroplanes or boats. Pieces of rope when found would be turned into swings in the nearby fields and forest. We now pride ourselves that out of that life came a sense of adventure. We learnt to improvise, adapt and adopt all of which took us into teenage and adult hood and stood us in good stead for what we are today.

My own childhood started out on a newly built council estate built mainly for the over spill from London after the war. Many of the men on the estate had relocated with the railways including my grandfather and my uncle. My family and that of my friends were very lucky as mostly all the men were employed although going without was the norm and sharing accepted. Our own home rested on the edge of the estate and was bordered firstly by the Grand Union Canal, then the allotments followed by open countryside. Beyond the canal we were only five fields away from a huge wood that formed part of the Duke of Bedford's Estate. The canal, the fields and the woods were all part of our giant playground. All the kids on the estate became one huge "gang" where we all looked out for each other the older ones helping the younger and we all learned to play and grow together. These early days were, I suppose my first taste of basic bush craft and self survival that would improve and follow me through the remainder of my life although at the time it was just simply called having fun. Boys carried sheath knives, matches and string. It was the norm. Our "gang" consisted of some twenty plus children. We would meet every day to go to school together. On term holidays or weekends, we would meet up to play. We taught ourselves basic rules of companionship, of a natural pecking order . Each child learnt its place either by age, ability or by imagination. Our mini society which we created would control our actions and our manners and our lives. These rules would stay with us long after leaving school and joining the outside world. It kept many of us together in a hidden bond that is still strong today.

Some of us joined clubs. I was in the Cubs and then the Boy Scouts. This guided us with the skills of cleanliness, washing and ironing. We learnt to tie knots, light fires and cook over those fires. We learnt to read maps, work a compass and read signs in the countryside. As scouts we would venture off to scout camps that are now referred to as wild camps. Here we would put in practice all the skills learnt. We would make all sorts of contraptions in the woods such as aerial runways, hides etc.

In my early childhood my father had left the RAF and had found local employment as a simple clerk in an office. My mother, to supplement the family income, took work in one of the local factories. It was as late as 1938 when the Holidays With Pay Act came in, and workers were entitled to one weeks pay. It would be after the War that the two weeks paid leave would become standard. Many firms insisted on dictating when these holidays would take place. They would shut the factory gates for that fortnight, and everyone had to take their leave then. The employers must have considered it cheaper to shut down entirely than try to run a skeleton staff. Luckily my father worked for Vauxhall Motors, and my mother worked for AC Delco, a subsidiary of Vauxhall motors. As such both companies would shut for the fortnight in July. This time also coincided with the school summer break.

As such our generation were probably the first to enjoy proper long holidays each year. The package holidays had been introduced to seaside resorts, and as working-class folks we all looked forward to our holidays each year. The only downside was of course the English weather which is so unreliable. Unfortunately, whether it was rain or shine, this was the time we had to pack our suitcases and head off.

CHAPTER 1

MY FIRST MEMORIES

I must have been no older than three or four and my father had just left the RAF and was now working in 'Civvy Street' as it was called then as an office clerk. My mother was also working at one of the local factories. Somehow, they managed to acquire discounted railway tickets which entitled them to travel abroad. As such my parents decided that we should take a trip to the South of France, where the weather would be guaranteed hot, as opposed to the unpredictable weather here in this country. The journey to the South of France would be long and arduous. The trains from home to London alone would take over two hours being by steam train. Transfer would then have to be made across London to catch the ferry boat at Dover. Once at Dover we would transfer to the ferry to take us across to Calais where further trains were waiting to take us south. I remember that this journey required an overnight sleep on board the train. In those days, the costs of a night cabin was prohibitive and so most passengers tried to sleep where they sat, but for a three or four year-old this was going to prove difficult. My mother tried first of all to hold me on her lap and cuddle me to sleep but this clearly was going to prevent her from having any rest. My father then came up with the idea that if they made it comfortable enough with coats etc., I could sleep in the overhead road luggage rack. And so, after laying out coats and an improvised pillow I was lifted up in the air and placed on the rack. As you can imagine being so young and being dark I was terrified and started to cry. My parents were worried I was going to roll out of the rack and fall some seven feet to the carriage floor. As such my father undid his belt and wrapped it round me and underneath the rack to give me some form of security. This was to have the opposite effect and made me cry and scream even more. So much so that this idea was abandoned, and I did indeed end up sleeping on my mother's lap. However, this early memory was to stay with me for the rest of my life and even today I cannot bear being "locked in" beneath the bed clothes and have to have my arms outside to avoid the claustrophobia.

When we finally reached our destination in the South of France, I can recall vaguely that the accommodation was a form of holiday camp. We were allocated chalets where we could sleep and be during the day. Meals however were taken at a central dining area that resembled an open air amphitheatre. The building was dome shaped and stood on the top of several stone steps. Inside was an array of tables and chairs where diners could indeed enjoy their breakfasts and evening meals. I don't remember lunches being served. I can recall the long thin cigar-shaped bread sticks that would take another fifty years before I could eat one again.

The beach from the camp must have been very close as we would walk to it each day. The whole site was very hot and very sandy. The beach led into warm Mediterranean waters where I could play on the water's edge happily. Of course, the sun was very hot so we were all covered in the sun cream to protect us. There was one particular day I recall when two young teenage girls came to the beach lay out their towels and proceeded to sun bathe to be able to boast of a suitable tan when they returned home. Sadly, the girls must have fallen asleep. I recall a crowd of folks standing round the girls and eventually medical staff arriving and carrying one off in a stretcher with first degree burns from the sun's rays. They were both taken to the local hospital for treatment but was a warning to us all of the power of the sun, and the dangers of falling asleep under its rays. What was ridiculous, as I came to work out years later, was the next day they were both back on the beach and back to sun bathing again. Just crazy.

This holiday was important to introduce me to all those continental smells of the cooking, the food and the wine and the smell of the plants and trees that only come from continental Europe. I would try continental cuisine and drink, and this would stand me in good stead for my future visits. I also did not understand what "foreigners" were they were just simply lovely people, whose speech I couldn't really understand. However, everyone I remember was very friendly, very nice despite their ages or their nationalities. We all stood in the same shoes of post war simplicity, and were enjoying being able to take a holiday and the place we were in.

CHAPTER 2

EARLY TRAVELS

I recall after the trip to South of France my parents had some friends in Holland and decided to go on holiday there. I cannot remember how we got from home to the ferry- port but I am aware that the trip was from Harwich to the Hook of Holland. It was probably through this trip that neither my mother or I have proved to be very good sailors since. The crossing was extremely rough. I recall that most folks spent their trip either hanging over the sides or inside the toilets including ourselves. It was absolutely awful. Holland itself is a very vague memory although I do remember being taken into a clog makers shop. My small feet were measured and some little wooden clogs fitted to me that I still have to this day. Since this time whilst I am now a reasonably proficient dinghy sailor my enthusiasm for larger boats is not very great with the shortest distance in them proving a priority. I have learned though, through my subsequent travels that if my ears and my eyes agreed with each other then I would not so easily be sea sick. When my ears are saying the boat is level, but my eyes are saying that actually it is rocking from side to side then the outcome is completely different. My safest place therefore is either right at the front of the boat looking forward out of the glass windows or if the weather is good sitting outside.

During my early childhood years my father rode a motorbike which had a tandem two-seater sidecar attached. The sidecar enabled me as a toddler to be tucked up nice and warm inside. If the weather was really bad my mother would abandon her place as pillion behind my father and retreated to the sidecar as well. Not having a great deal of money the motorbike and sidecar was used to try and get us away whenever possible. As a Lancashire lad my father would try to visit his family maybe once or twice a year. Given the awful weather that Lancashire can suffer all visits were arranged between late March round to late October. Each trip would involve a very long and difficult trip spanning anything up to eight hours on the old roads. The motorway system were not around then, and would be many years before the benefits could be felt. The route back then took us up the old A5 travelling through the potteries, the Black Country in Staffordshire, up through Cheshire and on to the industrial county of Lancashire including the mills in the north of the county. In addition to the amount of time it took, cost also played a great part. This meant we couldn't go as often as my father would have liked to enable him to see his family. I recall one such trip as being very miserable. It was raining when we left in the late afternoon. By the time we arrived, in the late hours of the night, the temperature was freezing, and the rain was torrential. I was happily tucked up inside the side car wrapped in blankets and the comfort of pillows. Mother had decided to travel as pinion on the back of the bike to keep my father company and try to help circulate some of his aching freezing joints and muscles in the long journey. At the end of the trip I know my father had to be physically lifted off the bike as he could hardly move his hands or legs. Needless to say, those trips were few and far between until with a little savings the parents were able to afford a Bond Mini Car. This was a three -wheel vehicle with the two wheels at the back and the single wheel at the front. In those days, it could be driven on a motor bike license which was all my father had. This gave us the luxury of all being able to travel inside the motor. The rear seat was more like a hammock behind the front seats and was extremely uncomfortable. The trips to Lancashire were not much shorter although a little more comfortable. With such inspiration and confidence the parents decided use Lancashire as a half way point and a few days break. We then headed off to Edinburgh in this poor little thing. Bearing in mind the car was propelled by an engine not much larger than the average motorbike, as such, it did its best to chug for the many hours it took to reach friends just outside Edinburgh. Luckily, we did have the little vehicle because it rained and rained throughout the fortnight we were there. I again recall at a very early, and impressionable age, hearing two ladies talking in the town itself and one remarked to the other what a lovely day it was. It was cold miserable and raining. I thought, even at that young age, if this was a lovely day I would hate to be here when it is a horrible day. My mother was never to return to Scotland, believing that this weather was normal and didn't want to be cold or wet voluntarily again. On the return trip sadly, the little car struggled as best it could but finally gave up the ghost just south of the Scottish/English border. After some temporary fixings the vehicle did get us home, but its days were numbered as a reliable mode of transport.

By the time the Bond Mini Car had given up the ghost my father had passed his car driving test. He had taken a job working as a clerk with Vauxhall Motors in its offices in Dunstable. This entitled him to a discount on a Vauxhall car. The first four-wheel vehicle to be parked out the front of our house turned out to be a Vauxhall Velox a monster of a machine, or at least it was to a seven-year-old. Where I sat, in the front, between father and mother on the plush seats I could not see over the dash. There was a huge bump in the middle of the dashboard containing the instruments, so I ended up sitting in the back with a far greater comfort and visibility. Seatbelts and child safety didn't seem to be priority in those days. With such a beast of a vehicle and with so much carrying capacity the parents could look further afield for our annual holidays. Also, with a little more money being earned rather than travelling north they decided to try South West and in particular Devon and the Torbay holiday area.

CHAPTER 3
OUR DEVON YEARS

For four memorable summers we would drive to Devon. Again, there were no motorways so we had to endure the cross country routes. We would meander through the countryside of Oxfordshire, Berkshire, Wiltshire, Somerset and Devon through some really picturesque towns. These journeys could take us up to seven hours each way to reach our destination. The route could take up to eight or nine hours and certainly was a full days driving. Once in Devon the parents would hire a mobile home on a static caravan park at Goodrington near Paignton. This wonderful site gave us great access to the lovely red sandy beach of Goodrington. We could also drive round to Paignton. It was the unwritten law then for a kiss me quick hat and evening entertainment of ice creams candy floss and amusements. We would go round to Torquay and watch the fishermen coming back with their sea fishing catches of mackerel and even sharks that were tied up on display. In those days Torquay was quite a centre for taking fishermen out shark fishing. Their catches would be hung up on hooks on the harbour wall on display. Some of these wonderful creatures could be up to eight or nine feet long and certainly must have given the fishermen a fight being landed. However, it soon transpired that our favourite destination would be Brixham. This beautiful little working harbour with its colourful houses strewn majestically either side of the harbour up the hills, its fishing fleet bobbing in the harbour was just a magnet for us all. In those days the old harbour was the only location that the fishing boats could land their catch. Because the harbour was dictated by tides the fishing boats would have to pick their times carefully to leave and to return. Along the side of the harbour wall was the fish market where the fish were landed, selected and boxed ready for transport on to London and other locations. Further along the coast road about half a mile from the town centre was a perfect parking spot. This car park led down to the rocky shoreline. Built into the rocks, which is still there today, is a tidal swimming pool. The pool itself would fill up with each rising tide and wash out all the old water with each lowering tide which meant it was always clean and fresh. Along the side of the pool itself was a pathway with a little café and some changing rooms that looked like beach huts. We had found ourselves sitting in an ideal little spot between two sets of the changing rooms that gave us protection from the wind on three sides. We at first hired deck chairs later to be replaced by our own to minimise costs. Arriving mid morning we could then spend all day lazily looking out to sea. I would quickly make friends with some of the other children and would spend hours exploring in the rock pools and splashing about in the swimming pool itself watching the big boys being able to jump and dive off the diving boards in the deep end. Lunch was sheer luxury. I was sent to the little café for three fresh warm pasties. With flasks of tea made earlier before our departure we had the most splendid lunches. On occasions, before we disappeared back to the mobile home in Goodrington we would walk down to the harbour and watch the fishing boats, both deep sea and day fishing boats return with their catches. Sometimes the day fishermen would come back with so many mackerel they did not know what to do with them so they would offer them to the folks lining the walls watching them. One day we were given three mackerel wrapped in newspaper. Now I should point out that my mother was and remained rather squeamish for all things that require cutting up and bits removed. My father washed his hands of the job not really eating fish. So, it was left to me as an eight-year-old following directions from a rather nervous mother shouting out instructions from the other side of the caravan. I had to top and tail the fish and then remove the innards to then allow the fish to be wrapped and cooked. It was at that point my mother was able to come forward and complete the preparation and cooking. I should add that like my father I didn't eat a great deal of fish then and have not really gained the taste or need for it ever since. Now about this time Brixham was building a brand-new sea wall that stretched half a mile out to sea. This wall protected the harbour area from the tides and foul weather coming in from the Channel. Later the wall became instrumental for a whole new industry of leisure boats, both sailing and cruising using Brixham as a large and expensive looking marina and mooring. Each year Brixham held a regatta in which all sorts of marine activities took place. One of these was the swim around the harbour wall or breakwater. The older youths and adults would start off at the little pebble beach beyond the wall swim out and then round the head and back the other side reaching the harbour side and completing a mile swim. For the less senior local swimmers they would start at the very end of the wall and swim back in on the far side completing half a mile. The humiliation and shame I felt that particular year, watching children my own age plunge into the water at the far end and swim the half mile back when all I could do was splash about in the shallow end of the tidal swimming pool. As a result, the very next day I was determined that I would make myself swim. Into the pool as soon as we arrived for our daily visit and splashing about making a terrible mess, I finally managed to propel myself forward by a grand two strokes. Continuing my efforts those two strokes became four, then six ten and by the time the end of the holiday arrived I had swum the entire width. With my newfound talent I would go on to pursue further achievements at home in our newly opened outdoor pool. I would learn not only to swim the width but then the length, learning to dive and be very proud of myself. Our times in Devon over those three years were wonderful as I remember. When my father was having a sleep sometimes in the afternoons I would sneak off. I would go down the camp site, through the underpass and up the other side of the road. Opposite was a row of tourist shops including what was an old-fashioned ice cream parlour. Inside I would spend some of my pocket money on a 'knicker-bocker-glory.' I would sit myself up on one of the highchairs looking out the window with this huge, long glass filled with ice cream, fruit and fruit juice slowly working my way to the bottom. To help the task there was also this special extra long spoon given with the glass which could scoop out the last of the ice cream and juice at the bottom and also the customary strawberry. I felt deliciously guilty having sneaked off like a schoolboy skipping school. After my first solo visit I was followed by my mother who was fascinated as to where I was disappearing to. Rather than a telling off she actually joined me, and it became our little secret adventure together while father slept.

As a family we also travelled over to Kingswear, the small town on the opposite side of the River Dart from Dartmouth. We would park the car on top of the hill looking down onto the river. We would then walk down the rather steep slope to the little ferry over to Dartmouth for a fish and chip lunch. The ferry was more like a pontoon that held six cars plus pedestrian passengers. The whole contraption was propelled by an old tugboat tied at the front to the side framework of the pontoon. By turning the boat into the direction of travel the boat would nudge the pontoon forward to reach the opposite bank. It was so eccentric but really fun to travel. It is still running to this day for those prepared to queue during the height of summer for six cars at a time to be transported over. In Dartmouth was a famous Cornish pasty shop that sold the most wonderful pasties with all various fillings. Buying these we could go and sit on the benches overlooking the river and watch the various boats travelling up and down the river. On the riverside walk was this most amazing building that was in fact a Victorian railway station. It was Brunel who was given the task of building the railway that ran from Paignton to Kingswear. He was so arrogant in thinking that the planners and elders would grant him permission to build a railway bridge to cross the river that he went ahead and actually built the station ready for the trains to arrive. Unfortunately, with the large Naval academy further up the river and with the status that Dartmouth held, his plans were thwarted and the trains to this day only run as far as Kingswear and then to travel onwards the small ferry had to be used.

I never seemed to remember rainy days as all children seem to recall only the sunny summer days. We would take the walks up from the Shoalstone beach swimming pool past the Berry Head hotel up the hill alongside to the old fort. This area was all developed during the Napoleonic wars. First of all, the Berry Head hotel was built as a military hospital to house the wounded from any possible defence against the invasion by the French that of course never happened. The fort at the top of the hill again built to repel any ships that carried the invading armies of the French. The Berry Head hotel then passed to a vicar who during his occupation wrote the famous hymn 'Abide With Me'. It has a fantastic location with views out across the entire Torbay and with all the palm trees and fauna is called the Devon Riviera. The Berry Head Hotel itself has always fascinated me being full of elderly rather middle class to rich folks with their expensive cars. I always wondered what it must look like on the inside and always said to myself that one day I would go inside. Little did I know that the hotel would become a regular visit in my later years.

On the way home after our third year of yet another wonderful holiday we were travelling our usual route home, across Somerset, Wiltshire and on, when we passed through this sleepy village with a steep hill. Approaching the top of the hill suddenly coming towards us on our side of the road was this huge monster of a car. It was a fast-moving Bentley which was never going to swing in and miss us. This monster hit us right in the middle of the front of the vehicle and by the time it had stopped had destroyed the front of our old Vauxhall beyond recognition. Had we been travelling in a smaller car we would have certainly been seriously injured or worse. Although we were all badly shaken and very upset, we were still in one piece. It turned out that the driver of the Bentley was the local squire. He was rushing because he was late for an appointment with his solicitors. Apparently, he was trying to complete the sale of one of his properties. As such he took unnecessary chances by over taking, on a blind hill and nearly killing us all. The car itself was a right off. I don't remember how we got home all that we were all shaken bruised and feeling very sorry for ourselves. I think this was the final decision for the parents that they would not return to Devon for another years vacation what with the narrow roads, the length of time travelling and the memory of that near fatal accident.

CHAPTER 4
OUR FIRST TRIP ABROAD

By now it was the early 1960's and package holidays had arrived. Those that could afford it were flying off to Northern Spain and indeed to Italy. The tourist trade had now reached as far down the Italian coast as Rimini a third of the way down the Adriatic side.

As I had joined the local cub group and was close to be promoted up to the boy scouts, I had a small tent that I would put up in the garden and pretend I was camping in all the remote places you would see on the films and magazines. In addition to flying, folks also started to travel abroad by car although they were very few and far between. My father had purchased a new Vauxhall. This time a more modern Velox that was very much the shape of the American cars. It had a lot more room inside and in the boot for the luggage. As such my father decided that he wanted to travel abroad. The weather would be guaranteed and the choice of destination greater. With a map and a pin, he literally found a place on the Adriatic coast called Cattolica. This was the next town down from Rimini where air package tours had just reached. Unfortunately, the luxury of the motorway system we have available today did not exist back then. It would be a long hard slog across country passing through the town and cities linking us to the route we wanted to take. Father devised a card system held to the sun visor with elastic bands. These cards had the names and roads of the twenty-two towns leading from Boulogne across to Switzerland.

Now at that time there were camp sites abroad, in fact the rest of Europe was far ahead of us in camping facilities and equipment. However, a family had hit the headlines by being killed on one of the French campsites. Deemed therefore as being highly dangerous places my father decided that we would find alternative means of camping away from the formal sites. Having worked our way down to Dover, across on the ferry and into France it became obvious that our journey was going to take a little longer than expected, bearing in mind we only had two weeks to achieve our goal to get to Italy enjoy a break and then get back in time for work again. We reached about two thirds of our way through France, it was late afternoon and we really needed to find somewhere to settle down for the night. We found a narrow track that led up to a woods about half a mile from the road. Here my little garden tent was pitched. We didn't have a sewn in ground sheet. An old second-hand ground sheet was laid out and our three sleeping bags laid on top of that. The car spare wheel became our table and all in all it was very adventurous and exciting. Finally we climbed into our sleeping bags and fell to sleep. During what would appear to be the middle of the night all hell let loose. There was firing, both rifle shells, artillery shells and all sorts of commotions. With the story of the French camp site still in our minds we needless to say lay very still and rather frightened. In the morning, after a night from hell we quietly packed up and hit the road. A few miles down the road we started to pass convoys of military vehicles, tracked vehicles, tanks and all the military personnel. It turned out that there was a full-scale military operation that had taken place on fields away from our cosy camp site the whole of the night before. In the future we would swallow our pride and head for the tranquillity of an organised camp site.

The next day saw us arrive in Switzerland and our next bit of excitement being the Simplon pass. The drive across the Jura Mountains from France into Switzerland was very pretty and pleasant. Although they call them mountains, they are really just a set of very large hills similar to what would be found in say the Lake District in this country with no sudden climbs drops or sheer falls. Once across we saw the true majesty of the Alps stretched in front. This range was so magnificent that I was corrected that they were not mountains in the distance but cloud formations. As we drew nearer so the clouds became very high and menacing mountain tops and my parents realised I was right. We skirted the Lake Geneva or Lac Lomond as the locals called it, to Montreux where we turned left and into the ninety mile pass that led down and up and over the mountain to Italy. As we travelled down the pass, so the sides got closer and closer to us. At the end we were surrounded by sheer high walls of mountains. The last town here was called Brig before the climb up and over the famous Simplon Pass. Now the Simplon is part of a very high mountain range with a very narrow thirteen mile road that lifts you up to its peak before an equally steep drop down and into Italy the other side. I should explain at this point that my father suffered from vertigo so badly that he could not climb a ladder without feeling dizzy. The very thought of crossing over a high mountain pass for the first time was just inconceivable in the wildest nightmare. It was simply not going to happen. He had done his research and it had showed that in Brig there was a connection by electric train whereby cars, vans caravans motor homes etc could be loaded onto the back of open trucks and then taken twenty two miles directly through the mountain to avoid the need to travel over. The train journey from Brig to Italy would take approximately thirty-five minutes as opposed to the two and a half hours over the top thus saving precious time as well. However, having arrived on the national route from Lake Geneva and along the side of the town there was little to no sign of the train terminal. What we did spot was this huge bill board, in French, advertising something or other but with a train and carriages with all the smiling faces at the windows. This we interpreted was the sign for the train, perhaps. What we didn't notice was that it was actually round a hair pin bend that started up hill away from the town. In the false comfort that we were heading for the station, further up the hill, we carried on. Before my father could realise it, he was already committed to climbing up the Simplon Mountain. I don't suppose I helped much by pointing out how small the cars and lorries were right down below us on one of the curves climbing the mountain. By this time my father had broken out into a cold sweat, my mother was wiping his brow and his hands while he clung to the steering wheel daring only to look forward. Now, most of us have watched the film the Italian Job with Michael Caine and the bus at the end snaking round the various hair pin bends winding its way up the road with very little to no barriers along its side. Well, this is exactly what the Simplon was in those days, the only added excitement was that instead of pretty little valleys round each corner we had sheer drops of thousands of feet and vehicles including the infamous Swiss mountain buses racing past us heading in the other direction. The journey from the top of the mountain, still covered in snow, and down the other side was no less dramatic as this time gears, brakes and nerves were at their fullest use and stress for the next hour as we snaked our way back down to sea level. Finally, after what seemed to be an eternity we arrived in Italy, crossed through the border check and made a very close note of the station on the other side for the return visit. I would not be going over the Simplon again for another forty years which is another story in itself.

Having arrived in Italy we were only about eight miles from Lake Maggiore. Nobody can explain just how beautiful this lake is with its trees, flowers and gardens. In the lake itself there are the three famous islands, the island of fishermen, the island of flowers and the island that houses the royal residence for the king during his summer residency. Beyond, nestled into the hills and leading up into the mountains were the pretty little villages with their churches and spires from centuries past. It was getting late evening on our second day of travel and so we had to find some form of camp site or stop over. In Stresa a most beautiful white stoned town with its very expensive five star grand hotels we found a little camp site. It was late and the owner in simple Italian my father could understand offered us a tent that had already been erected to save having to put up our little one. Also it had just started raining so this was going to be an added bonus. The tent itself looked like something from an Army camp that had seen better days. It was thick dark green and very old canvas that smelt rather badly of damp and mildew on the inside. It had cot beds erected but I volunteered to sleep in a frame bed we had bought with us. We ventured into the main street had something to eat in a little café and then after some drinks and a wind down back to the tent for a well-deserved rest from the days, and previous nights, activities. We all fell very quickly into a deep and sound sleep. Now, one of the customs that one finds in Italy especially on a Sunday is that the Italians like to proclaim their religious faith. Being very strong Catholics one can imagine an abundance of churches and holy places for worship and prayer. One such establishment, a very old and ornate church just happened to be the other side of the wall of the very camp site that we were camped in. Now of course every Italian church prides itself in its own array of church bells. The one day of the week when the pride becomes visibly pronounced is on Sunday mornings, and early Sunday mornings. These bells kicked off at before 6.00 am what seemed only yards away and were so loud they seemed to shake the very tent itself. We certainly did not need any other form of alarm clock as these had our full attention from the second, they commenced duty. We crawled out of bed, dressed and had even started our breakfast by the time the first peel had completed its dawn chorus to the populace. It started again shortly before we hit the road for our third and final day of travelling.

Once you travel beyond Milan, the pretty countryside that spills down from the mountains disappears. What is left is very flat, dry and indeed very hot open fields. The fields also have a tendency to be rather shall we say smelly. This is due to poor drains, sewerage and silage etc. on the fields. So the next few hours were rather taken up with trying to keep windows closed and the smell of the countryside more on the outside than the inside. Bearing in mind this journey was taking place in the middle of July the heat we were now experiencing was incredible so with no air conditioning in the car and the windows closed the journey was becoming a little uncomfortable. Finally, we reached our destination in the pretty little unspoilt town of Cattolica on the shores of the Adriatic. We arrived in a now very dusty car, the suitcases tied to the roof and we must have looked like left over refugees coming from the deserts of North Africa. Not knowing where we were or what facilities or hotels were available my father stopped the local policeman and asked him in his broken Italian where we could find accommodation. To our pleasant surprise the policeman got hold of his bike and gestured that we should follow him to his cousin's hotel. So we went down the narrow streets and into the main square only fifty yards from the sandy beach and we found ourselves parked outside a small 2-star hotel. The policeman disappeared inside and eventually reappeared with the owner, a small dumpy looking Italian gentleman complete with the dress moustache and wiping his hands on his apron. He gestured for us to leave the car follow him into the hotel. Inside we were warmly welcomed. We were shown up to a very simple yet very clean hotel room. He asked us if we had eaten which we of course we had not. As it was late lunchtime and we were invited into the dining room. The rest of the guests were just finishing up their lunches, but he was happy to prepare something for us to eat. Back in England my parents had befriended several Italian families that had arrived in our hometown sponsored by the local brick making company to work in the local brick kilns and factory. This was how my father first learnt his fumbling Italian and how we became familiar with Italian food. In return my parents would help teach the Italian families English in the simplest form. My father and the Italian husband and sons would spend many happy hours swapping translations of colours, hours of the day, numbers and other important snippets of tourist level conversation. So when the hotel manager asked us if we liked spaghetti this was a huge yes. A short while later he reappeared carrying this rather large silver platter heaped with spaghetti. Now for three days we had lived off basic breakfasts, rolls and tube squeezed spreads and in the evenings whatever we could force into our mouths to sustain our hungry needs. Freshly prepared spaghetti therefore arrived with such gratitude that none was left by the time we rolled our spoons and forks onto our plates. So pleased was the hotel manager that he asked if we wanted some more. Confirming that this would be no problem at all, another huge platter arrived. Now being our first time in Italy we didn't want to offend. We somehow managed to devour our second helping thinking that we could then retire to our room for an after lunch nap and to unpack. What we didn't realise what we had just eaten was the first course. The main course then arrived. Large lumps of meat accompanied by steamed vegetables. To say we were all stuffed would be an under-statement. We did have to apologise profusely and decline the large basket of fresh fruit that came next. What started off by being a lunch turned out to be a banquet. Needless to say, we didn't need to eat again for the remainder of the day.

The hotel itself would prove to be really friendly and would be our holiday home for the next three years. We would continue to travel over the three days through France Switzerland and finally into Italy. We had perfected the trip down by purchasing a better tent. We made regular stops at Grey, in south east France before the next leg through Switzerland to Italy. However, we were eventually able to extend the drive to Switzerland itself. Here just tucked over the border we reached Vallorbe a small Swiss border town. The second stop over would be on Lake Maggiore and the final leg to Cattolica. However for just two weeks it was a very long drive and rather exhausting. This meant by the time we reached home we were well in need of another holiday. However Cattolica itself was such a lovely unspoilt seaside resort in those days with just the Italians and few Germans visiting. Our hotel was literally five hundred yards from the very sandy and well kept beach. Being on the Adriatic there were no huge rolling waves just gentle sea lapping onto the beach. This was helped by a row of broken breakwater rocks a hundred yards from the shore. Every morning after breakfast we would wonder over to the beach. Here we would hire one of the beach seats with cushion and umbrella. I would spend most of my time either in the water or close to the water's edge. As the sea was so gentle and calm it made it all feel more like the side of a lake which made bathing very safe. Each morning vendors would walk the beach with buckets of iced water holding bottles of coca cola and soft drinks which we would gladly buy. One of these ladies accidentally stepped on my father's foot. Now one trait we seem to have in our family is that none of us like our feet touched or played with. To stand on our feet was a death wish. My father went crazy leaping about shouting in pain and whether it was accidental or on purpose, but he kicked a foot load of sand into the woman's bucket. At this point he was hopping around mad, she was hopping around mad, and they both became the entertainment and amusement of the beach. My father was not one to take jokes especially aimed at him so we had to stay very straight faced during this comedy act. Mother and I did fall about laughing when he was out of earshot. Now they say mad dogs and Englishman go out in the mid day sun. Well my mother being very dark skinned and myself obviously inheriting her pigmented skin didn't seem to be badly affected. Of course at Midday it was very, very hot. Most Italians had disappeared off the beach for their lunch and afterwards a couple of hours siesta. We had a set time to return to the hotel for our own lunches but afterwards we would return to the beach where my mother and I were virtually alone. We had great fun in the water, borrowing the 'pedalos' that were lying about and generally enjoying the lack of people till at least 3.30 – 4.00 pm when everyone reappeared. In the evenings after dinner, we would take a stroll round the town. Because everything shuts for several hours over lunchtime it means that all shops, bars and restaurants , stay open till quite late in the evening. This means that everyone is out on the streets and everywhere becomes very lively till quite late in the evening. The shops, cafes and restaurants were all very lively and full and the atmosphere was brilliant. A lot of folks ate out under the stars.

On one particular evening walk we rounded a street and found ourselves being approached by a couple of men, one carrying what could only be described as an inner tube from a car or motor bike converted into a bagpipe making the most awful din. As he got alongside us he suddenly produced this card which he handed to my father. Assuming this was an advertising card my father not wishing to be rude simply took it nodded at the chap popped it into his pocket and we carried on. However, this chap suddenly got extremely agitated and emotional and was waving his hands about. Assuming that he wanted money my father waved his hands to brush him aside and said he was not going to give him any money. The chap got more and more passionate until in the end he was pointing at my father's pocket where the card had been placed. My father took the card out as if to see what the problem was and the chap snatched back the card and stormed off. It turned out later, when discussing the evenings events with the hotel manager that the card was in fact the chaps begging license. By pocketing the card and walking away we were depriving him of his license and his trade which made sense as to why he got quite upset.

One picture that also comes to mind from those wonderful happy days in Cattolica was that after breakfast we would sit outside in the wicker chairs people and traffic watching waiting for our food to digest. Every morning, at the same time, a chap would cycle past us on his way presumably to his business. This was not unusual or particularly interesting apart from the fact that balanced between his legs from the bottom of the ladies bike he was riding, up and beyond the handle bars was this huge lump of ice that must have been a foot square and about some four to five feet long. He would simply peddle past with his ice dripping along the roadway and on to wherever the ice was to be served. It just seemed such an unusual sight at the time.

The hotel itself, being two star was very basic although spotlessly clean. The family that owned it must have been in the trade for some years as every day the beds were made the marble floors all wiped and the bathroom cleaned out. We felt really special because our bathroom had a foot bath which we had never seen before. Coming from a housing estate where we were privileged to simply have a bath, toilet and sink this really was a very special treat. Each day we would come off the beach with sandy feet, each washing in the foot bath so our feet were clean to put back in our sandals to be able to go downstairs. Each day the foot bath was cleaned for us and nothing was ever said so we were left in our ignorance to this little luxury. It was not until years later, and I was in my late teens having started my first job that having relayed the story to my work mates that I had my leg pulled as they all recognised the foot bath as being a bidet. I still laugh at our innocence! In the last year we travelled to Cattolica we took my school friend with us. Him and I just had so much fun as we were able to wander off on our own. One evening we came across a shop selling Moscato, a fizzy wine, attributable to a type of champagne. It was very cheap, and we could buy five bottles for a limited sum. Armed with our purchases we then passed an outdoor pizza takeaway. When it was our turn, we pointed to all these exotic tubs of various ingredients and the pizzas placed in the wood oven. My friend Barry and I then disappeared armed with our night's banquet off to the low beach wall and filled ourselves with this wine and pizza. We felt very grown up and yet naughty at the same time.

Before I move on I must just relay the story of one of the drives that we had once we passed the Swiss Italian border. First of all we have to drive through a town called Domodossola, a very old, antiquated town with cobble streets, old churches and buildings that all look like they have been there for centuries. Unfortunately, in those days there was no motorway, so it was a case of all traffic, local business and holiday driving right through the centre. My father always moaned at the time it took given that time was of the essence to reach our next destination. This particular day we seemed to be crawling even slower than usual. The traffic seemed to go on for miles. After what seemed to be a couple of hours we finally reached the edge of the town and found out what the delay had been caused by. There was a funeral procession, and the coffin was inside a glass coach pulled by beautiful black horses. The mourners were all walking, and we suspect the entire town had turned out. It went on for half a mile. At walking pace no wonder the traffic had backed out beyond the towns limits and the local police were more excited than normal. By default, this poor departed must have had one of the longest queue of mourners seen for many years. The queue must have stretched back at least 9 miles. Having finally cleared the parade we were soon able to get onto the motorway and head towards Milan and then on via the Autostrada Del Sol (motorway of the sun) for the coast. Sometime along the motorway my father asked my mother if she could take over the driving for a while. Now my mother was very nervous back in England but on a continental motorway on the wrong side of the road as we called it then put her particularly in stress. However she soon settled down, was doing very well, and we were travelling along not too fast but sufficient to allow my father the rest he felt he deserved. Nothing particularly peculiar happened until we approached what the Italians call an auto train which was a very long lorry and trailer. As my mother drew alongside to overtake so the lorry slowly started to come out into our lane. My mother braked and eased back thinking the driver of the lorry was overtaking something. He then pulled back into his own lane again. My mother accelerated but again the lorry started to drift out and so we had to brake and ease back. This happened several times till in the end my mother had become a bag of nerves not really knowing what to do. The lorry was going too slow to maintain a safe distance behind him but the alternative to overtake was just not worth the risk. Suddenly from out of nowhere two military police drew alongside on their huge motorbikes. One of the officers started waving what looked like a giant lollipop with the red "stop" sign on. Now one thing you don't do is argue with Italian military police especially not the ones carrying side arms and sub machine guns. My mother immediately pulled over to the hard shoulder. By this time her nerves had completely gone, and she was crying. She was thinking she had done something so terrible that she was going to be locked away in an Italian prison for the rest of her life. One of the police motorcyclists had sped forward and had equally stopped the auto train driver. By the time the military policeman had parked his motorcycle and walked back to us, the other policeman had virtually dragged the driver of the lorry out of his cab and had him more or less pinned to the back of vehicle and giving him a right dressing down. Our policeman approached our vehicle and instead of hauling my mother off never to be seen again, he was so apologetic. In Italian (which my father could just about understand) the policeman pointed out that the drivers behaviour was disgraceful, not acceptable and reflected very badly on the Italian people and their love for tourists. He hoped we would accept his apology. He assured that the driver of the lorry was going to suffer for bringing his people this humiliation and we were waved on to continue our journey. As we passed the lorry driver, he looked very sheepish ashamed and awaiting his fate from the two policemen the second of which had arrived to give his full wrath to this idiot and his driving.

In the years to follow, once I had my own children, we would travel numerous times to Italy for a camping holiday. By this time my parents had found an alternative camp site on the shores of the Lake Maggiore. Here they found six families of Italians who had static mobile homes on the site. Every year at the beginning of the summer they would all move to the site and remain till the end of the season when the site was closed. The atmosphere and the location were so perfect that my parents didn't bother travelling any further. Here they enjoyed many years of wonderful holidays amongst these friendly lovely families whom we would meet years later.

CHAPTER 5
THE BEGINNING OF OUR CAMPING DAYS

After the three years of travelling all the way to the Adriatic, my father had basically had enough. Three days in either direction only left 8 days of actual holiday. He also decided from our overnight stops that camp sites were not the dangerous places that he had first imagined when we first set off for our holidays abroad. In fact the continent had got the camping holidays down to a fine art. The camp sites were plentiful, were well equipped and clean with wonderful washing facilities, toilets etc. As such maybe we should invest in a proper tent and equipment to replace the small transit tent we had been using. This also meant it would be a lot cheaper in the long run with the overall costs of holidays. So, my parents invested in their first frame tent. Of course, it was a French tent as these led the field in those days for quality and design. We therefore acquired our first frame tent which consisted of two large bags, one containing the frame the other the canvas tent. Father felt that before launching ourselves off we should have a trial run to make sure we had everything we needed. Not far from where we lived and about twenty miles away was one of England's typical camping ideas which was the aquadrome come large holiday park. For the one night this was not too far to at least try out new acquisition. It took about forty minutes to drive over to the aquadrome. We then drove onto the camping field where we then needed to work out how this bit of kit came together. Having worked out how the frame fitted together and now balanced on its legs on its first level the tent was unrolled and laid over the frame and tied into the four corners. The tent was then stood up onto full height and ready to be pegged down. Now came the hitch. Where were the pegs. As much as my father hunted the peg bag they just would not materialise anywhere inside or outside the car. Now as suggested earlier my father was not one to be ridiculed so mother and I had to keep very straight faces. He was absolutely fuming. In his temper he got back in the car and had to drive all the way home for the pegs and mallet, still strategically placed in the shed so as not to be left behind. Once out of sight mother and I fell about with fits of laughter, left the tent and cleared off for a fizzy drink and ice cream.

We soon mastered the system of tent erection and folding away with each one of us having his/her own jobs to do upon arrival. We still had the task of travelling across country through the French road systems with the precarious law they had of having to give way to traffic whizzing out from the right, but we really had become seasoned travellers. It was decided that Italy was a bit too far, so we contented ourselves with Switzerland which had some wonderful camp sites amid incredible scenery. For the first three or four years my parents picked on a little camp site at a village called Cossonay which lay halfway between the Swiss/French border and Lausanne on Lake Lomond (or lake Geneva as most of us would know it by). The campsite sat tucked at the very bottom of quite a steep valley with the main road passing at the bottom. The site was very popular with the Swiss themselves who had worked out that by parking their caravans at the beginning of the season they could enjoy weekends as well as holidays and for those even luckier to live close enough to be on site every night after work. Eventually this would lead to actually pushing everyone else out of the use of the campsite. The site itself had two sections, the main section which held probably about forty or fifty tents or caravans then across the small service road a field that was really kept for transit campers or one nighters passing through on their way to grander locations. Between the two areas was the communal area that housed a bar with tables and chairs and a lovely clean modern swimming pool with its own diving boards at which I spent most of my time. The café had a flat roof terrace for folks to sit on if they didn't want to be down below amongst the tables and chairs, watching others drinking and eating etc. I absolutely loved this little camp site which I considered my second home as I knew it so well. Every year we would meet up with regular campers who would travel down from Holland, Belgium and some from Germany and it was like a reunion upon arrival. One Dutch family comprised of this rather large bellied middle-aged builder, his wife and their special needs child. The child was about eight or nine when we first met him and what a lovely little boy he was. The father doted his waking hours on him. The only indulgence the father had was this huge box of Dutch cigars which he brought with him and during the course of the fortnight he would slowly work his way through always keeping three for the return journey. Also, he seemed to have a stash of alcohol in every crevice of the caravan and awning. At any time of the day evening or night he would be able to pull out Dutch beers from one location, wines from another and even spirits from another. What a character he was. Up until the final year we actually thought that there were literally just the three of them till one year a very good-looking lad turned up in his late teens, early twenties. He had the long flowing brown hair, the sunglasses and all the modern clothes, riding an old American Harley Davidson which he had cruised down from Holland on for a short break. He was certainly the celebrity of the camp site especially amongst the young girls.

It was at the time of the Dutch lad's visit that Led Zeppelin was playing in Montreux, an old city on the Lake Geneva. He asked me if I liked the group and when I told him I had their album asked if I fancied going with him to the concert. He didn't have any tickets but hoped that maybe we could wing our way in one way or another. We set off the morning of the concert and arrived amongst a swelling crowd of supporters. Needless to say, all tickets had sold out months before and the security was such that there was no way we would get inside the concert with proper tickets. Being very disappointed we were just about to give up and walk back to the station and return to the camp site. At this point this very tall, beautiful girl approached the Dutch lad and asked him whether he would like to accompany her into the concert as she had two tickets and her friend had not turned up. He took me to one side and gave me the choice as to whether I thought he should return to the camp site with me or take up the offer. There was no hesitation. He must take up the offer. So, he wandered off arm in arm with this lovely vision of a girl with a huge smile on his face like a Cheshire cat. I made my way back to the camp site and basically said that he had been able to get into the concert and I agreed to head back without going into too many details. The next day he reappeared and came over to me to say how grateful he was for my generosity. He then told me how wonderful the concert was. He was more full of the fact that after the concert the girl asked him to go for a meal with her for which she paid. She then invited him back to her hotel where he spent the night with her. The next day she escorted him to the station and gave him some money to cover the train journey back. At this point I became extremely jealous having only heard of this sort of luck in romantic novels. Mind you, as I say he was a very good looking lad. The next day he pulled out on his motorbike to return back to Holland, and I would never see him again.

One day we had a couple of youngsters from England turn up with their back packs straight off the train that passed the bottom of the transit camp site and stopped the other side of the road bridge. They seemed a pleasant enough couple of young lads and while one set off to pay the site office and give them their passports for copying, the other set up the small tent and proceeded to get the little stove on ready for something to eat. Unfortunately, it would appear that the gas bottle that you screw into the bottom of the single burner cooker was empty so the lad simply unscrewed the old one put the new one into the slot and we assume started to push the bottom in. However, at this point the canister that was full of gas, leapt forward propelled by the escaping gas straight into the tent somehow igniting itself on the way. I have never seen a tent, or indeed anything else be consumed and destroyed so quickly by fire. The poor lad had enough time just to roll clear as everything they possessed just disappeared in a ball of flame. Nobody had time to grab extinguishers, or any buckets of water as in flash it was all over. These poor lads lost everything within seconds, their clothes, their rucksacks, their money, the tent, sleeping bags everything. All they had, luckily was their passports and a little bit of money. The community on the site quickly got together and arranged temporary accommodation for the night. Somehow the parents back in England were contacted to assure them that the youngsters were okay. The only thing these two could do now was to get home as quickly as they could. A collection was carried out and enough money was raised not only to buy them their return tickets but to give them a little money for food and refreshment on the way home. Their first outing on their own into Europe for a holiday of a lifetime was in tatters and they left with such sad looks on their faces. We never did hear any more and certainly didn't see them again.

Now the campsite being so close to the railway station and myself being a bit of a wanderer I decided it couldn't be too difficult to get on a train and go into Lausanne. I was after all now grown up and reached the old age of fifteen. Arriving in Lausanne I explored the city even taking the funicular from the top area of the city down to the port to look at all the boats. It was a great day out. The problem is that having returned and reported to the parents where I had been I then had to do it all over again the next day but with them in tow. I later went from Lausanne and ventured around the lake, stopping at this incredible little village called Morges on the side of the lake. It is the most picturesque French style little village with its magnificent French chateau type houses facing the lake. The small harbour housed the little sailing and motor boats used by those who wanted to explore the lake itself. Along the little streets of the town were the shops, restaurants and bars etc and even had horse troughs highly decorated with flowers and fauna. I just fell in love with this village so much so that I have been back on numerous occasions. I have even stayed in the hotel here overlooking the lake. Again, returning to the camp site later that afternoon and having told the parents where I had gone, it was in the car the next day and back to the lake this time dragging with us this Belgian family we had befriended. There was a pattern forming here.

Another incident that was played out while we were on the campsite involved a flat bed lorry coming down the hill from the Swiss/French border route across the bridge with the intention of travelling on towards Lausanne. Unfortunately, the driver clearly had not taken into account either the steepness of the hill or the sharpness of the bend just before the bridge. The first thing we heard was a screech of tyres and brakes before a huge crash and the sound of what appeared to be a thousand windows shattering. The Lorry had skidded across the road hit the kerb on the other side and had turned over sideways with its entire load of full beer bottles releasing themselves to shower down between the safety railings of the bridge, and straight into the river flowing below. Luckily the area was about fifty yards short of the entrance to the camp site and some way off the first tents or caravans otherwise a disaster would have been on our hands. As it was it was just piles and piles of broken bottles and even more upsetting a wonderful aroma of all that wasted escaped beer that had been spilled over the surrounding countryside. The glass was still there some years later having failed to be completely picked up. However, chaos reigned for a few days, while the road had to be cordoned off with traffic passing single file, while investigators came to inspect. Then heavy machinery came to right the vehicle and drag that away, then cleaners had to turn up to try to recover some of the broken bottles, boxes and debris scattered everywhere. It all kept us on the camp site entertained though.

CHAPTER 6
BACK TO ITALY

I had reached the grand old age of being only a week from away from my seventeenth birthday. My father decided that he would like to drive to Italy again, but this time try to head for the Mediterranean. My parents chose Via Reggio as a possible destination which I had never heard of and quite honestly was just a dot on the map. Nobody bothered trying to book camp sites in those days as they were plentiful. So, we set off in our brand-new Vauxhall Viva FB loaded to the usual gunnels with camping gear and food. After we left Switzerland, and into Italy we were soon on the Auto Strada Del Sol (motorway of the sun) heading south of Milan and down into the spine of Italy. By this time my mother had been demoted from map reader to passenger and my father put the map in my hands one day and said that this was my job from now on. "I want you to know where we are at all times, and it is the navigator's job to make sure he has an alternative route, and at the end of the day he should be as tired if not more tired than the driver". I think his military days were still coming through. I did learn map reading, quickly and the hard way but considered that I was quite successful at it. Often we would find ourselves in a jam or road closure and I would have to find an alternative route. This particular journey as we were speeding down the motorway heading for Florence I noted that there was a large red line indicating a road that seemed to take a much quicker route rather than the motorway that seem make a large semi circle and wasting time and miles. So we headed for the junction whereby we would turn off the motorway and onto the short cut. It was at this point that my father pulled over and ordered me into the driving seat to drive for a few miles. Whether folks these days would consider this fool hardy, criminal or dangerous I don't know. I was just seventeen years old and old enough to drive. I had applied for my provisional license but was not due to take my driving lessons till we returned home in early August. Now I should explain that I had been driving a two wheeled Vespa scooter for the past year and had passed my test on it so I was not a complete novice to driving and had even had a bit of a go on private roads and land. However, this was a foreign country, with different rules and the mere fact that we were driving on the opposite side of the road didn't really help my nerves much. We swapped over, I sorted out seat and mirror and slowly pulled away from the hard shoulder. The motorway was very quiet and soon built up my speed to sixty miles per hour which was fast enough for my limited experience. My father soon started complaining that I should drive a little faster. At this point I really felt I was not entirely in control of the vehicle. The top weight, and the internal contents made the vehicle very light to handle and I noticed that it actually was starting to weave very slightly from side to side. As I was not very confident, I was slowing down all the while with the car seeming to continue to slide and was now getting shouted out to put my foot down and go faster which I couldn't do as this merely aggravated the driving conditions. After some five miles or so my father's temper got the better of him and he ordered me to pull over as I was clearly quite hopeless, and he might as well take over again otherwise we would be spending hours of wasted time driving too slowly. When we got out of the car, me from the driver's side and he from the passenger side and went round the back of the vehicle to swap positions, to my horror I noticed the back tyre was as flat as a pancake. I had been driving for miles on a flat tyre. No wonder it went from side to side. By this time my nerves were shattered and after changing the wheel felt I couldn't do any more driving that holiday. We finally reached the turning for the short cut and having left the motorway behind us settled down for a quick cut across to our destination. Unfortunately, as the miles disappeared so a range of rather large hills started to get closer and closer. Soon we realised that the short cut was in fact a road that crossed over the mountains surrounding Via Reggio and the coast. Now I had explained earlier that my father suffered vertigo. We had successfully found the tunnel between Switzerland and Italy to avoid passing over the mountains. Unfortunately, there was no train this time. We started to climb, and my father's grip of the steering wheel became more intense. He started sweating and mother by this time sitting in the front was wiping his brow and washing his arms. We didn't mention the navigational decision at that point. We finally did climb over the mountains down the other side, but it was all a bit traumatic, and my father did go very quiet which was always a bit worrying. We found a lovely camp site right next to the sea put up the tent and settled in for our holiday. Shortly after arriving we nodded and passed the time of day with a German family. Now none of us could speak any German and likewise they could not speak English. The common denominator was Italy. My father by now was pretty fluent and the German gentleman had very good knowledge having served in the war mostly in Italy, so they got on like a house on fire. One evening we were all sitting on the beach and lit a small fire while all sitting round with beers and whatever nibbles folks had brought. During the conversation it turned out that the German gentleman had been a tank commander during the war. Now up to this point discussing the second world war was very painful and not many Germans would admit having taken part. Our German was actually quite proud to announce that he served as a tank commander and as a soldier doing his duty. The politics rights or wrongs were never discussed but he and his family were likeable. His daughter, about my age was a stunner. She had blond hair, was tall, slim and at the age I was my own hormones were really playing overtime. I was really trying to become friends with her even though the constraints of the language barrier were causing one or two problems. However, we were swapping hand signals and the usual murmurings and grunts to form some type of conversation. Her brothers kept disappearing and then reappearing with bits of wood to keep the fire going. During the evening the piles of wood seemed to get larger and larger till in the end we had quite a fire going. In fact, the fire was becoming more like a beacon. So much so it obviously attracted the attention of the local Polizia who arrived as a pair in uniform sporting their guns, and duly had a conversation with our

German friend. The conversation became a little heated and eventually they drifted off. It turned out that "someone" had been dismantling a beach hut further down the beach to the point where it had been virtually destroyed. We of course looked at our fire and putting two and two together realised that our young German lads had been disappearing to the ready supply of wood in the form of the beach hut and had been systematically dismantling it to keep us bright light and warm round our camp fire. Now the camp site at Via Reggio was lovely, I was hoping to form a relationship with the young German girl, so all was well. The area itself was quite pretty including the old town of Via Reggio. The only problem we had was the heat. It was now mid July. It was too hot and certainly too noisy, with the Italians and other tourists staying up till quite late. We were lucky to get to sleep much before midnight and by six o'clock in the morning we were literally crawling out of the tent for fresh air and to cool down. After a few days this began to take its toll and we were beginning to resemble zombies. The only relief we could work out was to take our little camp beds drive into the local woods and literally try to get some rest in the coolness of the forest. This was very successful for an hour before the local lads decided to try out their hands at off road scrambling on their very noisy mopeds. At least we did get some sleep but it meant we couldn't really continue as after all this was a holiday not an endurance test. Reluctantly a decision was made to return back to Switzerland before we all fried or became ill through lack of sleep. My budding romance therefore came to a very abrupt end before it had even started, we said our goodbyes and left.

On our way back to Switzerland we drove round the long way this time. Sticking to the motorway we retraced our steps back to Switzerland. We decided that our favourite camp site of Cossonay was no longer the ideal place to set up camp, so we kept going. We had known about another lovely little site in Vallorbe. This was the town that bordered the Swiss French border in the Jura Mountains. The camp site itself was a municipal site owned by the town. It was so pristine it was like someone's back garden. The grass was like someone's lawn. The hedges round the edge of the site were manicured and the manager made sure there were plenty of flowers in tubs and pots about the site. So, we put up the tent and settled down for the remainder of our holiday. I will describe Vallorbe and its camp site later in this book. The location of the town was perfect. It was only a mile from the border, and this meant an early departure would see us quite a long way up the country before having to find our last camp site before the port and return to England.

By chance we found another municipal site at a small town called Compiegne north of Paris. Now this did not mean a thing to me for many, many, years to come. Eventually the penny dropped that the woods of Compiegne was where the railway carriage was drawn during the first world war and where the Germans were made to sign the surrender to end the war. It was also where Hitler had dragged the same carriage back during the second world war and humiliated the French by making them sign their surrender to him. As far as I was concerned though this was merely the last stopping place before home. We always arrived around 4.30 pm which gave us enough time to get the tent set up, beds settled and tea consumed. The camp site itself was typical late 60`s French style which was very tired and rather run down. In the centre of the site were the washing and toilet facilities. Again, these were very antiquated. Each side of the block were metal doors leading to the old-style French porcelain bog which were for use by both men and women. Each end there were wash basin facilities for clothes one end and washing oneself the other. Now my father for some reason maintained this stiff upper lip and not wishing to be embarrassed insisted that I went with him whenever he visited the toilet. I would have to stand outside the locked door in case someone tried to get in. I have never understood his reasoning to this day. However, my father went in on the first day and I stood outside. Suddenly I heard the toilet flush and my father give a howl of sheer shock and indignation. What he failed to do and what I must confess did not previously tell him was that after one finishes one's ablutions one would step off the porcelain raised steps of the basin and onto the floor before flushing. Failing this the basin would flush itself and its contents with anyone still standing on the steps. My father didn't realise this and appeared outside extremely embarrassed and his sandals and bare feet were rather wet! Mother and I needless to say laughed about this for years. Another smile we shared again that came about at this site and again involving their wonderful basic toilets was when my father, escorted by me, on a separate day went for his daily ablution. In he went, door locked, and I stood patiently waiting for his reappearance. Suddenly there was a large bang on the inside of the door proceeded by laughing. When I asked if the occupant was okay he replied yes but what had happened, he had lowered his trousers and underpants keeping hold to avoid contact with the porcelain, had backed up into position, lowered himself to undertake his daily routine over balanced and had rolled forward so his head is now balanced on the door in front of him, his feet still in position of the raised steps and still holding on to his trousers and under garment. A position that he could not maintain without letting go of something to re position himself. Once again, I had to retain a very straight face and not allow him to see I was at all amused by his antics. I would wait until he was out of earshot to share this latest snippet of hilarity with my mother. One final story I must share, again back on the same camp site. I had gone off for my evenings wash. I arrived at the end of the toilet block that was open to the elements and the public, took my top off and started to wash myself in readiness for the evening. As I was busy sorting myself out a guy came in next to me, again like me grabbed the bottom of his T shirt and lifted it over his head to bare his upper body and proceed to dowse himself with water and soap to clean himself down. It wasn't until I had finished washing myself down and was now drying myself with a towel that I moved slightly sideways to now face my neighbour still vigorously attending to his washing duties. It was at this point, and to my horror that I realised that this half naked person next to me was not in fact a "him" but a "her" and did not have any embarrassment whatsoever that she was exposing everything to the now rather excited and shy fifteen-year-old standing next to her. By the time I had got back to the tent and blurted out my tail of excitement and my father had gone to investigate the young lady had completed her functions and had left. I thought about that picture for years.

Back in the 1960`s and still only twenty years after the second world war travelling through France and staying at various campsites one fact became obvious. There was always a lack of German cars and German visitors. The French were still very anti German. Any travellers through France simply used the country as a highway to other destinations and not stopping for fear of reprisals. For this reason, we rarely if ever saw German campers on any of the campsites visited. At the end of one particular holiday abroad we had left

Switzerland to drive back to the port for a crossing the next day but did not stop at our usual camp site. Whether we were early or what I cannot remember. However, we followed the normal pattern of reaching 430pm in the afternoon to then try to locate a camp site for the night. By this time we had virtually reached the coast of Northern France and assuming there would bound to be a camp site somewhere between Boulogne and Calais we kept our eyes peeled for our nights stop. Time was now slowly disappearing and by 5.30pm nothing had been spotted and we were now seeing the town and towers of Calais itself on the horizon. As luck would have it, suddenly, we spotted some tents and vehicles on the cliff line and feeling rather reprieved drove down the dirt track to the campsite which was quite busy with a good number of tents dotted about. As it was getting rather late, we didn't bother trying to find the camp owner or the site office but thought we could catch up later and book ourselves in paying for our one nights stop over. By now we had our set pattern. My father and I concentrated on the roof rack taking off the cover lifting out the tent and poles and setting them out ready for erection. The poles were first of all put together and the tent then rolled out over the top of the half height frame. Mother was busy unloading beds and sleeping bags and then came to join us to tie the corners and then lift the frame to its full height, whereby the tent could be stretched out and pegged down. While my father finished that off, mother and I laid out the ground sheet, I then sorted out the inner tent for the beds and mother would be working behind me passing beds then sleeping bags then pillows. This quickly followed with setting up the camp kitchen with its folding unit to hold the cooker followed by gas bottle kettle and pans. All in all, we could from arriving to finish have the tent completed within 40 minutes with chairs ready and cups of tea in our hands before starting the evening meal. It was at this point that I spotted a German registration car located not far from us. I remarked quietly to my parents at which point we then spotted another German car and another and another. To our horror we then realised that the entire camp site was full of German registration cars. The realisation then set in that this was not in fact a camp site at all. What we had blatantly put ourselves in the middle of was an entire ex German garrison that met once a year as part of their reunion from when they all manned the gun emplacements along the cliffs to repel the

English who of course never invaded at this spot. We were extremely embarrassed and apologised for our intrusion. The Germans found it hilarious and welcomed us on their site very politely although when we left the next day, we were rather relieved that we ourselves had not suffered any reprisals. Since then we have met many wonderful German families on numerous sites through Europe and relayed this story to them. Having finally crossed the channel and worked our way home after all those miles on the continent my father was less than pleased when we came off the M1 motorway with less than sixteen miles to home when the car boiled up. Checking the radiator, it was empty. Poor thing had boiled itself dry carrying us and all the camping gear all that way. I had to find the water bottle that we use on the campsite and go and bang on doors and find a kind person that was in and ask if I could have some water. Not such a brilliant end to an incredible holiday but at least it was a minor hitch and we got home in one piece and safe with another story to tell.

CHAPTER 7

RETURN TO SWITZERLAND

I had passed my driving test six weeks after turning seventeen. My second vehicle to replace an HA Viva with a twisted chassis was a Vauxhall Victor FB. If anyone was familiar with this model it was a big, hefty beast with a 1600 engine. The gears were operated from the gear change located on the steering column. The light switches and the windscreen wash were located on the floor next to the clutch. It was a real old tank, but I loved it and got me out about. As I was in the last year of the sixth form at school the car even took me to school and back as I was not to finish until the summer of that year. At this time, I had a girlfriend named Debbie. Although she was raised in England and for all intents and purposes sounded acted and was English, she nonetheless was born in the United States. She proudly still retained her American Passport. This particular year, the parents had planned to re-visit Switzerland, and I suggested that we take Debbie with us. It was agreed that as there were four of us we should travel in my car being larger than my father's car. My mother now had a small square Vauxhall box shaped viva HA. My father arranged to have the Vauxhall Victor mechanically checked out from end to end by a friend who worked at the nearby Vauxhall garage. The head on the engine was stripped and skimmed, a new head gasket fitted along with a thorough good service replacing all the usual parts filters, oil, brakes etc. A roof rack was fitted and come the day of departure the camping gear was loaded on board. Mum fulfilled her usual trick of introducing a mountain of supplies that had had taken six months to get together. The supplies included tins of salmon, ham, luncheon meat, potatoes, boxes of tea bags, sugar etc.

We set off early on the Saturday morning and having reached Dover crossed over on the ferry to Calais. From here we headed off across the Somme country for our doorway into Switzerland. Everything had gone extremely well until we reached Amiens some 100 miles into France. By now it was early afternoon. Suddenly, we noticed a grinding noise coming from the rear of the vehicle. This noise seemed to get louder and louder as we pushed further and further into France. Not wishing to go too far until whatever it was making this awful noise could be checked out we found a camp site just outside Amiens. Unfortunately, all the garages by this time had closed and would not re-open until Monday morning when we could ask a local mechanic to inspect it for whatever damage had been caused. Sadly, he diagnosed an area of the car that we could not have possibly covered. It transpired that the crown pinion in the back axle needed replacing. This is not a part that would come easily off the shelf of any parts shop in France and in fact had to be obtained from England. Luckily my father working for Vauxhalls was able to contact his source and conjure up some parts. These were brought down to Dover and crossed to France on the new hover craft service. The parts then quickly found their way to the garage and the rear axle stripped and the parts replaced. We couldn't have got more than 30 miles down the road when the whining started again. Clearly this was not going to be a successful trip and any further progress south was pointless. It was therefore decided that the best course of action was to abort the mission and return to England. We limped along the various A roads till eventually we arrived home very dejected. Once home the car was emptied with everyone now feeling rather sorry for themselves. Trying to resurrect some form of holiday break I suggested to Debbie we might try to find an alternative destination. Perhaps we could strap one of the small tents to a rucksack and set off, by train, down to Devon and visit one of the camp sites that I got to know from when I was a lot younger. As we were putting our plans together my father came out with an alternative plan of his own. Being a rather logical person, he asked me how I felt about having another go at the continent. The decision was unanimously made. All the gear from the Vauxhall Victor was re loaded onto my mother's very small Vauxhall viva HA. This was a little 1000 cc square box Vauxhall built vehicle. It was designed more for shopping than adventure trips to Switzerland with four adults and camping gear on board. Bits and pieces were stuffed in and under the front seats the rear seats and in every space that could be made available. The journey was not going to be very comfortable but at least it would hopefully get us to our desired destination. All my father did was to check the oil level, the water level and that the fan belt was not loose and off we went. We didn't have time for the comprehensive overhaul and service the Vauxhall Victor had undergone. I must say for a spontaneous decision and with a vehicle that was neither suited for or adequately prepared it all went remarkably well. After suffering cramped spaces and long driving hours, we finally reached Switzerland. We set up camp and were ready to enjoy what was left of the two weeks remaining of our holiday.

Debbie and I took the opportunity of wandering off leaving the parents on the camp site. We travelled by train from the station located next to the camp site down to Lausanne. From here we could explore Lake Geneva (or lake Lemon) and beyond. One day we decided to take the funicular that ran from the railway station down to the lake side. Here, just pulling in was the lake paddle steamer that served all the villages on the lake. We decided we could go as far as Geneva and then catch the train back on the same travel ticket. Unfortunately, we did not consider the length of time the steamer would take to reach its destination having to stop at all the little lake side villages, including my favourite village of Morges on the way. We arrived at Geneva three and a half hours later. The return ticket enabled us to get back to Lausanne in just twenty minutes. While we were on this lovely old paddle steamer chugging round the villages and wharves, at each docking we saw the most beautiful array of flowers sweeping over the sides of the jetty down towards the water and were all so inviting. On board with us amongst other passengers there was this one particular elderly couple who were both very well dressed in their Swiss clothes. It looked like they had been married for many years and were completely doted on each other. They had been holding hands for most of the journey on the table in front of them. It was such a lovely romantic thing to see that couples can still show their affections even after so many years being together. At one of the stops a local elderly lady got on board, and recognising the couple came and joined them to gossip the day's events with them. Politely they let go of each other's hand so as not to embarrass their new guest. However, we could see that each of their hands spontaneously passed under the table. They found each other's hands and clasped each other like a honeymoon couple. Even after all the years they had been together they didn't want to let go of the physical affection for one another. I must have made some gesture of approval as the gentleman with his silver white hair and immaculate dress looked over to me, realising we had been watching, simply gave me a wink, a smile and then looked back at their new companion. That is a look and a smile that I have remembered and brought with me for the past forty plus years.

At the camp site everyone was eagerly awaiting the 1st August. In Switzerland this is a very important date in their calendar. The Swiss will try to return to their country from all over the world for this day. It is of course in celebration of their independence from Austria. Every village town and city celebrates throughout the day and night. There are bonfires, fireworks, street bands and parades and folks dressed so proudly in their national costumes. Cossonay was no exception. The preparations started the day before with bunting being put up all round the village and the camp site. Folks would stay dressed in their national costume all day. As the lunchtime passed and the afternoon progressed so did the drinking and merriment. It was actually a date that Debbie and I were also looking forward to for our own reasons. Before we left England several of our school friends had prepared an old Comma Van and had set off for a summer holiday jaunt from as far away as Sweden to travel through Europe and end up in Greece. The idea was that they would try to reach Switzerland by the 1st August. Mobile phones or such easy communications were not available then and we had to just sit and wait and hope. Sure, enough mid-afternoon, this rather tacky hand painted battleship grey comma van turned into the camp site with hand painted names of countries already visited on its sides. Out came five very cheery beaming lads who up to that point were having the times of their lives. We helped them erect tents and then join the rest of the camp site for some liquid refreshments. We were able to catch up with all the tales of the countries they had visited so far and the mischief they

44

had got up to. Dennis, one of the group was being constantly teased for his rather outward eating habits. Apparently one morning they had run out of milk. This was not going to dissuade Dennis from his morning bowl of cornflakes to which he added tomato ketchup as a substitute. That evening, reasonably oiled with local alcohol we followed the villagers away from the camp site. The procession went up the hill behind the camp site to a spot above the village where a bonfire was lit, fireworks set off and speeches made. The local town dignitary was trying to put some coherent speech together but laced with alcohol was completely undecipherable to us. After the official ceremony had passed, we returned back to the camp site for the camp bar and more alcohol. By the time our weary travellers finally found their way to their tents they were very much worse for wear. In fact two of them never made it beyond the awning and my father later covered them up with a blanket to allow them to sleep it off till the next morning. The next morning the happy band then packed up, and with waves and cheeky comments left us to regain peace and tranquillity while they continued their adventure. They would finally reach the outskirts of Greece where the van would finally pack up and they all returned by way of public transport but with tales that would be told till their old ages.

As it was always so warm on the camp site in Switzerland, we would normally walk round in swimming trunks or shorts and T shirts. On a typical early afternoon suddenly, something thumped me on the back of the neck and not having much clothing on felt like someone had thrown a stone. As soon as I recovered from this first blow, others came in quick succession that were quite painful. Looking up we all quickly realised that we were about to be subjected to a summer hailstone shower. What we all didn't realise was the size and sheer volume of this shower. Whilst the storm was over very quickly the aftermath was incredible. Most hail stone showers take place in July/August but certainly in England the size of the actual hailstones are normally no larger than marbles. These hailstones were the size of snooker balls they were huge. Coming down with the force they were, was beginning for cause quite a bit of serious damage. Campers did not have time to pack away bits and bobs from around the caravans and items such as canvas garden chairs, umbrellas and children's plastic toys began to rip and break. As the storm intensified tents were beginning to suffer with ripped canvas and caravans were suffering their small windows on the top of the vans being smashed. When it was over the temperature had dropped dramatically and folks were still wandering around in what resembled a carpet of white shiny snooker balls and mopping up debris and broken possessions from the deluge. It was for the uninitiated quite scary for those moments during the storm.

At the end of a wonderful couple of weeks we reluctantly headed back to England on the long drive through France. We left early enough in the morning as to reach the coast without a night's stop. When we finally docked on English soil, we had to face the inevitable customs at Dover. The officer routinely pulled us over and asked us if there was anything we had to declare. Now my mother was pulling out some cigarettes, a bottle of half-finished spirit, a couple of bottles of wine and it was all very disorganised. The officer in the meantime having taken our passports and having checked them asked us to pull over to one of the enclosed bays whereby we were told to strip the car. My father was not amused. The roof rack was emptied, the tent taken out of its bag and rolled out across the floor, seats removed from the car and contents emptied and all left in a bit of a mess. All together we were over the limit by the half a bottle of spirit (the other half consumed at a camp site in Switzerland with a boozy bunch of students) and a small tin of tobacco for which we then had to pay the price of putting it all back. The reason why the customs officer had given us more attention than usual was because of Debbie's passport. Because it was an American passport, it had been stamped when we had returned from our breakdown ten days earlier unlike our British passports. As such they were curious to know why we had been out and back again in such a short period. Explanation was not asked for, merely let's strip the car and see what we find. It took us over an hour to put it all back by which time the sheds were empty with everyone on our ship gone. My father did not speak to my mother all the way home because she did not declare what we had, and he had to pay the fine on top of the humiliation of the search.

CHAPTER 8

LET'S TRY SOMETHING DIFFERENT!

By now the parents were earning a lot more money, my father drove a company lease car and the roadways abroad were becoming a lot more user friendly and faster. As I could now drive, I could take it in turns with him to do some of the driving abroad. It was time to try to travel a little further and Innsbruck in Austria came to the forefront for a visit. Now Austria, unlike Switzerland, was quite a long way and did require at least one stop over. This was not unusual given our early travelling to Italy in the days before motorways. The Estate Car that we now had was packed with the camping gear and off we set. Our first stop was going to be just over the French German border somewhere around the Black Forest area which we were not disappointed with. From there we could travel down through the mountains and down into Innsbruck. The first sight of Innsbruck comes from the pass that then snakes its way down to the plateau. It was a beautiful sunny day, and the first impressions were stunning. The mountains whilst not as high or dramatic as say Switzerland still gave a fantastic back drop and the meadows and fields below were lush with dark green grass. The city itself was very colourful with its domes and roofs. We were able to find a really lovely camp site on the edge of the city in a wooded area that stretched along the side of a rather fast flowing river. It was well into the season and the camp site was quite full with the only spaces left rather towards to end of the camp site. We drove along the camp road past all the other campers and found a nice pitch. This was some way from the toilet facilities but reasonably flat, clear and suitable for ourselves. We therefore launched into setting up our canvas home for what we thought would be the remainder of our fortnight holiday.

The next day we decided to explore Innsbruck itself with its splendid albeit expensive shops and were certainly not disappointed. On the way we drove past what was a large lido of various size swimming pools so we planned to spend the day here the following day. We reached the lido around late morning and I was in my seventh heaven with all the various size pools some with diving boards and even one with Olympic sized boards. By this time my swimming had become quite strong, and I was diving from quite high boards. Having said that I have never been able to go upside down for long as I lose my sense of direction and balance. My diving therefore followed a rather rigid pattern which did not involve flips, rolls or backward dives. I was still able to achieve some good dives and entered the water with minimum splash. I ventured up the boards first to the first level spring boards and then up to the top and launched myself off several times with what I was pleased with my swallow diving I was joined by a couple of German lads, one who looked like he had been in a fight with a donkey with front teeth missing and a rather bashed face. Now these lads were incredible. Not only did they perform forward and backward flips but rolls and dives from the half way diving boards encouraging each other to be more and more daring. They then took up the high boards for even more daring stunts. I remained at my rigid limit although admiring every dive they made. One dive, which my new friend who looked like he lost the fight with a four legged creature was not wholly successful and left him rather shaken and sore. It was at this point he admitted that the state of his face was brought about by dives that had not been successful as opposed to a boxing match with another creature. None the less they were both incredible. To see these two amateur lads diving off professional height boards doing the tricks of professionals was just mind blowing. I think this was the time I decided that I would draw a line in the sand and restrict myself to what I could do and remain contented with that. The lads and I spent the afternoon together but as the afternoon drew to a close the skies began to cloud over and clearly a storm was brewing. From experience we decided that it was time to retreat back to camp so that if any inclement weather did arrive we were at least on hand to button down the hatches so to speak. What a storm we had. It broke early evening and did not stop most of the night. Thunder, lighting and rain like I had never seen crashed, pushed and pulled us in all directions. Our efforts to secure the tent on arrival paid off and the tent remained unaffected aided with the guy ropes. The inside stayed relatively dry and we felt we were really lucky. The next morning, we couldn't believe our eyes. The camp site, from about 50 yards away back to the gates was on a very slight slope with us being at the top end. The water ended about three cars length away, so we remained relatively dry. The poor folks further down were not so lucky. One girl was walking round in high heel boots with the water still halfway up her legs. Tents, with their contents outside and in bits and pieces were in ruins. Folks were picking sodden belongings up and putting them down again in total disbelief of what damage could be caused in less than twelve hours. It was really sad. The river next to us which had been quite a fast-flowing torrent of water when we arrived was now like a raging bull crashing its way along the banks very close to bursting. Anyone or anything that got into the river would be swept away immediately and it was a very dangerous situation especially with no barrier to prevent entry. There was only one solution for us as the weather looked like it was not going to clear for quite a few days. We packed our belongings back into the car which included a wet tent and left. Given the security of Switzerland we decided that we would finish our holiday there and drove back to the little frontier town of Vallorbe where the remainder of our break was spent in glorious sunshine and very hot temperatures, so much so that the little field that we camped on which normally would be very lush grass was like a scorched farmers field of very dry corn stubble.

I should describe Vallorbe. It is a most pretty little French style town with rustic houses down the sides of the Jura hills that follow the roadway up to the border with France in one direction up and out of the town towards Lausanne in the other and follows the bubbling river to its source in another. The quite wide river is crystal clear with the water being fed from the mountains. In the river swimming quite free is an abundance of rainbow trout often caught by the locals to supply the evening tea. In the actual centre of Vallorbe which is located around the bridge over the river are little French style bars and restaurants whilst maintaining a very rural setting with farmers and farm vehicles coming and going to their fields beyond. The camp site itself sits at the back of the main square and is municipally owned. The manager of the site stayed for well over forty years tending the needs of campers and keeping a lovely clean and tidy site. Everything on the campsite was perfect. The toilets were clean and efficient with hot and cold water, showers that worked and toilets that were spotless. The camp was like a giant garden with a roadway that went along one side to the end turned for fifty feet then turned again back to the beginning and campers could choose to pitch along the outside edges or on back-to-back camping through the middle section all with easy access to the road. At the far end was a grand box hedge and the other side was the municipal leisure area with concrete ping pong tables, picnic tables and seats and a beautiful crystal-clear swimming pool. To the side was the clear river which led up stream for about a mile to the waterfall that was is source and that cascaded down from the steep banks of the hills that led into the Jura mountains. The entire place was timeless and beautiful. Above us, halfway up one side of the hill was the little railway station that greeted the trains coming in from France and departing Switzerland on their way back to Paris and beyond. We should have guessed that this railway line was a little more grand that we thought. Behind the camp site and municipal park and just before the river stood on display a huge railway engine that had four small wheels at the front, eight main driving wheels and four wheels at the back. This monster resembled something that would pull the huge trains across the mid-west of America. It turned out to be one of the steam intercontinental trains that joined the various countries of Europe. It was massive. It was not till two thirty in the early hours of Sunday morning that we realised how important our little station was. This was the time when the famed Orient Express train rolled into the station. As this was the first station over the border passengers had to be checked for passports etc. and it would make an awful din when it arrived and just as loud when it left. It certainly left no doubts of its grandeur and status. Of all the sites that I have camped over all the years I would say that Vallorbe is my favourite.

I have stayed at this site in Vallorbe numerous times over the years and never once regretted my stay. I have walked the riverbank to its source being the waterfall cascading from the mountain side. Some years after our first visit the locals discovered that behind the rock face there were huge caves with stalactites and stalagmites. The caves were opened with properly constructed steel walkways and flood lights showing the splendour of the insides. Following the little path along from the waterfall it cuts through the woods at the bottom of the cliffs with a steep walk up to the roadway above. The road either snakes its way over the pass to France or back down into the town and past the railway station. Having explored this my father decided he would like to come with me and see for himself what splendours I had uncovered. We wandered along the river, past a trout farm where a local had dammed off part of the river. Trout were bred here for folks to go and hire a rod and line to catch and take away. This fishery would still be here in years to come and feature in another funny story further into this book. It was fascinating watching the water bubble as each fisherman cast his basic line into the water and then take away one or two freshly caught fish for tea that night. You could never have more than two on the basis that you wouldn't eat more than two and also stocks would quickly diminish if you were allowed to take more. Also, the guardian was quite crafty in so far as he would feed the fish during various times of the day so that they were never over hungry when the amateur hunters arrived. We carried on to the source, watched the waterfall for a while and passed just underneath then entered the small forest that led eventually to the road. I can still remember to this day the smell of the forest floor and trees The man-made path then started upwards following the contours of the hill and just before the exit out onto the road came across a huge cave. Later the cave had a poster placed outside to announce that it was once inhabited by quite a few folks back in prehistoric times. It was then a final scramble up the path onto the road and the mile and a half walk back to the village. On my own I took it all as part of my exploration not thinking anything other than how lovely it was. However, I forgot that my father suffered with vertigo. It was not till we left the cave and started the slightly steeper climb up to the road that my father turned and was facing into the steep banks. Now I couldn't see any problems as the trees disguised any steep slope but his instincts were telling him that there was quite a slope and with that he started to lean forwards and if I had not grabbed him by the back of his shirt would have nose dived into the slopes below. I managed to get him up to the road where he regained composure. We then walked back to the village past the railway station. I don't think I remember him ever coming up to the forest again.

It was on this holiday that I met the "terrible twins", Freddie and his best mate Kurt. They were not related in any way and certainly did not look like each other. Freddie was tall thin and of Indo-Dutch parents. Kurt was that blond looking German type although they were both down from Holland. The pair of them were always into mischief and kept everyone laughing with their humour and antics. One evening they decided they wanted a memento to take home with them. What better from Switzerland than a Swiss cow bell. Now the shops here in the small town were mostly for day-to-day provisions. Certainly nothing as specialised as farm equipment to include cow bells. However along the river and up into the high meadows we could hear herds of cows by their bells moving around. A plot was hatched. After the evening meal, the three of us met up and we wandered off down the pathway by the side of the river. We passed the trout farm and to where the fields came down to the lane. We climbed over the barbed wire fence and started climbing up the field towards the sound the bells further up the hill. We didn't realise just how steep the meadow was until we were on it and was not helped at all by it now being dark. Eventually in the distance we came across shadowy four-legged creatures. As we approached, they became a little skittish to say the least. Now to try to undo a cow bell, quietly, after dark amongst a herd of skittish cows is not the easiest task. We did manage to undo one but by this time the cows were beginning to get a little boisterous to say the least. It was at this point that one of the boys commented in Dutch and the pair of them became a little hesitant. When I asked what the problem was, they both announced that we were not in a field of cows but rather frisky young bullocks and maybe we shouldn't stay around much longer. With only a very old tatty collar and bell we started to back away downhill away from the herd which started to follow us. As we sped up, so the herd seemed to speed up. In the end we were running for all our life's worth with this herd of very lively young bullocks close to our heels! Finally, we arrived at the boundary fence and not wishing to stand on ceremony or say fond farewells we scooted over as quickly as our abilities would allow. Unfortunately, the fence was barbed wire which caught hold of the top my legs just below the crutch and hung on to the material as

I was propelled forwards making a rather loud tearing noise. By the time I landed the other side of the fence I noticed a clear draft in my lower torso. I have learnt since that going near cows or bullocks at night is never a good idea in the first place and one thing you never ever do is run near to or from them. A lesson learnt nearly a very hard way. On the other hand, I kept that old rusty holy cow bell for many years that always made me smile of that night with those two terrible twins. Unfortunately, I lost touch with the pair of them and have no idea where they ended up.

The return journey was quite uneventful and we arrived home on a Saturday evening. As I was able to drive, I asked if I could borrow the car that had just done nearly two thousand miles to visit my new girlfriend. She lived some thirty odd miles away the other side of Aylesbury. We had a lovely evening together, but it was time to leave so I started the drive home. I decided I would take the back roads along country lanes. This way I would cut off the corner and avoid traffic. As I was circling the outskirts of Aylesbury on this very windy lane unfortunately, I had misjudged my speed and the road conditions. On this rather sweeping bend I lost the back end of the car. It whipped round and before I could right the vehicle it had plunged over a small brick wall on the opposite side of the road and into a ditch. All my nightmares came together in one event. Some nice people passing stopped and got me out of the ditch. It was then that we realised I had realigned the back end of the chassis by hitting the brick wall. I couldn't possibly drive the vehicle home all the way in darkness. The lovely couple offered me refuge at their home towards the end of the lane for the night and I could telephone home the next day. I did not sleep well that night having nightmares most of the night. I rang my parents the next day and confessed my sins. I expected the full wrath of my father's temper. However, he turned up inspected the damage arranged for the vehicle to be recovered and we just went home. He didn't speak much to me on the way home but I didn't get what I was expecting in a very heavy telling off. The vehicle was written off and my father ended up with a new company lease car. He took the blame himself saying he had lost the vehicle on a particularly slippery part of the road. Nothing more was ever said about this incident. It did teach me a lesson though, to slow down on country roads.

CHAPTER 9

GOING SOLO

As I was now working, I could afford to try to buy myself my own equipment. A chap that lived close by announced he had an old French frame tent if anyone was interested. Having gone back to his house one lunchtime and having taken a look at the tent poles and a few photographs I decided to buy it for my own adventures without parents. At about that time several mates were buying their own cars and had girlfriends. We therefore decided that we should try to organise a trip all together. My new girlfriend, Sheila, and I agreed to go along with the group to Bournemouth a part of the world I had not visited previously. We packed up our possessions and one bank holiday afternoon set off heading for the south coast. We found a really lovely quiet comfortable site just on the outskirts of Bournemouth and pitched the tent with the bedroom, cooking facilities etc waiting for everyone else to get settled and organised for a trip to the nearest pub and something to eat. It was just about this time, as it was starting to get late evening, that we realised that our quiet serene camp site was not going to be quite as relaxed as we thought. It seems that just over the other side of the hedge behind us, was the end of the actual runway for Bournemouth Airport. It was not then as popular or as international as it is today but still had its own fair share of traffic flying out at different times of the early morning through to late evening. We certainly did not need an alarm call each morning with the low level take offs just above our heads.

Apart from that it was a great holiday and with a group of youngsters such as ourselves let loose for the first time it was just brilliant fun. The drive home was full of stories of a great weekend, great weather and some great times on the beach, in the pubs and fish and chips shops. Unfortunately my little car which had been promoted to a pampas green Vauxhall viva HB by this time, complete with a pair of bright fog lights and the customary whippy aerial, reached as far as Aylesbury and then decided it didn't want to go any further. It had been playing up starting first thing for some time. It turned out that several of the valves that let the exhaust from the engine escape to the exhaust had turned oval instead of being round. The car completed its journey having to be towed back home for the head to be removed and the damage rectified.

Following this I kept with my parents for a couple of years more till I finally left home. At the grand age of 20 I met my first wife and then of course holidays were spent together rather than with parents. Our first trip together, again with my tent was back to my favourite haunt in Devon. We found a wonderful camp site above the town of Brixham at Upton Manor Farm. The owner who had turned his farmland into a camp site was really friendly and the site was very clean. It was just across the road from a Pontin's holiday camp. The camp site owner had done a deal with the Pontin's camp that his campers could have access to the club house in the evenings. This proved very successful. In the evenings we were able to walk over for a few drinks, listen to the cabaret acts, even get some food and it helped to give us a lovely holiday. Next to the camp site on the other side from Pontin's was a Devon clotted cream factory. We were able to buy pots of freshly made clotted cream cheap to put on our freshly baked scones bought from the town and have for late afternoon tea. The beach was only half a mile down the lane and down some very steep steps. Each day we would either wander down to the shore and just sit, sunbathe or swim. Occasionally we would head into town or across to Dartmouth leaving the car on the hill at Kingswear walking down the hill to the little ferry and cross over to Dartmouth for a few hours. Other times we would walk into Brixham and to the little working harbour that had not been developed as it is today. The various pubs were still very old-world sea shanty type pubs and a great atmosphere could be found in the evenings. One pub on the corner of the high street was a strange shape and had two levels one being the public bar downstairs and the next level the lounge which was in slightly better condition and set up than the bar. We decided to have a drink in here one night and we met a lovely couple that were from Bristol. As they loved the area so much and in particular sailing, they had sold their two properties, bought a flat together in Bristol which served them well during the working week and at weekends they would travel down to Brixham where they had purchased a sea faring yacht. After having a couple of hours with them they asked if we wanted to join them at the Sailing Club across from the harbour. I reluctantly agreed thinking it would be a bunch of hooray Henrys in their boating blazers. I could not be so far from the truth. All the folks in the club were proper sea fairing folks wearing comfortable clothes most of them just off the boats. There was one chap who looked a bit scruffy, not shaved and in fact quite dowdy and run down. When I told our new friends how I found the place and atmosphere so different to how I expected, they pointed out the chap sitting by himself at the bar quietly drinking. They then told me he had just literally just got back from sailing across the Atlantic single handed in his yacht. No wonder he looked so tired and worn out. Moral of the story is don't judge the book by its cover.

I don't think I have ever left Brixham Devon without being full of very happy memories. This holiday was equally as wonderful. We had met lots of lovely people, explored lots of pubs and cafes and got home safe and sound with happy tales to tell friends and relations.

CHAPTER 10
MY FIRST FLIGHT ABROAD

Apart from a short flight in a two-seater private aircraft round Skegness when I was fourteen I had never been on an aircraft before my first honeymoon. We had occasionally driven over to the local airport and watched the aeroplanes take off and land and often wondered what it was like to jet off somewhere exotic. Well, it was coming up to our wedding in August. As a wedding present, my grandma had bought us tickets to fly to Spain which seemed to be the in destination in the early nineteen-seventies. We were booked to fly with Clarkson's who operated out of Luton. Now Clarkson's had two very famous aeroplanes nicknamed "Pinky" and "Perky" as they were both painted bright pink. These aircraft would fly backwards and forwards to Spain carrying holiday makers on the cheap bucket price package holidays. I was quite excited at my first prospect of flying. Unfortunately, in June, two months before the wedding, Clarkson's suddenly went into liquidation, and we became part of the many victims of the fall. It would be some time before we were able to recover any money at all. What was more important we were going to have our honeymoon completely ruined. My Nan made enquiries with the travel agent as to anything that could be done. It seemed that Thompsons had jumped in to help and were offering "square deal" packages. You paid a set price turned up at the airport for a destination airport but didn't know what resort or hotel you would be staying at till you arrived at the other end. It was of course a way for the operator to fill up seats on the planes and rooms at the various hotels. We managed to book a holiday to Majorca and on the Sunday after the wedding duly set off to Luton Airport. We boarded our own flight with Pinky and Perky both parked just across the tarmac looking very alone forlorn and abandoned. They had of course been seized by the bankruptcy company put in charge of overseeing Clarkson's. When we took off the plane levelled out and we were able to relax. My new bride suddenly recognised one of the stewardesses as being a girl that had attended her school. They had a quick chat as the girl was on duty and off she went. After an hour of serving out various refreshments and other duties she came over and asked if we would like to go up and look out of the cockpit. She had spoken to the pilot and advised him we were newlyweds and that she knew my new wife. I jumped at the chance and the next few minutes saw us shaking hands with the pilot and looking out the cockpit windows. I asked a very stupid question based on hearsay that I understood that in the air you could only see about ten miles maximum. He politely pointed out Majorca in the distance with Minorca and Ibiza all some fifty sixty miles away at the very least so that rather educated me on that point. Now both Luton and Majorca airports were both built with short runways. This means the planes that took off and landed were designed for steep take offs and steep landings. As we approached Majorca it seemed the plane just pointed at the ground and descended at a rapid rate. I had never experienced decompression like it and thought my ears were going to explode. The pain was awful. When we landed, we were met by the ground crew of Thompsons and ushered onto the coaches waiting outside. Luckily my first wife had flown many times herself round the world to visit her parents who were stationed abroad at various locations over the years so was able to guide me the novice as to what to do next. On the coach we were given the names of the hotels and locations we had been allocated. We had been booked into a lovely hotel in a quiet but expanding village called Magaluf several miles down the coast from Palma where the airport was located. It didn't take us long for the coach to pull up outside this wonderful modern tall glass fronted hotel. I was just over the moon as I had not stayed in many hotels in my life up to that point. The hotel itself had three meals a day, was a very short distance from the beach and the small-town shopping centre. It was very quiet and very peaceful but then on honeymoon that is really what you want. We would go to the beach each day. I would snorkel and see the incredible number of fish just below the surface. I came up for air at one point close to this girl who had her arms wrapped round her boyfriend and they were both laughing at me with my mask and snorkel. I simply laughed back and said "you wouldn't be smiling so broadly if you saw the size of fish that are swimming about just below you." He didn't wait for her, he was off out of the water and up the beach before I could raise my mask.

While we were in Majorca we took the organised coach trip to the north of the island passing huge private mansions such as Harry Secombe's villa. They were magnificent. We stopped at little ports like Porto Cristo a typical Spanish fishing port with its highly painted fishing boats dotted in the harbour. We visited the caves of Drac where you go down these long stone corridors in the bowels of the earth where a massive cave opens up with theatre seating. Everyone takes a seat then it goes absolutely pitch black to the point you cannot see your hand in front of your face. Suddenly from the right-hand side comes this eerie music that seems to get louder and louder. Suddenly there is a faint light that gets brighter and brighter till you can make out two small rowing boats on the natural lake in front of us. In each boat is a man holding a candlelight over folks playing either a violin or guitar as the rowers take them slowly and eerily past you to the left where they disappear again. It was like watching mythical characters taking the dead across to the afterlife. It was so strange to watch and hear that we all had goose bumps. Then the lights come on and the tour continues through the stalactites and stalagmites. All very memorable. We also went to the false pearl factory where the famous Majorcan pearls are manufactured. What did fascinate us was the small shanty huts and boardwalks that made up the main shopping areas of the small town. Only a few shops and bars existed so shopping and souvenirs didn't take very long. Now to see the descriptions of what Magaluf has turned into and the night life etc., it is so different to the sleepy little place that we first visited.

There was a lovely couple with their son at the hotel who we became friendly with. We did in fact keep in touch with them for several years after the holiday. They lived near Birmingham and ran a textile company making curtains. They were very useful in helping us kit out our new home with bedroom and lounge curtains. The flight home was just as exciting as the one going out. The descent into Luton was equally as steep and neither my wife nor I could hear properly for quite a few days.

CHAPTER 11
OUR FLIGHT TO CYPRUS

By now, our son, Leigh, was born and we did not have a great deal of money. My first wife had to give up a very good job with the bank to look after our new-born. It was left just to my own wages to support the family. So I took a second job several evenings a week driving taxis to the early hours. The money was quite good especially with tips. The problem was of course that trying to work all day then work into the early hours, the toll was being taken on health and stamina. By the time late spring came I was beginning to feel the pressure, so much so as the remainder of the family noticed. My wife's parents who were stationed in Cyprus on one of the military bases, asked if we wished to join them for a holiday staying at their home. I was now working for a Local Council Authority. I was able to stack up my holiday entitlement, and so with their agreement took a whole month off.

The year was nineteen seventy six and the weather was about to turn unusually continental. I remember going into our local town and into a men's clothes shop to ask for clothes for a hot climate. The shop assistants comments were "how much hotter do you want it?". At this time the roads were melting, and new build estates were turning into a nightmare for developers. Brand new sub-surfaces were drying out cracking, and the final top-surfaces for the roads were again all melting, meaning they had to be completely remade in many instances.

Our flight to Cyprus left at the beginning of August from Heathrow which was absolutely wonderful. Even today I consider this to be the best airport to fly from. We were allowed to take the baby buggy as far as the plane doors where the stewardess took possession to place in the hold. In those days harnesses etc was not so strict. We were given a baby crib that hooked onto the wall in front of us. Leigh was absolutely brilliant and slept most of the journey just dressed in a light baby grow. Sadly, the political problems were still very difficult between Turkey and Greece. As such our flight was not allowed to go over Turkish airspace. Instead, we would have to fly right down to the tip of Italy where we then turned left and flew the entire length of the Mediterranean putting an extra hour on our journey. We arrived finally at Larnaca airport in the early hours. Due to the conflict, it was not possible to fly into the capital city as this was now forming part of the restricted territory by Turkey. As such the British had to very quickly put together an airport that could cater for international travel. Larnaca was chosen and within a few months the British Military had been able to construct a suitable airport. This temporary airport was to remain for a further forty years before a more substantial airport more suitable for international flights would be open.

Trying to make a reasonable impression on my in-laws. I had dressed in a shirt tie and a light-coloured suit. When we arrived in Larnaca at something like two thirty in the morning, it was so hot that I had difficulty keeping the jacket on. When they opened the door for us to leave the aircraft, I made the comment to my first wife how hot the air coming from the engines was. She laughed and pointed out that the engines were at the back of the plane and it was the heat of the night coming in it being the beginning of August and the hottest month of the year. By the time I had got down the steps of the aircraft and reached the tarmac the jacket was over one shoulder, by the time I reached the terminal the tie was off, and quite frankly by the time we exited the terminal I could have happily have walked out in just my underpants it was so hot. The journey from Larnaca to Episkopi near Paphos was going to take another three hours minimum along the newly completed road they called the A5. I should explain that when father-in-law was first in Cyprus in nineteen sixty six they had just started this road. The road itself was no larger than the normal

A roads in this country and certainly was not even a motorway. Ten years later they had just finished it. Talk about a laid-back country!

The next morning after a rather disturbed night's sleep in the heat and the ensuing month I was not going to be disappointed about the weather. It was absolutely scorching. Everything around us that may have resembled grass at one time had turned to a burnt crisp scrub. Each day we would take the bus down to the private beach. The bus was run by a private company but for the sole use of the inhabitants of the estate who all formed part of the personnel on the military base. The journey was only eight minutes but because of the steepness of the climb down and back was too far to walk especially in that heat and pushing a baby in a buggy we used it. It always amused me that approaching the valley floor next to the beach lay the sports fields. Everywhere else as far as the eye could see was completely burnt and parched except these several acres. This area containing lush grass cricket field, tennis courts and leisure field looked so out of place. The British Army in its improvisation had piped in all the waste water (and treated effluent water) to be channelled out through pipes onto the fields giving it such a lush appearance. It really did resemble the old colonial days of the Raj in India. The bus took us through a little tunnel carved out of the cliffs by the British military many years before going onto a pebble beach. The nearest beach previously was some miles along the coast. As such the army opened this previously inaccessible beach by digging the tunnel to it. On this very pebbly beach were three very long huts divided only by three low walls. Each of these three areas had a sign at the entrance. Each sign authorised the rank by which the occupants could enter the areas. Officers on one, NCOs on the next and the non ranking personnel on the last. I find this quite daunting personally given that I was not really used to this form of authoritarian division especially out of work. One day two young children were playing with each other on our particular patio in front of the huts when one asked the other where he lived, and the youngster replied whatever the name of the estate was. Straight away the youngster recognised that the father of the child playing with him was a lesser rank than his own father and without hesitation shouted, "Get off this patio you are not supposed to be here". I just found out the justification why I could never have been a military person. Now the beach we were sitting on had quite a significance several years before our arrival. In nineteen seventy four, some two years previously, the Turks had risen up against the Greeks and swarmed the whole island and would have taken the whole area had the British not been able to administer some form of reason and diplomacy. However, the leader of the Greeks had to flee for his life. The British managed to get hold of him and quickly brought him to the military base then on down to the beach we were lying on while the Turks swarmed the cliffs above and even started shooting at the helicopter as it was taking off carrying the president. What a political mess the whole situation made.

At the top half of the vast military camp where we were staying, protected by barbed wire and guards was this huge open area. Inside this area lined up in military fashion were lorries, buses, vans, cars, hand carts, bikes and anything that was mobile that could be loaded to the full with peoples possessions. These were the abandoned vehicles of those that had to flee their homes during the uprising. Clearly, they were not going to make it with the vehicles so they had to be left behind along with all their possessions by the roadside. The British military gathered them up, put them in this large compound until such time as the conflict was over so that people could regain their possessions. I went back some twenty years later, the compound with its barbed wire is still there, the vehicles etc are still lined up with their cargo that by now has been decimated either by weather or by rodents. Such a terrible shame.

The island of Cyprus has a magnificent history having been occupied from as far back as the Greeks and Romans through to the Crusaders. About twenty miles from the military base and close to the town of Limassol is Kolossi Castle. This was built by Richard the Lion Heart as his country retreat from the holy wars. The small castle is in quite good condition given its age and is now a tourist attraction. At the time of our visit and from the top of the tower looking down over acres and acres of fields below stood what could only be described as American Union type military camp. There were white tents as far as you could see all occupied by the refugees that had fled from the Turkish section now cordoned off from the rest of the world. This was to be their homes for years to come. On my return home I would visit a barber for a haircut and chatting where I had just returned he confessed he was in fact a Greek Cypriot. When I narrowed the conversation to the encampment and what an impact it had on me he said that his own sister was one of the refugees still living there. He had only full praise for the British Army who without them there could have been greater bloodshed.

Although my first wife's father was based in Cyprus to work most days, during his spare time he would show us what I think probably was his favourite places of interest. We would have evening dinner in Limassol at one of the Greek tavern restaurants. Here we were allocated a table for the evening. on the table were displayed old bottles of whiskey rum and any other wine or spirit bottle that would hold spirit. this random assortment of bottles were fill with the local red and white wines. as each bottle was emptied so it was replaced. it was so cheap to buy anyway. in addition we had the task of trying to wade through seven courses of food. However, these were not ordinary courses. on the table with the random assortment of wines were bowls of various salads such as tomatoes lettuce onions cucumbers etc. again as each was emptied so it was replaced. then came the daunting task of each course being put in front of us. the first course was half a chicken. I thought this was wonderful and dutifully ate mine down without hesitation. what I did not realise was that we were then presented with two pork chops each. these chops were huge. following the chops were three skewers of barbecued squares of lamb. this was followed by liver and several other dishes. I really don't know how on earth we were able to consume such a vast amount of barbecued food salads and drink. We would visit Ladies Mile, a peninsula jutting out from Limassol and a short distance from Kollossi Castle. At the end of the peninsula was the RAF base of Akrotiri. Apparently, Ladies mile took its name from when one of the British generals was stationed there years ago. One of the lower ranks would have to exercise his wife's horse along the straight sands of the peninsula. This gave access to the sea which was so shallow it was good for the horses. It was indeed so shallow that you could wade out a hundred yards and still only be up to your waist. If you then sat down in the crystal, clear water small fish would then swim around you.

As for the remainder of the Cyprus area that we could explore

I was just blown away by its beauty and its history. I was of course only mid twenties at the time and still quite young to appreciate the history of the place yet it would all leave a lasting impression on me. We had driven down to the rather scruffy town of Paphos for lunch. The town had not seen anywhere near the investment of wealth and construction that was about to benefit it. The main road was literally a scruffy road past small taverns, cafes and shops to the harbour and beyond. After lunch father-in-law drove beyond the town a short distance and stopped the vehicle. He pointed out the edge of the sand dunes and told us to walk over and look out for the holes in the ground. We were just blown away to find was turned out to be the ancient ruins of the tombs of the kings. These burial chambers that were huge and laid underground were laying unprotected without fence or guards just laying there for anyone to investigate open to the elements. These huge tombs were laid in solid stone with separate chambers holding several coffins. To have them just open to the world was quite incredible. Of course, today these are a massive part of the tourist attraction to Paphos. Not only have they uncovered more burial tombs, they are within the boundaries of Paphos. Folks are charged to walk and explore the area. Inside the area there is the most magnificent roman villa complete with its exquisite large mosaics. These mosaics are under cover now to protect them, but the colours are still retained after several thousand years.

One day John my father-in-law asked if we wanted to accompany him down to Limassol as he had to visit a tailor he knew. We went down with him and while he was in the tailors we had a wander around the shops and stalls along the street. We ended up picking up a huge leather suitcase the size of which I had not seen before. The price was ridiculously cheap and would certainly get all our belongings back to the UK. John then reappeared carrying a suit bag with a suit inside. It turned out that he had been in Cyprus in the mid nineteen-sixties and had called at the tailors for a new suit to be made. He was duly measured but after the second fitting and before he could bring away the completed garment he was to return back to the UK. He advised the tailor that he would have to leave the suit with him but that he would return and would the tailor hold on to it on the basis that John would pay for the completed garment. Here we were ten years later and sure enough the suit had been kept all that time safe and protected. What is more interesting is that it also still fitted him.

Several miles south of Limassol sitting on top of the cliffs overlooking the Mediterranean Sea lies the ancient city of Kyrenia which had been mostly destroyed by earthquake during roman times. The researchers had systematically over the years exposed the walls and the mosaics. On the other side of the now modern road from the ancient ruins lies the fully re-constructed roman amphitheatre. Parts of it were discovered after years of being buried. Each piece was removed cleaned and systematically replaced in the order they belonged. The amphitheatre was carved out of the side of the cliffs where live performances could be shown. Now, after its reconstruction it is still used for live performances with the ocean as its backdrop. All in all I fell in love with Cyprus. I have revisited the island three times now and each time I learn more and more about its history.

Life as military personnel was not all bad, I must confess. First of all there was the little bus that took folks either to the beach or to the facilities on the camp free of charge. At the top of the estate was a shopping area with an open-air cinema, shops and a supermarket. Everything was subsidised. On entering the air-conditioned supermarket, it resembled our own type of mini-markets back home. One would push a little trolley round selecting the shopping needed, return to the till for paying. Here one chap rang up the totals while another packed the shopping into boxes. Payment was by way of card and then the shopping was left while we caught the bus back home. Within a couple of hours there was a knock at the door and the shopping was delivered by one of the drivers from the supermarket. In the officer's mess close to the shops every Sunday there was a buffet type lunch offered for a very small charge. Here long tables covered with starch white cloths held dish upon dish of various salads, fruits and other add ons for the curries that were served or other tasty offerings. Each person was served by non-ranking personnel again in best uniform all in something like thirty five degrees of brilliant sunshine and heat. It was for want of a better word "cuckoo land" no wonder so many couldn't settle when they finally go back to England and found they were not going to be treated as special and as cheaply. Many folks ended up buying properties in the village close by the base. Again, you could tell by what ranks those retired homeowners were by the location and prices of the houses bought. The military discrimination was still maintained in the cafes and bars of the local Cypriots. One story that did bring the personnel together despite rank occurred shortly before we had arrived. The countryside was so dry that it caught fire. The fire slowly spread and came towards one of the three housing estates on the base. Needless to say, the men of the estate gathered together irrespective of rank to fight the fire. I say the men of the estate but this did not include one particular character who refused to help. His reason was simple. To fight the fire you have to be in front of it as it approached you. Now Cyprus is renowned for its infestation of snakes. Apparently, Cleopatra introduced wild cats to the island to try to combat the problem. The cats are still there today and you should expect visits from the feral creatures should you visit the restaurants and cafes. Anyway, our reluctant volunteer had the theory that if the fire was coming towards him and he was standing there trying to put it out then the fire would drive the snakes towards him and that was a fate he was not willingly going to face.

Being located on a military base it was easy to quickly get to meet and socialise with the neighbours who were also military and worked there. One pair of such neighbours who lived several doors down had come for a barbecue one evening. The wife was asking Rose, my mother-in-law some advice regarding a vegetable they had found growing in the bottom the garden. They didn't recognise it as such although it had been purposely sown and grown presumably by the previous occupants. The plant was quite tall with green leaves etc., and for all intents and purposes was intended to be cooked and eaten as a vegetable with a main meal. However this couple had found that the vegetable had very little to no taste and was very tough to chew and eat despite boiling for some time. Rose being even more curious as the story unfolded asked them if she could see what this vegetable was. The husband disappeared and came back with a stem sample for Rose to inspect. She unfortunately burst out laughing. What had been grown and what they were trying to cook and eat was in fact a loofah, which when harvested and dried is then used as a back scrubber in the bath or shower. I think they both had red faces for some time to come.

Our month soon passed, and we were back at the airport for our flight back to the UK. Although I am fair coloured my skin seems to have the oils of my mother. As such I had tried vigorously to return home with some form of tan that friends would spot. However, within a few days home I was greeted with "well for someone who has been away for a month you haven't got much of a tan". I now have accepted that I turn three colours. I start off white, turn red then to a rust colour and soon revert to white. Hey ho! at least I can go out in the sun and the only difficulty is that I must wear sunglasses to avoid the glare.

CHAPTER 12
OUR "WEEKEND" ANNUAL HOLIDAY

I suppose if any reason could have given for not taking an annual holiday in this country, your next such holiday would be the justification. By now my son was eighteen months old. We didn't have a lot of money as my wife, who gave up a very good job with the bank to have our first child, was not working so it was merely my money supporting the family. I had downsized our family car to a small Vauxhall Chevette hatchback which was still large enough to break down the pram for the base frame and the cot section to fit in the back. We still had the camping gear and camping then was still quite a cheap holiday. Various friends had recommended us to go to Wales and in particular the Gower Peninsula. I had never been, but looking at the map and studying the camping books, it did look like an ideal holiday for a family with a young toddler in tow. We set off late Friday afternoon and soon cleared the Bristol Channel and the Severn Bridge. We were past Swansea and Cardiff and heading for West Wales. It was early evening, and I suppose that did not help what was fast approaching us. The sky became a dark dirty grey colour with the surrounding landscape to match. The roads, the adjoining fields, the houses and surrounding buildings all seemed to be a mix of dirty brown or black, mixed with grey and dark dank colours. To make matters worse there seemed to be an abundance of chimneys spewing out flame, smoke and fire which seemed to be mixing with the already horrid landscape. We were approaching the area around Port Talbot.

If ever one wanted to describe a picture of hell this must surely, be it. How anyone could have existed in these awful surroundings I have no idea. My heart sank thinking this was Wales. I have never ever forgotten that experience. We did eventually pass through and arrived at Tenby and having found the camp site pitched up the tent and settled down with the youngster for the evening. During the night it started raining quite heavily and again into the next day. This was not over useful with a very lively eighteen-month-old who wanted to simply get up and run around. We tolerated a day inside the tent but then discovered this weather was likely to be with us at least for the following week. This would be a disaster. So, a quick re-calculation and we decided to abort the mission. I was up early packing away, we put the wet tent back on the roof rack and we set off back to England. We passed through that awful Armageddon which didn't look any better in daylight to arrive on the English side of the Bristol Channel. We were only ninety miles from Devon, so we turned right and drove down the M5 to Brixham the place of my youth. It was a nice sunny day and so we had a stroll round the harbour, having lunch before we set off for the camp site. It was not till we were about to leave the town when the heavens opened and it poured. Local knowledge confirmed that the weather that had hit Wales was now covering ourselves and again not expected to go for at least a week. This now was a catastrophe. Reluctantly we had no option, we packed our little fella back in the car, and set off for home. He happily slept in the back until just after Oxford and bless him for the last three quarters of an hour before we reached home did cry quite a bit. Given the time and distance we had travelled he had been very patient and had done very well. We arrived home very late that Sunday evening. I didn't bother unpacking the car till the next day. However, the sun came out and we spent the remainder of our holiday in the comfort of our own home and back garden taking day trips to fill in the gaps. This simply reiterated the decision taken many years ago by my parents to abandon holidays in this country if fine was weather was required and head to the continent.

CHAPTER 13

CARAVANING AT THE WITTERINGS

By now my daughter was born and as we were still not able to afford an expensive holiday, we jumped at the opportunity of a friend of a friend's mobile home at the Witterings on the South Coast. I had never heard of the place and had to look it up on the map. We only had a week, but the weather stayed fine, and we had a really good bucket and spade holiday with the children enjoying the freedom of the safe camp site and on the lovely beach. A chap next to us had a small sailing dinghy. Now with all the things I have tried sailing was indeed one sport that had eluded me. I asked him if he wouldn't mind taking me out one afternoon to suit his time scale. The afternoon arrived and we wheeled the dinghy down to the shoreline. The chap ran through the procedure of putting up the mast, adding the sails, the rudder and all the paraphernalia. Soon we had launched, and he showed me where to sit while we sailed parallel to the shoreline up and down and up and down. I couldn't believe that you could get lost so close to the shoreline or indeed that time disappeared so quickly concentrating on the importance of keeping the boat upright and steering it and controlling the wind at the same time. It only seemed we had been in the water for about half an hour when the chap told me it was time to turn round and head back to the beach. The poor chap was absolutely shattered. When we got back, he really was beat. I had to take over dismantling most of the dinghy. The chap was in his sixties and we had been out over three and a half hours, so I felt really guilty for my enthusiasm at keeping him out so long. He did tell me afterwards that he had really enjoyed our trip together and was one of the best he had while on that holiday. I had now really got the bug for sailing and was to shortly enrol for a sailing course on our own local lake and eventually purchase my own dinghy for my own use and enjoyment.

The area itself is very flat and ideal for young families to have a nice, relaxed holiday near the sea. There is not a lot of seaside amenities or amusements but for most that re-visited the area this was an ideal location for them. We certainly had a lovely rest albeit it for the week. We took the children to the beach each day which meant they slept very well each night. I always think that when a lovely restful time is had on holiday the time goes very quickly This was the case of this short but very beneficial holiday.

CHAPTER 14
OUR FIRST CARAVAN TRIP

Having been a camper all my life one golden rule when arriving on a camp site we would always look out for any caravans and avoid camping near them like the plague. Caravan folks always seem to have this belief that once inside their tin house on wheels nobody could hear them moving about. Of course the old caravans being made of wooden boards etc., the flooring sounded like a ball room dance floor on a Friday night at the local church hall and we have had a few nights "suffering other's noises". The thought of even owning a caravan put us all in dread with the accidents that we had witnessed together with the actual problems of towing etc. It was therefore somewhat against the grain when I actually decided to purchase my own caravan. I had been given assurances of a very good friend of mine who had bought one and was having a wonderful time. I was assured that all the problems of the past were now ironed out with the new modern designed caravans. Having now two young children I thought this would be ideal weekend and holiday breaks for the future. Something that helped make up my mind was the thought that we would remain dry inside if it rains, be able to keep warm and have a cooker and all the mod cons onboard. We looked round and found a CI Musketeer which was quite a lump of a caravan. It had two dining areas one at each end that could be made up as beds. The idea would be to make one end up as a double for ourselves, the children sleeping in sleeping bags on the singles at the other end as needed. The caravan came with its own awning and looked perfect for what we were looking for. I had bought a Vauxhall Cavalier with a 2 litre engine that should be more than capable. I bought the customary wing mirror extensions and we were all ready for the off. I was later to discover that the Cavalier was more of a sports model than a towing vehicle as it hand soft shell big ends and was not designed to tow. Just as well I did not know this prior to setting off. As a destination we chose a camp site, in North Devon that was an area that neither of us had been to before. The brochure that advertised the site looked lovely. It was a large friendly site with a club house, children's facilities including a play area and we thought this would be ideal with two youngsters under five. Now the journey down I must openly confess was not the most comfortable of journeys nerves wise. All the nightmares I had heard about came true. The caravan was larger than I thought and it was difficult to manoeuvre round corners. Everything that went in the opposite direction shook the caravan violently. On the motorway lorries, coaches, vans and everything else that passed seemed to give the caravan a mind of its own. The snaking of a heavy caravan behind is quite unnerving. Someone had given me the advice to keep an eye open for fast travelling coaches and lorries. As these large vehicles approached and could be seen in the tow mirror to slow down and as they appear to pull along-side and you could feel the "wash" of air they push before them to slowly accelerate with them. As they pass you are still maintaining a pulling momentum to help. It did, slightly. The problem was that even with extended mirrors you didn't spot the blighters till they were virtually on top of the caravan. I couldn't brake and by the time I had tried to slow down and then accelerate again the caravan was off once more heading for the hard shoulder. It was a nightmare and travelling down the M4 then M5 on a Friday evening with the amount of traffic didn't help one bit. By the time we arrived in North Devon having the final excitement of narrow roads and lanes to navigate pulling the monster behind I was somewhat a bag of nerves.

We arrived on site, in one piece, luckily with nothing damaged. We found a spot slightly away from the cliff edge and set the caravan up with the awning on the side furthest away from the cliffs. All seemed wonderful and our journey was quickly put to one side worrying about the return home in a couple of weeks. We settled in for what we hoped to be a great fortnight in our new home on box on wheels. The children really took to it well going to bed and sleeping through. I was slowly becoming converted myself being able to go inside where it was warmer, drier, quieter and more cosy. The camp site was as it was made out to be with the children's play areas and entertainment and the beach was just as lovely. All went well for a couple of days. One evening after a couple of nice days we noticed the wind was getting up. We weren't too worried as we had the caravan and felt safe and cosy inside. Some of the tent owners were beginning to roll out their extra guy ropes and storm straps just in case the weather turned nasty. That night all hell broke loose. The wind and the rain coming in off the Irish sea was not going to be kind. The caravan rocked furiously. The awning was still up and was squeaking and rocking like an old whore's bed. This particular design had spring suckers against the caravan walls. These suckers took a lot of the shock of the wind effects thank goodness. The children were fast asleep, and I lay there, in the dark listening to the rain, the wind and the squeaking thinking how lucky we were not to be in the old tent. I was all cosy warm and tucked in. The next morning the storm seemed to have passed as it was a lot calmer. It was then that I looked out of the window and saw the carnage that had been created during the night. There was a lot of activity with car doors banging and folks stomping around with what sounded like lumps of metal banging against each other. I couldn't believe what I was looking at. My first impressions was that the camp site had been turned into a first world war battlefield enactment. There were trenches dug, piles of soil, peoples' possessions, bit of tents, poles and all sorts of debris strewn everywhere. Folks had been hanging on for dear life to their tents. It required at least one person hanging on to each corner where they could. Others had been digging trenches in the dark trying to keep water from the insides and the whole scene was just chaos. During the course of the morning the early birds that had been up all night trying to save their possessions as best they could had packed away and were slowly leaving the camp site. They were quickly followed by the remainder of the campers forming an orderly line exiting the field throughout the morning and early afternoon till in the end there were just a few of us left, mainly caravans.

We stayed for a few more days, although the weather was not

fantastic and then decided to make a run for it ourselves. We packed away the relatively dry awning and ground sheet, made sure everything was secure inside the caravan and pulled off the field back into the narrow lanes heading for the motorway. To add insult to injury I had not gone many miles when a vehicle coming the other way either had a grudge against other road users or perhaps caravanners in particular. Whatever his motives were, he was not going to share the road with us and clipped the side of the wing mirror cleanly taking off the extension mirror to beyond repair. This left me blind on that side for the remainder of the journey making the preparation time of over-taking vehicles even less and adding to the anxiety and pressures of getting family, car and caravan home in one piece. We did get home, after quite a few hair-raising hours with the vow "never again". We later found out that the storm that we had suffered while caravanning on the cliff tops of the North Devon Coast was to become known as the famous Fastnet disaster. The storm that had arrived from out in the Atlantic was vicious. It was so severe that out in the Irish sea ocean going yachts taking part in the Fastnet race were being blown off course, having their masts destroyed and in quite a few cases lives were lost with the boats actually sinking. From a nautical point of view that night turned out to be an absolute disaster.

The caravan was positioned on the front lawn where it remained till it was sold. Luckily not long after advertising it, a lady came round to look at it fell in love with it and asked if she could have first refusal at the asking price. She then told us she hated the tent she had bought and wanted to sell it with all the gear before she purchased the caravan. A few questions and photos later and we clinched the deal that I would take the camping trailer, which was about a metre square, and half meter deep. Inside the trailer was a brand-new tent all the camping gear including camp kitchen with cooker, the air beds and sleeping bags. In fact, everything we needed. The lady swapped and gave us in addition the sum of £400 for the caravan. I would have paid her the £400 had she known. I was absolutely over the moon and with the money banked started planning our next holiday which was definitely going to be abroad.

CHAPTER 15

BACK TO THE CONTINENT

With a virtually brand new large frame tent we were ready to head back abroad and have perhaps a wonderful memorable holiday. The tent was one of the best I had ever owned either before or since. The tent had all the mod cons including sleeping areas for the four of us; a kitchen area, a massive inside porch area, plus all the gear. We were ready to have a holiday of a lifetime, especially given the recent year's disasters. Where else could we guarantee warmth and sunshine, but in Italy. My parents by this time had found a wonderful camp site on the shores of Lake Maggiore south of Arona and invited us to join them. I engineered that we would arrive, within a few days before their own departure back to the UK. This way they would not get bored with us and vice versa. I had my customary month off work so booked the ferry and was ready to go with car trailer and all the camping gear.

At the beginning of the summer however, I managed to fulfil another dream I had since our weekend away in the Witterings. I had fallen in love with a sailing dinghy that someone I knew was selling cheap, and purchased it - the Proctor Merlin sailing dinghy which was a one off special. It had been designed by the mast and sail expert Proctor. It had proved to be a huge success as a family boat as opposed to a primary racing dinghy. It had a large area inside for everyone to sit in as well as a large mast to take two sets of sails, one for touring and one for racing. The boat itself came on its own road trailer. For myself to handle it was perfect. I could launch and retrieve the boat myself in our local lakes and was an absolute beauty to sail being very user friendly. As we were about to go to one of the largest lakes in Italy, and I wondered why we weren't taking the dinghy with us instead of the new camping trailer. The cockpit area was larger than the trailer, the boat sturdy enough to withstand the camping equipment and the road trailer perfectly adequate to tow the boat and its contents. A quick phone call to the P&O Ferries to ask a change of ticket to accommodate the larger trailer and the whole thing was booked ready to go. The camping equipment and all the children's toys including bikes were loaded everything covered and tied down and we were ready for the off. Friday night is always difficult for travel to any seaport especially Dover which was very busy all the way down the motorway. In those days the motorway finished some miles short of Dover, and the last sixteen miles had to be driven on normal coastal A roads. We were in a line of traffic, by now on the downward slope heading down into Dover when the steering wheel started to play up showing there was something wrong. Now to stop on this road, was going to be pretty dangerous. The verges either side of the road were high banks, there were no lay-bys as such and the traffic in and out of Dover was very busy. However, I had no choice when I encountered a grinding noise and the trailer seemed to be wanting to overtake me. I stopped dead. The traffic came to a grinding halt. I got out of the car and revealed that the inside wheel of the trailer had collapsed inwards. The bearing had completed disintegrated. This left the wheel hanging on the inside of the axle with the outside of the axle resting virtually on the floor. I began to panic. I couldn't drive backwards or forwards. I couldn't leave the car stranded or indeed the trailer on its own at the side of the road given the volume of traffic now building up. Lucky for us some students, with backpacks were walking up the hill and spotted our dilemma. There were enough of them to be able to lift the back end and using it as a wheelbarrow resting on the right offside tyre could propel the trailer forward as I drove very slowly and sheepishly to the lay-by that was in fact only a couple of hundred yards in front of us. We eventually reached the lay-by much to our relief and probably that of the traffic most of which were heading for the docks for scheduled sailings. I thanked the hikers who all shook our hands and set off up the hill once more. Another stroke of luck was that a police car was now with us having come across our dilemma. He was able to radio the local garage, who happened to be an AA repair garage, to come out and retrieve us from what was still a very precarious car park. He took car and boat on the back of the lorry and us into Dover. The driver very carefully reversed off the one-way street under an archway between shops into his garage (a mean feat in itself) dispatched trailer then car and we unhooked the car from the boat. We then through the aid of the AA located a local hotel for the night. The garage could not do anything until the Saturday morning when spare bearings could be bought. We got the children into the hotel, had something to eat and trying to make light of a rather disastrous situation put the children down for the night. We eventually joined them but needless to say my mind was going overtime as to the repairs, the cost, the time lost, the missed boat. So much so that at midnight I had to get up, get dressed, left my first wife with children and drove to the dock to enquire what would happen now we had lost our sailing. I was assured by a lovely lady that all was not lost. This was a calculated situation that happened regularly, and all boats catered for late arrivals and non arrivals. I went back to bed a more contented man.

The following day we had breakfast then contacted the garage who were now having problems locating replacement bearings. The nearest would be a supplier in Ashford quite some miles back inland. There was also the problem as to whether the supplier would remain open on a Saturday long enough for a driver to go and collect. By one o'clock we were in luck. The bearings had been located, fitted and the trailer, with boat was all ready for departure. I signed the docket to clear the payment through the AA; cleared the excess and completed the short distance from the town to the dock. Within the hour we were boarded and heading for France. Even though the garage had done a wonderful job you still have this nagging doubt as to whether something else was going to go wrong. I would worry whilst travelling all through France, as to whether we were going to break down again but I needn't have worried.

It was mid afternoon by the time we had cleared the docks at Calais. We had a long way to go and very little light left to do it in. I decided to take what was then the quickest route on motorways via

Paris. This meant the dreaded Perifique. I should describe this as a four-lane ring road round inner Paris. The motorway was always very busy and very congested although the traffic still seemed to scream along at breakneck speeds. Normally there wouldn't be a problem overtaking but now I had the car and eighteen feet of boat and trailer on the back. The drivers do not take prisoners. The journey round was an absolute nightmare. In the end I took to tagging behind the lorries who were heading south and would get me through. Eventually we found the sign heading south and exited the dreaded nightmare to carry on towards our destination. We got through France and into Switzerland. We were able to catch the late morning train from Brig in Switzerland through the mountains to Italy. Within a couple of hours drive in Italy we were hugging and greeting all friends of my parents on the camp site on Lake Maggiore.

We had an added problem this holiday. The two children were under 5 years old, and both had blond to virtually white hair. The Italians just fell in love with them. Every where they went it was "Bella Bella" and touching their heads and stroking their faces. The children were not used to this type of attention, and were a little frightened at first. I say at first. My daughter soon worked out she was on a winner here. Putting on the hang dog expression with those big blue eyes and blond hair she had them totally melting in front of her. The pair of them would come back with sweets, biscuits and all sorts of treats. I was so worried one day that they had helped themselves that I marched them to one of the couple's holiday home where the lady apologised thinking she had done something wrong.

The children had a wonderful holiday. The camp site was split into rows of tree covered plots where tents and caravans could pitch. At the end of the rows the little track led to a gateway. From the gateway access could be gained to the edge of the lake where a beach had been formed. Access to the clear crystal warm water was safe and secure for the children without any dangers. As for me well I had the sailing dinghy. I didn't get out every day and when I did it was normally late morning. I quickly discovered that the wind on Lake Maggiore had a timer with it. Every day, at 1.00pm the wind would disappear. I know I wasn't a complete novice, but I really couldn't work out what I was doing wrong. I had the largest sails on, yet the boat was going absolutely nowhere. Yet other sailors seemed to be motoring along without any difficulty whatsoever. Motoring was the operative word, because when one of the blighters drew close, I noted he, and afterwards all of them had small outboard motors attached to the back ready for such eventuality. I had to resort to getting the oars out and rowing back. So humiliating!

One afternoon, with children on board having sailed down about four miles towards the Swiss border and where the lake extends into the larger area, the wind suddenly died. We had stopped at a little resort on the lakes edge for a spot of lunch and let the children play. However, with the wind now disappeared it was a case of out with the oars and having to try to row the several miles back to the camp site. The children were fine no problems at all, waving at the swimmers, waving at other boats, waving at the sun worshipers on the shorelines as we passed. In the distance however, behind them but where I was facing, there were some rather nasty dark sinister clouds that seemed to be settling over the Alps dividing Switzerland and Italy and rather angrily racing towards us. So much so my rowing became a little more urgent as the clouds and pending storm approached. I was extremely grateful to reach the little beach annexing the camp site and even though the children were wearing life jackets lifted them off and onto terra firma to await the inevitable storm. By this time the winds had arrived. The locals had all gone into a semi panic. They had retreated off the beaches, folks were crossing themselves while trying to drag ashore boats and other floatable objects. As for us having beached and got the children safe I saw this wonderful opportunity of getting some serious sailing in. I had the racing sales already up which gives a far greater sail cover. I donned my all in one sailing suit which has rubberised water proof sleeves and neck line, my sailing Wellingtons that seal below the knees put my life jacket back on with the obligatory woolly fisherman's hat on my head and launched myself out into the lake. The faces of the Italian onlookers was amazing. I am sure they thought I was crackers. As for me, the winds came hurtling down the lake, I just sailed from one side of the lake to the other and back again. The whole dinghy literally rose to float on top of the surface as I absolutely flew back and forth. The opposite side of the dinghy was virtually dragging through the water as I put my whole body out as far as I could reach while holding on to the tiller in one hand and the sheets or ropes with the other. The most amazing couple of hours sailing I would ever probably experience before or after. I loved it and didn't want to call it to an end.

This part of the world is an amazing, interesting and varied country. There is so much history here. The first umbrellas were made not far from our camp site so there is literally an umbrella museum up into the hills. There is a large statue of Saint Carlo on the hill above the town looking down to the lake below. Any visitor can first of all climb the spiral ladder to the skirt of the statue. For those brave enough there is a ladder that can be climbed inside the body of the statue right up into the head. The head is large enough to hold a couple of adults or in my case an adult and two children. From here to look down through the nostrils and out the eyes and ears and there was the most amazing view of the lake and surrounding mountains beyond. In the vicinity of the lake there are old churches to visit, old towns and markets, it is all just wonderful. There are boat rides and all to keep the tourist fully occupied. We had a wonderful month. The people on the camp site were just so friendly. We were fed and watered by so many families who invited us to their various tents and caravans to join them for evening meals, barbecues or just drinks. The characters here were wonderful. There was one guy who was a huge character. He would get up very early three times a week and his job was to deliver supplies to the local high security prison. He was then finished for the rest of the week. He would take his little wooden canoe out on the lake first light and laying down paddle with what looked like a pair of pink pong bats and slowly work his way round the edge of the lake between the reeds sometimes fishing sometimes hunting and whatever he caught he would bring back and cook that evening. The trout he caught would be wrapped in tin foil having first laid butter spices herbs rosemary into the inside and the final offering was just exquisite. He was sat there one day and with a very strong local Italian dialect summoned me over to sit on his veranda and eat what to me looked like Twiglets. I asked him what they were and gave me a name that I didn't recognise and asked if he meant chicken. "chicken" he laughed and shouted to some of the other folks close by that I thought I was eating chicken. My youngster then came over and rather curious asked if he could try. Brazilio, the guy, looked very serious and waved his finger that the youngster should not eat these as they clearly were not good for children. What the hell was I eating. Eventually my father came over with the dictionary and having looked up "rarne" discovered this was in fact frogs legs, they crunched like Twiglets, tasted like nothing I had tasted before and needless to say didn't bother finishing the basket. What we did though was to open up his huge basket that held bottles of red wine and were soon joined by the other local Italian campers and ended up having a very jolly evening with home-made Italian wine. At about one o'clock in the morning Brazilio slaps his bare belly and shouts in Italian "hungry" looks at me "you hungry?" I think he said, so I said "yes". His wife suddenly disappeared and half an hour later returned with the largest stainless steel cauldron I have ever seen full of white spaghetti which is basically cooked spaghetti in butter. What a feast to finish off a wonderful evening.

The next morning it was a tradition that if you were up first you wandered up to the café at the edge of the camp site. Here you sat away from those you had been with the evening before. Quietly sit, have your coffee and your cake taking in the thoughts of the day and quietly waking up. You might nod but nobody interrupted your space - nor did you interrupt others space. Within an hour of returning to the tent and life fully returned to the camp site everyone laughing and enjoying the day.

Now in those days the Italians were a bit like the French. They were not over enthusiastic about the Germans. Most Germans passed by anyway on their way to the coast so very rarely did they stop. However, there were the occasional night stops. The Italians had a special field set aside for them. What they called the transit camp. Now our camping spot was situated between two large trees which had been specially planted along with all the others down the entire avenue on both sides of the track which gave each tent or caravan the shade and coolness necessary in such intense summer heat. The transit camp was open to the elements and was extremely uncomfortable for anyone to want to stay beyond a night. We did have one family who strayed into the avenue and found a space down the bottom close by the toilets. That evening the chap who occupied a form of chalet opposite suddenly opened up with a snare drum. This drum was accompanied by some awful singing which went on to the early hours. The next night the same. Eventually the Germans left and we never heard the snare drum again. He convinced himself that he had helped drive the family out. I disagreed with this doctrine myself but being a foreigner in another country didn't express my approval or distaste just accepted that this was their way.

We had got quite friendly with Paolo the head of one of the families living in these chalet type mobile bungalows opposite our tent. He asked if he could take us out for the day. The children were more than happy staying with my parents so we could be free for the day. We left first thing and drove off back towards the mountains leaving the lake road at Stresa and headed inland. We had to cross over some rather steep wooded hills. It was here we passed through a village that held the famous umbrella museum that I had often heard and read about. When we dropped down the other side we were in a beautiful forested valley with its own lake. We headed to the north of this lake called Lago D`Orta to the little village at the far end. Here we had to leave the car at the top of the village as the entire village was for pedestrians only. We then descended down stone steps into this most beautiful yellow stone village that must have been over a thousand years old. We passed along its narrow-cobbled streets past houses, little cafes and novelty shops. There was even the smallest church I had ever seen beautifully adorned in bright colours of golds and reds etc., the church couldn't have been much larger than a corner shop, nestled between houses. It dated back to the 11th century and was just breath taking. The little cobbled street then took us into the main piazza. Here on three sides were cafes, restaurants, tables and chairs where morning coffee could be taken overlooking the lake. The sun is late arriving here due to the high mountains but had just crept up and was now shining its brilliance down on us. As we sat there looking out over this picturesque tranquil lake there in the middle is a small island with what looked like a castle built on it. It was in fact home for a closed order of nuns. As we sat and watched so we could see several nuns being rowed the short distance from the island back to the mainland. It all in all was the most wonderful view to remember. I would re-visit this area many times and still find it as beautiful and peaceful as the first visit. Paolo wanted to get on so we retraced our steps back through the village up the stone steps to the car and headed off. He took us even deeper into the mountains. Here the region is called the Monti Rosa Mountains as they take on a pink effect in the sunshine. He wanted to take us to what he described as a lovely restaurant in the mountains for lunch. Now the Italians have a different viewpoint on the word's lovely restaurant to us. We would expect a lush building, expensive carpets and furniture, pristine waiters and service. So when we walked into what looked nothing better than a motorway café we were both rather disappointed. However, when the food arrived, we could see why he had described it so well, the cuisine was just amazing. Now the Italians don't rush when they are eating, and two hours can easily slip by which was the case today. By the time we left it was mid afternoon. We were expecting to start heading back. Instead, we headed even deeper into the mountains. First of all, we stopped off at a small textile factory owned by Paolo where he wanted to show us what he manufactured and where. The textiles he produced was of very high quality in fact he gave me a roll of cloth that I was supposed to take to a tailor back in England for a suit to be made. The cloth had the words "Tuscini" written on it. After forty years I have still got the roll of cloth and still can't afford to have the suit made. Paolo also gave me what looked like some form of wooden boat. This was in fact a weavers bobbin. It would shoot backwards and forwards carrying the thread between the cloth as it moved up and down on the machines. Paolo suggested I had my name scrolled onto the tin plate on the front which again took some thirty years to do. In the meantime, the bobbin has sat proudly on my office desk in all the places I have worked, and now on my antique desk still holding pens, pencils, paper clips etc., We left his factory after a walk round and again headed deeper into the mountains. It seems that Paolo and his family owned a mountain refuge, a form of stone building with a stone roof, that they could visit in the summer. Obviously in the winter it wouldn't be accessible due to deep snow and adverse conditions. At the refuge we were joined by a friend of Paolo's who brought with him the customary home-made wine and mountain cheeses. We had a wonderful picnic there on that glorious location amongst the pink mountains gorging on local Italian wine and munching on a selection of salami meats and mountain cheeses. Paolo's friend gave us a medium sized mountain cheese to bring away for ourselves from the mountains. It was saved till we got home and when we could celebrate the most wonderful holiday at home with a bottle of wine brought home with us. From the mountains it didn't seem to take any time at all to drop down to the lakeside and back along to Arona and the camp site. The children were absolutely fine having been spoilt rotten by the Italian mums and my parents.

Eventually all good things come to an end and it was time to

leave. I think everyone was in tears. The children were crying because they didn't want to leave their new friends, the mothers were crying because the children were crying. We were crying, because we had been shown such a wonderful time and so the drive back to the train taking us back through the mountains was in very sullen silence. We travelled through Switzerland stopping the evening at my favourite site in Vallorbe putting the tent up and settling in to complete the final leg the next morning. Once we had eaten, we put the children down and then sat in the evening warmth talking lightly and drinking a few glasses of wine brought with us. Vallorbe was not very large and I suppose for the teenagers the excitement was to gather at the gates of the campsite to see what girls/boys had arrived for them to chat to. This evening was no exception and soon we had a gathering of some eighteen teenagers. Some of the youngsters were riding these irritating mopeds that they rev and think are Harley Davidsons and eventually became more than an irritation. The camp steward had gone home so we were all rather left to the mercy of these noisy gatherers. Now having young children trying to sleep does drive one to get up and say something. I walked over to this group and basically told them by pointing at my watch that enough was enough. With gestures I suggested they should keep quiet. The most extraordinary thing then took place. Every single one of these noisy "louts" both males and females came over to me, offered to shake my hand and apologised for the inconvenience and noise and then quietly disappeared. Remarkable. I still think to this day what reaction you would get from most youngsters in our country if you went to ask them to be quiet or even worse to go away.

We left at a reasonable hour to make the final journey back to

Calais. There is a set schedule to keep so not too much time can be spent site seeing or stops. We were well ahead of our time to catch the ferry back to the UK and I had put behind me the nightmare we had suffered on the way down. Suddenly there was a huge explosion and the boat trailer started rumbling. Oh lord, not again. Pulling over I discovered that now we had a puncture. Out with the jack up with the axle, off with the wheel, on with the new wheel and then off again. We were now behind schedule. I drove as fast as my situation would allow. We arrived in Calais and racing through the streets overtaking with my long load of car and twenty-foot trailer we raced to get to the gates. Before the entrance we saw the boat that we should be catching with no vehicles on the quay so my hard drive for the past eight hours was down to minutes and looked like I was going to lose. We reached the gate, my heart was pounding handed the tickets to the guy sitting at the window who calmly, quietly and gently looked at me and simply said "calm down sir, no need to rush, you have plenty of time" I didn't know whether to laugh, cry or swear! We caught out boat and got home safely from what was one of the most remarkable holidays.

CHAPTER 16

HOLIDAY IN AUSTRIA

In nineteen-eighty my then parents-in-law were getting prepared to enjoy retirement. Unfortunately for them, their plans had to be put on hold as they ended up having to take a very urgent posting to Austria. The chap that the father-in-law was to replace had been diagnosed with terminal cancer and had to return to the UK quickly. The parents in law departure was very rapid and they were gone within weeks. They did send word however that the house that had been rented for them was large enough for members of the family to go and visit should any of us desire. I had started a new job which came with a company car, a Granada 2.8. This was powerful enough and comfortable enough to take us as a family to Austria and back even though it was a very long way. The destination was situated in the far east of Austria close to the border with a then communist country. We set two weeks aside for our vacation and booked the ferries. My father-in-law said it should take me two days to drive and suggested various overnight stops given we were not camping. Having travelled since I was very young and over long distances without breaks other than comfort stops, I studied the maps and worked out the best times to leave. If I left for early afternoon, the children would enjoy the excitement of the trip down, the boat crossing and then by the time they got bored we could put them down in the back seat to sleep. The ruse worked brilliantly. We caught the early afternoon boat, cleared France by four am and was through Belgium and into

Germany by seven that evening. We stopped at a motorway service area for something to eat and drink then setting the children down for the evening sleep, I could press on. I drove the entire motorway of Germany arriving in Salzburg in Austria for three in the morning with still the width of Austria to clear. We finally arrived at the city of Graz in the far east of the country. We came off the motorway heading up towards the hills where the village was located. Finding the house just before seven in the morning and knocking on the door my father-in-law came to the door and you could see he was physically bowled over that we had in fact driven the fifteen hundred miles nonstop. At that moment I still felt I could drive on being fuelled by my adrenalin and chewing gum. However, having gone inside I sat in the armchair awaiting my cup of tea. The last thing I remember was my elbow slipping down as I dropped into instant sleep where I stayed for the next couple of hours.

To say we had discovered a wonderful new beautiful world would be an under- statement. This part of Austria is very rural. Most of the locals still dressed in traditional costumes and drove about on their tractors. It seemed so peculiar to see the women arriving in the village for their morning groceries astride a tractor. Indeed, the lady across the road, who was single-handily building an Austrian style chalet home while her husband was away during the week in Vienna. She would take us and the children down to the village in the metal box that sat on the back of her tractor and was large enough to stand up in but secured with metal mesh to stop goods (and people) from falling out. I remember talking to her one day asking what she considered herself to be, given her husband was a banker. I expected the answer to be either middle class or upper class. What she confirmed absolutely threw me as she quite proudly said she was a peasant. I explained that we no longer use that expression given its stigma as a low-class citizen. She explained that in that part of the world anyone who worked on the land ate from the land etc proudly called themselves "Peasants "which clearly had a whole different meaning to ours. In the villages themselves and in the local shops it was strange to walk in and find a complete array of all the various costume dresses complete with pinafores etc ready for the local females both old and young to buy. The Austrians are all very proud of their nationality.

Now Austria can be described as a country of two climates and lifestyles. In the winter months everyone including the animals live inside. Some of the houses have the cattle mangers on the end or underneath their houses to utilise the warmth from the cattle. The logs would have been stacked during the summer/early autumn ready for the log fires. Folks would only venture out for necessity and certainly not for social occasions apart from church or perhaps the odd trip to the local café. Summer however was an entirely different ball game. First of all the houses, streets, cafes shops and hotels etc were all adorned with the most brightly coloured flowers. Everyone tried to keep outside for as long as possible. The very large pond in the village centre which we would describe as a small lake was in fact also the local swimming pool. Families would gather mostly at the weekends but occasionally during the evenings for children and adults to swim in the lake. By the lake the locals would have their food and drink and play all sorts of games. Televisions were rarely used while daylight could be enjoyed outside. Also any excuse was used for the village, and we noticed other towns and villages also, to stage a party. There was always some form of stage assembled adorned with flowers etc and folks would gather with normally a local band for a 'knees up' on a Saturday night. The one occasion I did ask what they were celebrating. they looked at me as if I was crackers. "We are not celebrating anything" they said, " just that it is not raining, and we can have a fun evening together" was the reply. What a wonderful existence they had. Everyone knew each, other looked out for each other and the general atmosphere was one of sheer harmony, something we have lost in this county many years ago. Hunting was still very much a big thing in Austria. One piece of advice I was given was to be careful if I was to walk in the surrounding woods and certainly avoid taking the children in. One morning quite early not heeding such sound advice I decided to take a stroll given I was the first up and the house was still quiet. I wondered out the back garden and through into the local woods. I had not gone too far in when I heard a noise and thinking it was an animal went off to investigate. A strange whistling sound ran past my ears which I later discovered was a bullet. When I looked in the direction from where the whistling came I saw a guy carefully and slowly stalking along carrying his rifle. Without making too much noise to disturb his quest but sufficient to draw attention to myself, I did a quick u turn and doubled back the way I came rather hastily. I didn't bother venturing into the unknown again after that episode. What I did find fascinating though was at the local shops you could buy virtually every kind of killing, maiming or decapitating device most of which were advertised in the front windows. In this country it was fast becoming very frowned upon to have these things on display and of course not so long after that were banned. The other strange sights were in the hardware shops. One could still find traps and snares but also hanging up were these long wooden handles. Alongside the wooden handles were long blades of different lengths and sizes. Because the folks still cut their grasses by hand they could go and be "measured" for their own scythe to ensure the handle was the right length and the blade the correct gauge. I certainly have never seen before or since such articles on display apart from the odd museum.

I absolutely loved Austria, and have always set myself a goal that one day I would return to that particular part of the country. One place I wanted to visit was the silent museum. We came across it one day while out on a drive. We noticed a sign, turned off the main road, drove down a track and parked in front of what looked like a few very old houses forming a small hamlet. What it actually turned out to be was a museum created in the open spaces within a small wood. Here the Austrians had re constructed some of the very old traditional houses from around Austria which had been dismantled and re-erected here. The houses themselves were stocked out with all the equipment, clothes and furniture for that period and looked as if the couple living there had popped out for the day. The houses even had gardens with vegetables growing, and in some cases chickens and small goats running about. What a wonderful find. Unfortunately, it was late afternoon and the chap on the gate didn't charge us knowing that we would only get half a dozen houses down before everyone would be asked to leave. The houses we did get to visit were just incredible and really opened our eyes as to how basic and how poor folks lived and survived all those many years ago. The little cots that folks slept in, the clothes they wore and the clogs that they put in their feet showed a very hard life endured. I often told the story of this open museum and longed for the day I could go back and see it all in its full glory. Sadly, that has never happened as the parents moved back to England before we had a chance for another visit. I was to discover years later an identical project created by the Swiss at Brienz just off the shores of Lake Interlaken and have visited that museum several times.

One of the trips we did go on was to one of the many lakes that are found in Austria. On the lake was a large town that we parked up and wandered round. The children were hungry, so we called into this restaurant for something to eat. Having chosen we were waiting our turn for our food to arrive. While we were waiting we kept the children entertained by pointing out the large fresh water fish that were swimming around in the huge aquarium that sat right next to our faces along the entire side of the restaurant. The children were completely taken by the fish and their movements. However, all of a sudden, this huge net came plunging into the water what seemed right next to Kelly my daughter's face. The net retracted as fast as it had appeared but unfortunately on its way back out had captured this large fish that was now flapping for its life. My daughter was heartbroken to learn that this was the chosen food for someone's lunch time dinner. Even we were quite perplexed by the actions. She reminded us of that for many years to come. On the way back as you can imagine we had to pass over several large hills and mountains to get back to the parents village. One such pass came down a rather steep road with numerous hair pin bends. Now I should add the vehicle I was driving was a large powerful motor which had no problems finding the momentum of getting up such large slopes. However, like all vehicles it had to be stopped on the way down. Now this particular vehicle was an automatic. I never really did understand the mechanics involved in automatic transmissions only that as the car slowed so the lower gear was found and as you accelerated so the car went up the gears. Obviously on steep mountain roads the brakes were used as opposed to brakes and gears as I had been taught in manual transmission vehicles. It would appear that this particular pass was rather longer and steeper than the vehicle was used to. By the time we reached close to the bottom suddenly the brake pedal went to the floor. There were no brakes. Now being in a foreign country, with a company vehicle that itself was rather foreign for me to drive to say I was stressed was an understatement. I used the hand brake and the second gear lever and slowed the vehicle right down and finally stopped. We must have been stationary sufficiently long enough for the brake fluid that had turned to steam, to gain some of its strength to return me to some normality sufficient to complete the journey. My first trip once we had reached the safety of the parents-in- law house was to go to the local garage the next morning. With a bit of sign language and the odd sounds thrown in the chap got the gist of the story. He immediately diagnosed the brake fluids which he changed and also checked the brake pads. He assured me the vehicle was fine and would have no problems now getting us home. From my part I was very cautious from then on using the lower gears whenever I could to slow the vehicle down and up until recently I would never drive another automatic transmission vehicle.

The parents had given us a wonderful holiday. We had numerous barbecues, drunk lots of Austrian wine, sung, danced and met the most wonderful warm kind people. Before we departed, we had to get one of the local costumes for my daughter. At this time, she had beautiful long blond hair and was so cute. We went to the local shop, and they had just the right colours to show off her fair skin and blond hair. My first wife went off with the assistant to help get Kelly dressed. When she came dancing back into the shop like all little girls dressed up in their new clothes do she looked an absolute picture. We bought the outfit and until it was just far too small for her to wear, she would insist on wearing the costume. I still treasure the one photo I have of her in the dress complete with the little pinny and all the colours.

Unfortunately, the drive back home was not going to be as easy as the drive out. I had contracted some virus while out in Austria which meant for a couple of days, I had been bed ridden. I was not really fully over this by the time we left. I drove as far as I dare before finding a small chalet style hotel for the night and finished the journey the next day back to the coast and home. I was not really right for a good week after that which was such a pity as I had so thoroughly enjoyed our holiday with such wonderful, warm and friendly people.

CHAPTER 17

COACH TRIP TO CALLELLA SPAIN

In my previous book "It Shouldn't Happen to a Lawyer" one of the stories I shared was when a friend of mine and his wife took us out to dinner. We had all dressed up in smart clothes and while I was at the bar talking to a contact of mine a couple came in and mistook me for one of the waiters. Well, the chap I was talking too was a local insurance agent that recommended work to me from time to time. He was also the chairman of the local resident's association close to where I used to live. Some years later he approached me and asked if I wanted to go with the club on a trip to Calella in Spain. I asked my then wife if she fancied the trip. The cost of it was going to be very reasonable, as it involved a coach as opposed to a flight. We agreed to accompany the club on the basis that we would not be tied to any demands for group attendances. If we wanted to join in any particular activities we would but we wanted to be free to enjoy the holiday to do just what we as we wished as opposed to the group decision. Brian agreed and so we paid our money, and awaited the day of departure. We got a lift down to the club premises and there was this rather luxurious coach waiting for its passengers to embark. Off we set and soon on our way to Dover and the channel crossing.

Now, the intention was that we would travel most of France during the night to enable us to sleep. However, coaches are not that particularly comfortable to travel in and sleep on when going long distances. At the southern end of France, we pulled into another service station for a comfort stop. It was obvious by then that most of us were not sleeping and most of us were suffering from stiffened joints and legs. However, this was the start of the holiday, so it was all laughed off and on we travelled. We passed through the French/Spanish border in the early morning and the sun was now rising and it was getting hot. There was a toilet on board but after some seventeen hours of travelling it was getting shall we say rather ripe to visit. We eventually arrived in Calella in Northern Spain just after lunch having travelled for twenty four hours. Most of us felt like death warmed up and I must confess it was not the most enjoyable experience I have ever had. In fact, it was quite horrid and we still had to face the journey home. The hotel itself was very pleasant but did remind me a little bit of the "Brits abroad" type hotels from the mid sixties advertised with English all day breakfasts and Spanish attempts at English food for dinner. The room was clean, and the outside had a very nice pool. It was only half a mile walk to the beach so all in all we settled down for a relaxing week. As expected after twenty-four hours the club, which always has its "leader" started organising times and trips to the beach to the restaurants etc. We did try to be polite and diplomatic at first simply making up excuses not to tag along. It did get a bit silly when we were somewhat ordered to report to reception at a certain hour after breakfast to join the merry line to march to the beach. This we turned down and were told quite plainly that as a club guest we were expected to join in and tag along. At this point I reminded the leader that we had only joined on the strict understanding that we would not be ordered about. We did however by our own choice go to the beach later that morning. We joined the group that was already there and enjoyed each other's company in the glorious sunshine. Suddenly, the leader slaps his stomach looks at his watch and announces that everyone should get their things together as it was nearly lunch time. Like sheep they all, without murmur packed up their belongings and joined the procession back to the hotel. Everyone of course except us. I could not believe that folks really react in such a way. I suppose in all the years I have travelled it has been solo, so I was not used to a group mentality. I certainly was not going to conform now.

One of the places in Calella we liked to go was a little bar a few hundred yards away. I think on these types of holidays you find a particular bar, get a feeling for it and return throughout the remainder of the holiday. We sat there one evening and it was getting quite dark when all of a sudden, a bunch of English lads walked in. Looking at their appearances it would seem that they were all working on a site close by as they were all covered in builders' dust and grime. Needless to say we thought it was going to turn noisy. The lads had a few beers then one of them egged another that he should get up and sing along to the karaoke that had started up. The poor lad was so embarrassed. His mates kept on and on until eventually he reluctantly stepped up on the small stage and choosing a song launched himself into the accompaniment. Wow! we were so pleased his mates had persuaded him. The lad was incredible. The voice that came out of this young man's mouth was beyond wildest expectation. He was just amazing. He was also very embarrassed at the ovation he got when he finally finished his second song having been persuaded through popular demand to sing again. The next night we went back to the bar hoping the lads were re appear and we were not disappointed. In fact, the lads came back several nights and entertained us all with the crowd each night growing bigger at this young man's fame spreading. Whatever the lad was doing on the site was clearly not his true vocation and with a voice like he had should be using it to his full advantage.

I have always been fascinated by tattoos. I have never wanted one and can't see the point of agreeing to undergo unnecessary pain for the privilege. However, on others that is fine. I am curious as some of the designs and reasons why folks have tattoos. There was a young lad with us in his early twenties. I noticed that on his arms, on his legs and on his torso front and back he was covered in tattoos. I asked him why he wanted so many. His answer was that when he gets bored, he gets another tattoo. I asked him if there were any tattoos that were a bit peculiar or located somewhere that he could confess about. With that he rolled his bottom lip forward. There behind his bottom lip was a inscription tattooed along the inner skin. Now I should imagine that one did hurt and one that I definitely would never wish upon myself.

One of the trips we did agree to go on was a visit to a water world located out of town. Having had breakfast we loaded ourselves and our belongings onto the coach and off we went. Now the coach itself had two young drivers who shared the driving down and back to

England. It was too far to return home and back for the week, so they stayed with us. As such they were able to organise a few trips out for those willing and wishing to join in. As we left the town and about to hit the main highway we were suddenly pulled over by the local police. The police officer came on board to check the driver's paperwork. As we all sat there the discussion between the police and our drivers started to turn into a bit of an argument. In fact, at certain points the discussion became quite heated and seemed to stretch on for ages. Of course, being in Spanish none of us really understood what was going on so we all sat there patiently with towels and day things on our laps. Eventually the driver who was a little red faced turned to everyone apologising that there was a problem and we all had to return to the hotel. The police followed the coach back to the hotel. Once everyone had disembarked the policemen who were still shouting at the driver took a piece of chalk from his motorbike pannier. He then drew a line on the pavement and onto the front tyre and waved his finger at the driver and pointed to the line. We were all rather perplexed at what exactly what was going on. It turned out that these two drivers only had a permit to bring the coach full of passengers to the country and then take them home again. They were not authorised to take anybody out on day trips or travel beyond the hotel and were in fact moonlighting without consent. It was therefore a bit of a sensation that these two had been organising trips for various members of the group throughout the week to all sorts of locations and clearly pocketing the profits without authorisation from their head office or from the authorities in Spain. Having confessed their sins both to the club and even worse to their employers they had both come to the conclusion that upon their return they would both be out of work.

Not wishing to be completely stuck in the resort we discovered an alternative form of transport very close to the hotel which was the local railway. Now as a child I was fascinated by the stories that my Gran told us of her and my grandfathers' trips to Spain in the mid nineteen-sixties. They were part of the first "Brits abroad" package holiday tourists. One of the places that my Gran loved was Lloret De Mar which happened to be very close to the resort where we were staying. We took the local train and got off in the old town of Lloret and what a lovely place it was. It lived up to all the expectations of an old Spanish resort town. It wasn't run down at all as expected but indeed from the architecture and antiquity of the place you could tell it was very old. It had a lovely array of shops and a market which was open the day we arrived. One strange sight which I have always recalled was the jewellery shops. Now, these shops were very expensive and stocked some very high-quality jewels and antique clocks and watches etc. What they also stocked was a full collection of Japanese swords which seems a strange offering for a jeweller and for a seaside resort town. It turns out that the Spanish are world class sword masters, the Toledo blades are some of the most prized swords in the world. The factory itself was not far away from here. Now the Japanese are very jealous of their swords which actually form virtually a religious following. So much so that the Japanese swords are not allowed to be made anywhere else in the world and can only be produced in Japan. However, there is one exception and that is a special license granted to Toledo who are in fact the only ones that can reproduce the swords. The quality is so high that they only places that really justify their sales are in good quality jewellers thus the displays we saw. I was in fact studying martial arts at the time including the Katana (Japanese sword) so I had an extra interest. We therefore went into one of the jewellers and asked to inspect some of the swords on display. What I saw was very, very impressive. The Japanese Katana is made up of seven pieces all held together with an ivory pin. The Toledo replicas also made up of the same delicate parts but held together with a nylon pin. The cord that so delicately entwines the handle of the original is replicated on the Toledo blades. Even the water line that runs the length of the blade is also reproduced. All in all they were things of beauty as well as being a live working weapon. At least it would only be true enthusiasts that would purchase these objects given the prices of them.

Another trip we took was to Barcelona. Here we explored the harbour. From the harbour we climbed the hills beyond and at the top could look down onto the whole of Barcelona, its port and of course the ocean. The site we were standing on would become part of the site used for the Olympic Games. We then travelled down into Barcelona itself to its famous architectural streets for a late lunch in one of the street restaurants. We were led downstairs to a dining room below ground. Here we were all seated, and the most magnificent banquet was presented to us representing Spanish dishes. This was all washed down with the local wines which always taste better than that bought in bottles back home from the supermarkets. After our meal we were transported to where the palace is located. It was now late afternoon, early evening with dusk settling. It was very warm and dry. As we stood on the steps leading up to the palace. piped music started playing. In the large square that was in front of us were quite a few large fountains. Each fountain had a series of waterspouts firing water into the centre. As we stood listening to the music, so these shoots of water started to change colour. The fountains started to "dance" to the music with shoots of water getting stronger and weaker with the tempo and the waters changing colours around the various fountains. The display lasted at least half an hour. The selection of music was completely varied from classical to modern from pop to orchestral. It was so well presented that it all became very mesmerising. The atmosphere also became very emotional. So much so that it was an experience I would never have again, but one I will always remember with affection.

Eventually the end of the week arrived, and it was time to depart. We dutifully placed our luggage in the hold took up our places on the coach and off we went. To say that this was the most awful journey I have ever been on including being strapped to a luggage rack on a French train when I was a child, is an understatement. It was a nightmare. This time we had no anticipation or excitement to a pending holiday to look forward to. Most of the travelling took place by day and the journey up through France has to be one of the most boring events you can dread. For mile upon mile upon mile in southern France all there is to look at is flat fields and sunflowers. When we did finally pull up at each service station we were all just so relieved to be off the coach. I did say when I got home that I would never ever travel on a holiday involving a coach again. It was horrendous. Not a good end to a rather mediocre holiday I must confess. We did some years later take my mother back to Calella but our return trip was from Luton Airport some thirty five minutes away by car, and flew to the local airport which was less than the hour from the hotel. My mother loved it so much in Calella she had been back herself several times herself after that.

CHAPTER 18

TRIP TO ALMERIA SOUTHERN SPAIN

Our trips to Calella would open up a whole new chapter of trips to Spain. A very good friend of mine and now ex-neighbour had purchased as an investment with his father a lovely first floor apartment. This apartment was in a row that looked like houses along the sea front only yards from the beach and the sea. It was a new development in the village of Roquetas some twenty miles south of Almeria in southern Spain. My friends used the apartment as their own holiday retreat but lent it to relatives and very close friends when they were not using it themselves. My friend and his father had taken a trip out to Spain especially to see what was available as an investment. Finding this lovely development they decided to buy the one we were to borrow. The apartments that formed the complex were in the shape of a triangle. The apartments along the sea front and one rather grand hotel and other apartments on the other two sides of the triangle. In the middle was located two fantastic large swimming pools separated by a sunken bar with restaurant. These areas were surrounded by sun lounging areas with sun loungers all exclusively for the sole use of those within the complex.

Having purchased the apartment, my friend and his father returned to the UK bought a whole lorry full of John Lewis furniture and the pair of them then drove all the way back to southern Spain to fit the apartment out.

Having agreed we could take the apartment for a fortnight, we duly booked our flights from Luton to Almeria. The father always boasted that he could be having his breakfast at home early in the morning and be at the resort and having his lunch by lunchtime. We took the early morning flight and after two and a half hours arrived at the little airport of Almeria. Now this was a wonderful little airport with the runway sitting parallel to the shoreline. One's approach was over the Sierra Nevada mountains down towards the sea, turn and then land. The little runway then gave us access to the arrivals lounge. This was no more than a large room with a hole for the luggage to be pushed through. There was a small conveyor belt where the luggage was then collected. We went past the customs chap that looked like a ticket collector at the local railway station and then literally through the door straight into the arrivals/departures lounge which again resembled a British railway station. I was so impressed at how relaxed and low key it all was. We had been given a set of apartment keys in the UK. There was also a set of keys for the family Jeep that the father had bought, and again driven over to Spain. This was really strange coming out of an airport in a right-hand drive vehicle straight onto the wrong side of the road. I had driven many times abroad but at least coming out of the port it gave you a chance to acclimatise. It was a case of out of the car park straight onto a busy road to a roundabout and into the city port of Almeria. Character building to say the least. Now anyone who could drive one of these bone shaking little cars for more than an hour had my vote. To drive down all the way from the UK was heroic to say the least. It was so uncomfortable. I would also add that Almeria is an old port that serves Spain to north Africa. There is the hustle and bustle of foreign vehicles both small and large. The smells of the oil, diesel and other mechanical devices along the port entrance plus an assortment of nationalities making their way to and from the port. All this in the middle of a working week midday morning. Hectic is rather an under- statement.

As we drove the coastal road out of Almeria, we were told to keep our eyes open on the cliffs above us and in particular the caves. In those days, not so many years ago, these were all lived in by whole families and had been occupied for many, many years. It was rather tragic to find people still living in this environment in modern times. The next town to be passed was called "Aqua Dulci" or "Sweet Water". Nothing could be further from the truth. What a total dump.

This place even had its own cardboard city made up of cardboard constructions which were people's homes, all lined up along the sides of the roads leading in and out of Aqua Dulci. It was quite menacing and quite frankly glad we didn't have to stop for any period at traffic lights or pedestrian crossings for fear of all sorts of illegal approaches. Having experienced both Almeria and now Aqua Dulci our spirits were beginning to dampen to exactly what we would face when we reached Roquetas especially as we were going to be marooned here for two weeks. The countryside was very dry and desolate especially given it was the hottest time of the year being early August. The dust was everywhere which seemed to create its own clouds up to the nearby mountains that seemed to stretch down virtually to the few fields before arriving at the sea. We eventually arrived at the old quarter of Roquetas and again it looked rather sorry for itself. However, as we drove further into the centre all of a sudden it was like going through a magic curtain across the road. All new buildings, shops hotels marbled footpaths walkways, palm trees restaurants. It was absolutely beautiful. The directions found us at the hotel on the triangle and parking the vehicle up in the allotted parking spot we walked out onto the block paved walkway running parallel to the sea to the last apartment, up the short flight of outside steps through the door and into the apartment itself. Wow, how beautiful it was. It had three balconies. The one at the front over-looking the sea, was large enough for a small table and possibly three chairs and a built in barbecue, at the very back there was a small balcony large enough for a couple to stand there looking out over the glass partitioned wall to the swimming pools, and to the side a huge balcony which could take at least eight sun loungers that had a view over the land to the side and out of the village as nothing had been built beyond the edge of this complex. The apartment itself was just ideal. Three bedrooms fully furnished with our own recognisable English cutlery, furniture and all the trimmings. This was going to be a wonderful holiday.

Our expectations were not wrong. What a lovely location and a lovely town! A place that one could really relax and have a wonderful holiday. After twenty four hours the routine was set. After breakfast we would have a wonder into the huge pools. At lunchtime we would cross over the little road in front of the triangle and find one of the many busy bars for a Spanish lunch and in the afternoons a couple of hours out of the sun sitting on the front balcony in the breeze watching the sea and the passers-by. There was a German guy who every day appeared without fail at 12.00pm pushing a potato oven which happened to have been made in Britain. From the oven he would spend two hours selling hot jacket potatoes with various fillings. He was always busy. We got chatting to him one lunchtime. He confirmed that living out there most years he would be bored after a few weeks. Buying the potato oven meant he had a purpose each lunchtime, would get to meet lots of wonderful people. He would also get to practice his various languages in addition to German to include French, English and Spanish. He only worked weekdays and on the days he worked, he made enough money to sustain his and his wife's lifestyle. This would include running the car, buying groceries, alcohol and spare cash for evening meals etc. He was having a wonderful time. We saw him for several years until finally ill health meant he was going to sell the oven and the apartment. His plan was to move back to Germany which was something he really regretted, loving his life there in Spain.

In the evening if we were not barbecuing from the apartment barbecue we would again visit one of the other bars or restaurants. The food offered was very good quality and very reasonably priced. The children in particular loved the huge ice creams that came with sparklers to the table. If we felt adventurous, we would wander along the sea road up to the old quarter and the harbour. This area had been renovated and up graded to a lovely marina with its Spanish restaurants offering seafood specialities. The Spanish love their seafood especially on a Sunday when all the family would gather at one of the harbour restaurants. This was encouragement enough for us to try, if it was good enough for the locals. One Sunday after lunch we wandered onto the harbour itself and spotted a rather sorry looking sailing yacht and overheard the couple on board who were speaking with broad Scottish accents. We introduced ourselves as being English and struck up a very interesting conversation with them. It turned out that the boat was looking rather sorry for itself as they had spent the past three and a half years sailing round the Mediterranean, and it had been their home for this duration. Having spent all this time visiting some wonderful places they had decided it was time to get back to the real world. As such they were making their way down the coast to Southern Spain where they would turn right, hug the Portuguese coast, then off across the Bay of Biscay past France up the English Channel and via the North Sea home. The idea was once home they would tidy up the boat and then sell it. We had a light-hearted bet that having reached home, having spent several months back in the real world they would decide not to sell but indeed set off again for another great adventure. I wonder if they ever did.

One trip over to the local restaurant one evening meant we passed one of the travel shops. In the window was advertised the film set from the spaghetti westerns, in particular the "Good the Bad and the Ugly." These films had all been filmed in the Sierra Nevada mountains not far from Almeria. We decided to take the children on a day trip and booked the air-conditioned coach. We left mid morning and after a short coach trip arrived at this very dusty area right in the Sierra Nevada desert. The desert is located over the other side of the mountain range from the sea which of course meant it was very, very hot and dry and very dusty. The film set of the town with its bank, sheriff's office, shops and sidewalks just looked like you see on a Hollywood film. Stood there, suddenly we heard the clatter of horses as the "baddies" rode into town, were quickly set upon by the Marshall and his deputies and then a gun fight broke out. The baddies needless to say lost with several of them falling from their horses pretending to be dead. A couple were captured and led off to the gallows. Up the steps with the noose over their heads and hung (obviously there was a wire down the backs to support them) but the undertaker turned up with his horse and cart and a couple of coffins to carry them off in. It was really good fun and the children were enthralled to watch not only a gun fight but a hanging as well. The films seen later on the television, really couldn't be taken seriously knowing where they were actually filmed and the buildings with their false fronts etc.,

Because the area is close to the Port giving access to North Africa a lot of vendors come over selling various wares. You will see them along the sea front selling anything from leather belts, to towels, T shirts and beach wear equipment. Most of the articles on sale are counterfeit and have the name of a well-known brand marked on them. I did point out to one black African boy that the leather belt he had on display with others had the name of "Levy" printed on incorrectly. This was very quickly removed and hidden. If the police should appear along the waterfront of course these vendors quickly pack their wares back into their suitcases and just disappear. In the main streets there are of course the pedlars that try to sell more exotic souvenirs. You can be shown watches, wallets, gold rings and bracelets etc. One evening the boys that were with us came back really excited. They had been stopped by one of these street pedlars and offered some cheap jewellery. Of course, they were attracted to the necklaces and the rings which they were offered really cheaply. They fell for the old trap that these were all "good quality gold". So much so were they fooled that they asked if they could borrow some more money to go buy some more while the bargains were still available. I didn't have the heart to destroy their fantasy. It was not till they got home that their gold started to turn a funny colour and green rings started to appear on their fingers and round their necks that they realised that they had been tricked.

Even though the apartment was open on three sides with the doors and patio shutters it nonetheless could get very hot during the height of summer. Very often the evenings themselves would still prove very hot and sticky. We would sit on the front balcony overlooking the sea with the sea breeze coming on to help cool us. Sometimes it would be so hot we would stay up looking out to sea till the early hours. We watched the small fishing boats come out from the harbour and lay their nets a couple of miles offshore. They would be bobbing up and down with their red and green lights glowing trying to net decent catches to be sold to the restaurants for the next day's menu. It was a very tranquil, peaceful setting and many of the world's troubles were put to rights as we sat there.

One of the items that the travel agents don't mention about this particular part of the world is the fact that they are prone to earthquakes. We only came to discover this hidden secret one morning, sitting in bed drinking our very English first cup of tea before rising when all of a sudden I felt like I had very minor shakes. At first you do try to convince yourself that all is fine that you are not shaking and it is your imagination. However when the arms and legs join the brain in this eventful occurrence and the cup of tea you are holding actually has a tidal wave crossing from side to side then reality does slot in. This occurrence has happened two or three times over various visits and to be forewarned is to be forearmed is a very true saying. So visitors beware!

I have always admired bilingual people. Anybody that can switch between one language to another has an incredible talent and ability. For myself I can mutter my way through a bit of German, a bit of French and reasonably well in Italian. However, It does take me several days if not a week before I become acclimatised as it were to be able to stammer a few words back. It therefore always amazes me in tourist resorts where the barmen waiters etc., can switch from their language to English. There is a particular bar in Calella that we used to go to. The owner himself would always great us with a smile and a cheeky slightly London cockney accent including some of his favourites sayings. One particular evening we were sat there having a drink and chatting to the owner. A couple came in next to us and he simply turned his head and asked them in Spanish what they would like which he then served and returned to us. This happened several times, with the owner switching from his soft cockney English to Spanish, French, German and even Italian. Suddenly this rather tall good-looking couple both with blond hair came in and the owner got most excited. He left the bar went and greeted them like long lost cousins and was chatting away in a language that sounded at first to be German but had a "singing" dialect and words I didn't recognise. I then discovered that this pair were in fact from Holland and our owner was speaking to them in fluent Dutch. Wow this guy is talented. I got an opportunity of asking him later how on earth did he managed to pick up all these different languages in addition to English. He looked a bit bemused at me and then confessed that he was not in fact English. English was his second language and in fact he was himself from Holland. What a talented fella.

When it was time to leave Roquetas we simply bundled our belongings in the back of the Suzuki jeep drove along the coast road back to Almeria airport parked up in one of the bays allocated and then went into the departure lounge. The next couple that went out would have a spare set of keys both for apartment and vehicle so as long as we had left adequate amount of fuel in the vehicle everyone was happy. Now I did give a short description at the beginning of this chapter of Almeria airport. It was to say the least very basic and very friendly. The departure was equally less traumatic than back in other airports I had departed from. The luggage was lifted onto a platform passed through the hole in the wall to the chap on the other side who then loaded onto a trolley to be pulled out onto the tarmac. We in the meantime went through a very basic passport control through the gap and into the departure "lounge" only it wasn't a lounge more like a cage. The outside walls were only about 3 feet tall with angle iron reaching some 15 feet off the ground at intervals around this wall with chain link fencing to keep the passengers inside. Even the "roof" was chain link fencing. To sit on, there were literally concrete seats. I very quickly realised that we all resembled some form of primates in a cage which I always felt amusing. When it was time to leave, the chain link gate would be swung open, with the padlock removed and we would shuffle off to the aircraft. There were only a few flights a day as it was very much an under used airport in an area that wasn't really over visited. This would change however because the Chinese promised the Spanish that if they were to invest in a more substantial airport that could take larger intercontinental aircraft then the Chinese tourist board saw a very lucrative market. The Spanish spent millions. They upgrade the runways to accommodate larger aircraft requiring longer distances to land and take off. The terminal buildings were re developed into an international airport with numerous checking in desks a full and proper customs area duty free areas with their own coffee and food outlets and the whole rebuild was absolutely splendid. The only problem was, the Chinese never did arrive so all the money spent was rather in vain for the promised outcome.

I did travel back through this area a couple of years ago when driving back from Morocco in the Land Rover with my grandson. I noticed that the whole of Roquetas had been vastly developed and much of the old quarters had disappeared. Sweet Water that we used to laugh at as we passed through with its derelict buildings and cardboard huts for the homeless had all been swept away. The area had become very much up market investment developments with wonderful apartments and sea front houses, shops and restaurants. The road approaching Almeria itself now is a proper motorway and the caves above that used to be occupied by the gypsy families were all now empty and the gypsies moved on. Almeria still runs a very basic port that still supplies north Africa and thus retains the smell of oil, fish and diesel, but the remainder has become very cosmopolitan.

CHAPTER 19
FIRST SKI HOLIDAY

I was about mid-thirties and thought it was time that I tried my hand at skiing. I had always imagined that skiing had been a reserve for the rich and famous, the upper classes, public school boys etc. However, this sport was now fast becoming more and more of an interest to the middle and working-class folks trying to escape the boredom and depression of the long dark miserable, dreary, winter days. Once we had decided that this was something perhaps, we should try the next question would be where? As novices we needed something simple and ideal for beginners. There was no point in organising a trip where there would be an abundance of testing black runs and red runs or off-piste skiing. We didn't even know how to put ski boots or even skis on let along throw ourselves downhill. Another deciding factor was of course the price. One of the High Street tour operators had a special deal called a "ski pack." This was designed for first time skiers. Another deciding factor was that these holidays were mostly in Italy my favourite country. The deal we seemed to be able to secure was very good and was going to include the flights, the coach transfers, the hotel half-board, the lift passes and all the equipment hire plus lessons. This seemed a great deal.

Having now booked our holiday the next task was to try to find suitable ski clothing. Back in those days ski equipment was few and far between. The only place we could find was an outward bound shop in Northampton some twenty miles away or a C&A outlet that had just started to stock basic clothing. We trundled off to Northampton and had a session stocking up with thermal underwear, ski socks, ski jackets etc. The prices were very reasonable, and if it was a venture that we really would never bother with again, then it would have not been a waste of a lot of money.

The time finally arrived when we set off driving down to Gatwick to catch our early morning Sunday flight to Italy. I must confess that walking into the airport for the first time my heart sank. There they all were, my worst nightmares. All the fur coat brigade with their expensive fur boots, designer ski wear with their designer bags and matching luggage. All frightfully posh and all rather established as well as confident. Exactly what I really didn't want. However, it soon transpired that most of this lot were heading off to the expensive resorts and the slopes saved for the upper classes and seasoned skiers. The C&A crowd as I called ourselves, of which we were happily part of, headed for our flight. A couple of hours later we landed in Milan transferred to our coaches and headed north to the resort. The coach was destined to take nearly five hours travelling on part motorways and part ordinary roads. Our route was to take us round the beautiful Lake Como that I had never seen before. We stopped off at a wonderful friendly café serving fresh Italian coffee, rolls and meat for breakfast. Even though it was winter, and everything was dull overcast and grey you could just feel the beauty of the surroundings of this place. The lake itself was as calm as glass and the surrounding villages so picturesque.

We arrived at the resort mid afternoon which sadly was too late to go up the mountain for a recce. Our lift passes were due to start the next day. After seeing the numbers of people coming down off that mountain that Sunday afternoon, clearly it was a better idea to leave it to the next day in any event. The resort was not too far from Milan and other large towns so was a great place to drive up for a Saturday or Sunday ski day out. As from Sunday night all the Italian tourists and all the locals had gone home and back to work. The hotel we stayed in was fantastic. It was only a small two-star hotel run my a young couple Marrisa and John-Franco. They were helped by John-Franco's parents, father in the kitchen with brother cooking, mother helping out at the desk and above kitchen duties. It worked very well.

The other stroke of luck we had was that the hotel was feet away from the chain link fence of the car park for the lifts. Literally, two hundred yards past the fence were the two massive cable cars, each capable of carrying sixty people straight up to the top ski station a mile uphill in what seemed to be the clouds. Some of us were a little daunted by the height and the prospect. We didn't need to be. That evening we were to meet in a local convenient bar in the town halfway between where we were located at one end of the village and the other end of the village where one of the three hotels selected by this tour company was situated. At the welcome meeting we were given our welcome packs with our ski passes and timetables of where, when and how we were to start our skiing experience. After a few drinks we all left, trudged back through the snow and very cold air to our hotels.

After a good night's sleep from all the travelling, the excitement and the mountain air, we were up washed dressed and ready to roll. A short walk over to the cable car where only a small handful of folks were waiting for the lifts and then ascended up to what looked like halfway to heaven. The ski lift itself was amazing. Suspended by this thick cable but with a drop at any given point of over a hundred feet minimum it slowly pulled itself up the mountain with the village behind us getting smaller and smaller all the time. At the top we walked out of the station across a flat section to a couple of wooden Swiss chalet type buildings where the rep was waiting for us. Now, for reasons I have never understood the ski equipment is always stored downstairs. This is all very well at the beginning of the day walking down in ordinary shoes and boots but clunking back up in the most unimaginably uncomfortable ski boots carrying these long stiff pieces of wood and ski poles was quite a difficult task. Added to this we had folks trying to get up and down the stairs past us. The whole thing was a nightmare. Finally, we had our feet measured, our boots fitted, and our skis selected for height and weight and we were back out in the fresh air. I had been very lucky that back in the summer I had been on an open day organised by an insurance firm to a dry ski slope. I had some idea on how to walk in the boots, how to put skis on and take them off which compared to some was like I had been skiing for many years. Anybody that has ever tried skiing will never forget their first experiences. The skis seem to have a mind of their own going most of the time in the direction not actually desired. Eventually we all lined up, some hundred yards away at the bottom of the nursery slope. Now looking back at this nursery slope it was so gentle that most children would find it difficult even getting the momentum to even get going. For first timers this slope resembled something equivalent to a downhill race. We all lined up and took it in turns to push ourselves forward, try to turn and point ourselves downhill. This then allowed the skis their freedom to go whichever direction they wanted. Many of us ended up in a heap just beyond the last person in the line. Eventually we were selected into the "useless" and the "even more useless" groups depending on how far we had slid before falling over. I was lucky that having been able to slide down a dry ski slope I was selected for the less useless group. We were then dragged onto the next torment being a "rolling carpet". This has to be described. Basically, you shuffle your way forward up this slope trying desperately not to slide backwards. Once at the end there is a long rubber mat that is moving on a flat bed that you are expected to push your skis onto. Once the skis find the mat they are then sucked on and upwards irrespective of whether you are ready willing to follow or not. By this time many of us are becoming experts on how to stand up from falls wearing skis. That is the first nightmare. Secondly while these sticks on your feet are heading uphill, not necessarily parallel to each other the body has this inclination to want to lean backwards. The only thing to hold onto is this rope the size of a skipping rope that runs about knee height from one pulley at the bottom to the pulley at the top. The pulley rope itself does not actually move at the same speed as the mat. This is a bit like an escalator in one of the department stores where you have to keep adjusting your hands on the moving handrail otherwise you tend to start leaning forwards till you fall into the moving stairs. Well of course on the rolling carpet your feet seem to be glued down, your body is trying to fall back and your right arm is taking off in a different speed and direction. This experience really should be bottled for posterity as one of the most unnatural wonders of man's creation. Then comes the finale, getting off at the other end. The rope disappears round the pulley back in the opposite direction, the rolling carpet seems to end some way in front of that and suddenly the feet and skis are jerked forward onto a section of snow that has been highly polished by all the previous victims gone before. This leaves most folks slipping and floundering with arms and legs flailing in every direction. The good news is you have now reached the top of the slope, there is only one way to go and that is down. Now to the Italians this is a an area that young children as small as say three years old learn to ski. In their minds there is nothing to be afraid of, no dangers and it is all second nature. They don't realise that for us Brits first time on skis, anything that moves by itself is quite daunting. Suddenly from the top of the slope now looking down it all becomes even more steep than imagined from the bottom. At this point the love of skiing and everyone who has the remotest idea of what he or she is doing becomes your enemy. The horrible children who have been skiing since the day they were conceived are whizzing past. They are actually chatting to each other while you are still trying to hold on to some form of dignity just standing still. You start to move. All the training and exercises that have been shown early that morning have gone out of the window by the time you reach ten feet. At this point the only steering seems to want to come from arms that resemble someone trying to wind down the windows of their cars, the feet are crossed skis going in different directions and the question really is how long, rather than how far you are going to get. After several falls you finally reach the bottom and lo and behold you then repeat this fruitless exercise numerous times till it is time to go for lunch or until the brain says, "the mind is willing – but the body is clearly weak". Three days later, you have made such progress that now you are touring to the top of the nursery slope on the rolling carpet without fear or favour and snow ploughing down to the bottom of the slope and actually able to look at other folks and smile. By now you have turned from novice to expert downhill skier. But then comes the next nightmare. It is called the 'Prima Vera.' This is the second nursery slope which disappears off the side of the first slope. You haven't noticed this one until this point. You have not dared go near it for fear of falling over what seems to be a sheer edge and drop. If a guy had a ladder propped up against it you would not be that surprised. Your instructor is smiling and waving you over to the edge as this is going to be your second level of torture. You are advised that you are not allowed and will not be taken to the top of the mountain until the prima vera is conquered. The teachers have by now already taken from you the ski sticks. Whilst experience later shows they don't really serve much purpose, to a beginner they are safety props to have In your hands. All you now have are the skis themselves. You are shown how to shift your weight from one ski to the other and in this way and in theory the ski will turn . To be more specific the art is to lower the body with arms in front facing one side and as you come up the arms change direction to the other side which, apparently shifts your weight from the inside edge of one ski and puts it onto the inside edge of the other ski and that is how to traverse the slope. Unfortunately my skis seemed to have a mind of their own and at various given attempts, mostly when facing straight down hill they would take the shortest line. At the bottom we then had to try to stop, then shuffle over to another form of lift, the button lift that would drag us back to the top of the second nursery slope. The method is to shuffle forward to another rope that went up and down the slope. Attached to this rope was a metal bar with a round plastic "button" attached to the bottom. As it came round to head back up hill you got hold of the bar pulled it down on a telescopic spring till the button was between your legs. Holding the bar with one hand you waited for the tension to let itself out and then it would gently pull you back up the slope. Feet have to be kept parallel again for fear of falling over and not to sit on the disc as gravity takes over again and you will fall over. Having reached the top of the slope, or should I say, nearly the top of the slope the button with its umbilical cord disappears off to the right as you shuffle out of the way of the person coming up behind you to position yourself facing back down hill for another run down. We had spent two days on the first nursery slope to gain our confidence of control. The next three days were spent on the second nursery slope and time seemed to pass very quickly.

Lessons were for two each day from ten until twelve then everyone stops for lunch. Leaving our skis and poles outside we would shuffle inside the large restaurant. The restaurant itself seemed very much like a motorway services style café. As the visitors arrived so the floor got wetter from the falling snow and ice. This means the floor got slippery and to try to walk on it was difficult enough. Having queued into the line again similar to a motorway service station you shuffled your way round taking the dishes that you fancied along with a drink and made your way to the check out. Here you paid for the food and drinks picked up the knives and forks and then very, very carefully tried to manoeuvre your way across the floor to a suitable free table and sit down. Many a cheer went up with someone sliding over and their tray with contents going flying. After lunch which could last up to an hour and a half, those that still had the strength could carry on for the remainder of the afternoon. The resort itself would start to close at four pm with the lift operators and instructors leaving the furthest slopes and skiing down checking everyone was off the mountain. At the cable car we were then shuttled in and back to the village. However after two gruelling hours of ski school and the use of muscles you just don't use at home, tiredness sets in very, very quickly. The mind says just one more go but the body is so tired that you have to give in and head back. I don't think of all the days I was there I stayed beyond three pm. Carrying the skis back to the ski school hut, down the stairs and positioning them where you would remember they were the next day we then took our boots off. The strangest feeling is taking ski boots off after a day's skiing and putting back on normal footwear even if they are heavy walking boots. The feet seem so light and free away from the ski boots. Making your way back to the cable car it was then a case of waiting for one to arrive, pile in with up to sixty people, waiting for the doors to shut and then off it would go. Now the first hundred yards the cable car runs parallel to the floor of the nursery area. After that it goes over a gantry sticking out over the mountain and falls down the other side. As it passes over the gantry it gives a gentle rocking backwards and forwards. Now to the initiated this is not even noticed. To those that have never travelled on one of these before it is really unnerving. Bearing in mind that as it rocks forward all you see through the front windows is the sheer drop down with the village looking like small match boxes a mile below. Once the village is reached I think all us beginners had a large but silent sigh of relief.

Now there is a custom with all skiers that comes about from necessity not from anything else. When you get to the bottom of the lifts, and you are free from the days skiing you find a bar. Preferably a bar that is the closest. Here you order a very large drink of alcohol and amongst all the other pretenders boast how well the day has gone and what a wonderful time you have had. You fail to mention the bruising, wet trousers and aching limbs. Of course, tomorrow you are going to do it all over again.

By the fourth day I was doing really well, the Prima Vera or second nursery slope had been cracked. I was rewarded by finally being allowed to hold the ski sticks and was reaching the bottom with some form of style and control. The instructor therefore decided that some of us could go with him to the top of the mountain the next day. My nerves returned. When you have never really been to the top of a mountain and especially on skis, the imagination takes over along with the trepidation.

That evening we had the presentations of our medals and certificates of the standards of where we had reached. It was back to the restaurant we had visited that first day and sat there while each group, each class and each level passed through receiving their certificates and medals be it bronze, silver or gold. First of course, we all had to endure watching the video that one of the instructors had taken of us on the slopes. I have to say we did all rather resemble the ape position while skiing down the slopes. Unfortunately, I was late the next morning and by the time I got to the slopes my class had already left to go up to the top of the mountain. I hung around with the less confident group. They had finally progressed to standing at the top of the second beginners' slope, the Prima Vera, looking very fragile. Others were still struggling up and down the first nursery slope. After a couple of hours, my group returned and my tutor having spotted me came over and asked what had happened. I apologised and confessed I was a little late arriving. He then told me not to worry and announced that as I had not been with them it would be a shame not to experience the whole mountain. So, if I cared to report to him after lunch he would make a special visit with me up the mountain for a one to one lesson. I spent the lunch in nervous silence. We met and made our way over to these rather ancient looking two-seater gondola cars and climbed inside as best we could which is not easy wearing ski boots. The skis were put into special slots on the back of the bubble car. The door is locked by one of the ski operator assistants and we were pushed forward to catch the large circular cable and off we went. To say these little bubble cars were old, when I looked down there were holes in the floor where the welding was going, leaving a view of the snow fifty feet below us. The bubble car then went straight up the side of the black run to reach the top. Any confidence I had built up had now disappeared. Having reached the top, in fairness to the tutor, there was the first slope that was only slightly steeper than the first nursery which we eased down. At the end of this first little slope instead of heading over the edge and down the black run we turned and snow ploughed our way down through a series of little slopes and turns, onto a plateau some several hundred yards below. At this point we had to be careful to negotiate a very interesting turn to place us onto a narrow ledge. On our left was a very steep drop so concentration was very necessary. At the bottom of the ledge we then had to drop over and traverse an edge onto a flat and safer area of ski run. This was the point when the prima vera training had come into its own albeit that the drop was only half the distance. Once onto the flat and wider area that looked like a wide lane of some thirty yards wide the instructor came next to me. Both our sets of skis now were parallel, and we were holding our ski poles like a pair of professional down-hill skiers. I was feeling like an experienced skier. The adrenalin was pumping, and suddenly for the first time all week the whole ethos of the skiing world came together. I was the master of the slopes, and it was fantastic. After about a mile of parallel skiing and getting round the corner all that remained was this long curving wide slope where the tutor helped to show me the racing stance of leaning forward, bending knees down with poles tucked up behind and allowing the skis to run and enjoy the whole exhilaration. Did I have a tale to tell at the café that night.

What a wonderful week we all had. Yes, it was hard work, yes we were all tired at the end of each day, we slept well, we ate well and we played well but what incredible teachers we had. By the end of that first week we felt we had really achieved something. One of the characters that we met was an elderly gentleman from Chelmsford called John Osborn. Now John was a real character. He had travelled all over the world and had worked for the foreign office. When he was stationed in the far east he would find out the weather conditions of the snow in Europe. Choosing the best resort he would fly over for a skiing holiday. This was at a time before most of us were affording a bucket and spade holiday at one of the English coastal resorts. John had been there done and seen most of it and was a wonderful warm colourful character. He had long since retired and his children had decided that they would buy him a ski holiday. Taking into consideration his age they chose Chiesa for him as it would be an ideal safe place for him not being too taxing. John was one of those characters that very quickly made friends within the hotel and village. He loved the village so much he re-booked year after year. John even left his skiing gear in the hotel to return home travelling light knowing he would be back. John and I got to know each other very well and he even persuaded me to take up learning Italian seriously which he was doing himself. He sent me the BBC tapes of Buon Giorno Italia and helped me find the backing book. He had taught himself to speak out of respect for the Italian people and to be able to converse with them each year on his return. John would arrive shortly before Christmas stay over Christmas and new year leave his equipment in the hotel returning home to check mail and any urgent tasks, then drive back to Italy staying perhaps a month. While he was in Chiesa he would not rush to rise each morning preferring to slowly get himself sorted have breakfast then appear on the slopes for a few hours. He would then disappear down the mountain where most of us couldn't venture as the slopes were a little more difficult. Halfway down he had found a little restaurant on the mountain where you could leave your skis outside, go in and sit down at the pretty wooden tables with table cloths and enjoy a typical couple of hours Italian lunch. After a couple of hours having lunch with one set of friends or another and of course a few glasses of wine it was very rare that John would make more than a couple of runs that afternoon preferring to wander back to the hotel. Some days he never appeared at all as he had gathered some local friends bundled into the car and drove off to another resort for a days' skiing. He really lived the life. At the end of the ski season which in Chiesa was quite late as being very high up the snows were still falling in early April, John would try to purchase his season ticket for the following winter. Every year they refused and every year he would argue with them and have to return empty handed. Every end of season his skis and gear were packed away by John-Franco our hotel owner and he would toddle off back to England to play golf during the summer waiting for the season to start again. Tragically the inevitable happened. One day while playing golf John suffered a heart attack on the golf course and had passed by the time his body hit the green. His family returned to Chiesa that Christmas to celebrate John's life and love of skiing and pick up his ski gear to return home. That was the last I saw or heard of them but will always remember John as a friendly lovable old character that touched the hearts of those that got to know him.

After several years revisiting Chiesa we became quite friendly with the villagers and the staff on the mountains ourselves. The second time we returned we had my son and daughter with us. We had taken them previously to Scotland for the Easter holiday to see if they would enjoy skiing and they were both like ducks to water. Wanting to make sure they were not frightened or in danger in any way we were like mother hens ourselves when we got them to the hotel and went through the paces of having them measured for skis boots etc. We had attended the evening welcome drink for their sakes and now we were standing in the group waiting to be selected for their lessons. Because of Scotland they both ended up in the higher of the groups. I knew they were in safe hands so by now being reasonably proficient and familiar with the mountain skied off to re-explore the slopes further up. Now with Chiesa if you were to stand somewhere round about the Prima Vera for long enough everyone on the mountain would pass by. The resort was a giant figure eight and you would end up back in the middle of the eight which was the second nursery slope that I found so daunting on my first ever visit. It was at this point some chap came over to me in sheer horror wanting to spill the beans on the mornings activities and in particular "Do you know what your son has done?". Oh lord, here we go, what has he been up to now. He was in fact only eleven years old, my daughter nine so I know he couldn't have got into that much mischief. Well it turned out that the group he was in was so successful with mastering the first nursery slope (kids don't you just love them) they quickly progressed to my nightmare the Prima Vera. On this slope there were several instructors who were taking lessons. One in particular had a more experienced skier showing her the ropes. What the instructors tend to do is form a snow plough but backwards, so they are skiing backwards right in front of the pupil who they can catch, stop or turn if in difficulty or give encouragement and tuition if they are doing well. My son however only saw the instructor going backwards. Oh what a good idea. Turned himself round and with a whoop and a yell skied the prima backwards, after his second or third ever descent. To others he became a hero, to me he obviously had to be kept on a very tight verbal and visual rein for fear of what else he might try to do.

119

By the end of the second visit to Chiesa, he wanted to try the black run, which was right in front of us and down the tree less steep slope. He was quite competent by now so I took him up the new chair lift that had replaced the old rickety bubble car. I made him promise he would stay right behind me in my ski tracks not do anything flash or different. We slowly worked our way down till we were about three quarters of the way down then we opened our skis and down we came. My stomach and adrenalin were pumping having got him down safe. He simply turned to the others and muttered "bit boring really."

Everyone that goes to Chiesa, or indeed any other Italian resort is warned to look out for "the yellow perils" these are a special collection of local children that have proved their skiing ability. They are selected to be able to go to the mountain each day for a few hours to obtain special racing skills. The idea is that with each child selected eventually there may be one in particular that would then go on to represent the resort or even the region. These children could be particularly identified as they all wore yellow jackets and leggings. They had no fear whatsoever. They would launch themselves off the sides of the black runs steep sides etc. the only problem is that they had priority at all the cable car stations. So, if you were politely waiting in a queue to get onto a chair lift or button lift these dear little mites would simply ski to the front of the queue and get first choice of the next lift back up to the top. Over the we watched these youngsters grow from small children to lanky teenagers who really were sensational.

It was always sad leaving Chiesa to return home. The resort was just a perfect safe and now familiar place to ski. The hotel became like a second home and the owners were so friendly and made us feel so welcome. The ski instructors were all now known to us along with the operators of the various lifts etc. Sadly. the last time we visited they had shut down the old cable car from the back of the hotel. The alternative was a brand new station further down the valley. This made it impossible to walk to and the ski buses were few and far between. The large cable car went to the top of the mountain but from there it was necessary to catch a small funicular type of train down to the nursery slopes. It was a nightmare and after a few poor experiences we decided we wouldn't go back again. However, some very, very happy memories were made here, and I thank Chiesa for is ideal conditions and simple slopes that gave me the confidence that went on to help me ski some rather more difficult resorts.

CHAPTER 20

FIRST TRIP TO SCOTLAND SKIING

Having spent a very successful and enjoyable week at the beginner's resort of Chiesa, suddenly we got the ski bug. We felt we now had the confidence to try skiing in other resorts. As such we decided that we should try Scotland where we could drive up and save all the fuss of flying etc. At this time, we had become very good friends with Sue and Chris. Chris by our standards was already a very good skier although Sue was a novice. By taking them with us not only for the company but also for Chris to keep an eye on us we thought it was a very good idea. We planned to head for Scotland for the Easter break hoping that the season would extend, and the snow would be good. Unfortunately, the motorways at this time were not as efficient and as long as they are today. The M6 at that time only stretched as far as the Carlisle area. The terrible disaster involving the air crash at Lockerbie had just taken place and so the roads were blocked with repairs and road works which meant our journey was going to be rather longer than hoped. We decided that we would leave at the end of the working day on the Thursday and travel up as far as we could making a stop-over at Carlisle which seemed to be about halfway. Finding a suitable and reasonably priced hotel in Carlisle we arrived late evening. After putting our cases in the rooms we met in the bar for a bar snack and a couple of well deserved drinks. The hotel was lovely for the price. In the middle of the lounge bar was a glass dome which stood about three feet off the ground. Standing over the dome it turned out to be a well that had been covered over for safety's sake although lights had been installed down the well which made it a really interesting feature. To one side of the hotel was this old bit of wall that did seem out of place. When we asked the proprietor, it turned out to be an actual part of the Hadrian's Wall which went more or less through the grounds of the hotel. The hotel had preserved this particular piece and highlighted it within the structure of the hotel which made the building even more interesting.

The next day having covered half the journey we continued on past Edinburgh, Perth and on to Blairgowrie. By this time the famous Scotland scenery had taken over and it could only be described as beautiful. The slopes of Glenshee where we were heading are part of the mountain range that are extremely guarded and protected against any development or change and for this reason no houses, hotels or structures are allowed within miles of the slopes. Our nearest base we could find was in fact halfway between Blairgowrie and the Glenshee ski slopes. This still gave us a thirteen mile drive each way each day. The hotel which actually was an old pub/inn but had been extended was very isolated but had a fantastic atmosphere. The owner was a tall slim elderly chap originally from Kentucky who spoke with a deep south drawl. He called us English "you'll tea drinkers" as we all drank far more tea than coffee which was his preferred beverage. The rooms were adequate for our purposes although a little old with shared bathroom facilities. The girls wanted to freshen themselves up before we went down for the evening meal and so took it in turns to use the bathroom. Sue went in first but soon appeared much bemused and agitated. It seemed that when she run the bath all that came out was this light brown water. Of course, being isolated most of the water came from natural sources i.e. from spring or well and being in an area of peat the water would naturally be of a slightly brown colour. Sue was not going to immerse herself into this for all the tea in China. Now because the hotel and bar were halfway between the ski slopes and Blairgowrie it was the perfect stop over for all the visitors and instructors leaving the slopes for a quick beverage before going home. By the time we came downstairs the bar was heaving. It was strange as we seemed to be listening to two dialects. There was of course the local Scottish dialect from the instructors and lift staff from the slopes but there was also a very strong New Zealand dialect. It seems that during our winter season the Scots and the New Zealanders all work the slopes together. At the end of the season, of which Easter is the normal cut off point, they all pack up their bags disappear off to the southern hemisphere where they then start the winter season together. What a wonderful life they all seemed to be living. All of them were as brown as berries with the benefits of the sun and wind. One chap who we all got to know very well, was young Graham, a rather well built local ski instructor. Now Graham was not that old and being single was not in a particular hurry to get home. During the evening Graham consumed shall we say a little too much alcoholic substance to really be any good travelling home. So, our Kentucky host got Graham under one arm helped him outside and round the corner where a mobile home was waiting for Graham to sleep off his evening's entertainment. The next day, as right as rain, Graham was duly picked up and driven to the slopes where he then spent another day teaching. That evening the same thing happened as the previous night resulting with yet another sleep over in the mobile home. The following evening Graham turned up at the lodge, this time for only a quick light beverage before departing for home. The problem was of course that whilst Graham was on the slopes all day, and in the bar all evening then slumping out in the mobile home, he did so wearing his ski gear including his ski boots. His boots had not been taken off for three days. Now anyone who has ever gone skiing will ratify that at the end of the skiing day one piece of clothing that is quickly removed and placed somewhere beyond the living quarters, preferably submerged in soapy water, are the ski socks because of the odour that they emit. After three days (and nights) the results can only be imaged in the worst nightmare. I certainly would not have wanted to be his parent that night being presented with his undergarments including his socks.

The Glenshee slopes themselves were very basic. Because of the ban on development there was the simplest of car parking arrangements on a flattened area opposite a basic building that housed a ticket office and a small café area for teas and coffees. That was it. We put our ski boots, gloves and hats on in the car park carried our equipment to the drag lifts and then we were off. Down each side of the slopes, we noticed this sheep fencing that literally seemed to go from top to bottom. It was explained later that the reasons for the sheep fencing, which certainly we had not experienced in Italy, was because the weather can turn so quickly that any walkers in the summer or skiers in the winter that are caught out by this sudden turn of weather and visibility can be left in life threatening conditions. The idea therefore is to find one side of the fencing or the other and slowly descend the slope using the fencing to find ones way down. Obviously if you are wearing skis these are to be removed and carried while side stepping down the mountain. The thought actually was quite daunting. However, this particular weekend visit we had lovely clear skies and our skiing experience was really enjoyable. Chris skied like a professional to our feeble standards, but we were still able to explore the green and blue runs either side of the mountain. The conditions on the slopes were very basic and, in some places, we found ourselves paddling across heath and heather where the snow had melted and disappeared, to reach the next piece of snow to continue.

We left Scotland again feeling we were now even more expert that when we arrived. Having timed our return early we decided we would try to make the long journey home in one go. Now Chris to this day has a wonderful habit when travelling. Being ex-military, he was always advised to rest and sleep whenever and wherever he could. He took that advice very literally. Most of the journey home he would simply snuggle down, arms folded and doze off. By the time we finally got home he had slept most of the way and was certainly the most refreshed of us all.

Our next trip to Glenshee was a few years later. We stayed in the same hotel but this time only two of us. Our experience was a lot better now so we could venture further afield. We decided to take the small button lift beside the car park up to the top of the first slope, ski down to the bottom of the first gulley then again button lift to the top down into the second gulley then take the final lift to top of the third slope where there was a wonderful huge crest that went out then curved back in on itself. However, by the time we reached this top level the wind had picked up, the previous sunny ski had turned very grey and clearly bad weather was coming in. I had heard about the infamous Scottish weather patterns and how dangerous it was in the highlands, so having carried all our bad weather gear we changed glasses for goggles, donned our hats, put on thicker gloves, adding scarves etc and headed back towards the car park. By the time we came off the last slope the snow was falling quite heavily to the point we were using the sheep fencing either side of us to give us perspective on the steepness of the slopes as well as distance and direction. Having reached the car park, we quickly took our ski gear off stowed it all in the car and departed back down the mountain. It was still snowing quite heavily when we reached the accommodation some twelve miles away. By this time the road going up and over the pass was closed to all traffic. The poor folks that were actually still on the mountain were now all snowed in. It took quite a few hours for diggers to physically dig out the car parks to get the vehicles off the mountains. There were many folks still stuck up there as later afternoon and dark approached.

Having skied successfully, the next day we decided to avoid the mountain and take a road trip to Pitlochry. As we seemed so close, well on the map that is, we carried on after Pitlochry to Aviemore. What a disappointment that place was, it was horrible and reminded us a bit of a neglected mid-west town out in America. Rather than go back on the route we had come, we found what seemed a bit of a circular route that would eventually come out near Balmoral. What we didn't realise was that this route would take us right over the bleak mountains, in winter, and be over ninety miles before we reached Balmoral. The weather had turned sunny but crisp and I must confess the heather and moor of the Scottish mountains in winter was just beautiful. I had never previously been to Balmoral so by the time we reached the hotel we had covered nearly 300 miles round trip and were pretty exhausted. We had got our first glimpse and taste of true Scottish mountain beauty. We only remained at the hotel for that night. The level of service and standard had dropped terribly. We left the next morning and headed back to Aviemore and try to find accommodation close by. In Aviemore itself there is a tourist office that has the facility of linking with all the bed and breakfast facilities in the area. We were quickly allocated bed and breakfast about twelve miles outside Aviemore. When we arrived it was a pretty bungalow owned by Mr. and Mrs. Grant in a small holding of some two or three acres. Mr. Grant was a sheep farmer and in the field next to the bungalow were all his sheep dutifully protected by the good old sheep dog who we discovered later would rather lie with the sheep than be indoors. It was late afternoon and Mrs. Grant suggested if I wanted to really enjoy the last of the afternoon sun and see some really lovely views to take the little path down through the silver birches to the river which lay hidden at the back. I wandered out of the gate down a narrow path leading through a copse of silver birches and came back out into the sunshine next to this most beautiful shimmering Scottish river. It wasn't very deep and as the waters flowed down it passed over stones and rocks leaving shimmering colours in the sun. in the background were the mountains topped with snow. I just had to sit on the bank soaking up this amazing atmosphere. On the opposite bank was a fisherman fly fishing for salmon. This was all just too perfect. However, way, way off in the breeze I am sure I heard the distant sound of bagpipes. They were so far off that the sound was very intermittent and carried on each breeze. I really thought I was imagining all this. After what seemed to be ages sitting there in this perfect location I returned back through the silver birches to the bungalow. Mrs. Grant greeted me at the door and was pleased to hear I had just soaked up the wonderful experience. However, when I told her about what I thought was the sound of Bagpipes she confirmed that I had not imagined it. She explained that the Lord Provost of Scotland lived just down the glen. He often practiced his pipes especially if the queen was going to visit Scotland where he would have to officially meet her. What a memorable experience.

Whilst at Mrs. Grant's lodging we did make the effort to go up and see for ourselves the ski resort of Aviemore. This turned out to be as basic if not more basic than Glenshee and was very disappointing. The equipment was real hand me down. Now it seems that top resorts like Switzerland and Austria when they come to replace their ski equipment like cable cars etc, sell them to second rate resorts. After the second-rate countries finish with them then they are passed on again to third rate countries such as those in Bulgaria etc. Now Scotland is not able to invest as the ski season is very hit and miss and very short. As such their equipment is very much third hand. This was very obvious it was so old and rickety. The only memory I have of the actual skiing was the effort I made to try to ski the "White Lady". There was an old-fashioned T-bar that dragged myself and another up the side of this rather now infamous black run. As I climbed the temperature got colder and colder till in the end I could hardly feel my hands and face. The guy next to me I don't think had skied much as he was fidgeting and moving about which didn't give me much confidence of reaching the top. I was rather glad to say goodbye to him at the top before turning to head back down. Now the White Lady was actually an awful awkward difficult steep run. It was made up of soft snow, hard snow moguls and very difficult to turn. I couldn't wait to get down and found the whole experience not enjoyable at all. After this experience we called it a day and headed home for the two-day drive back. We did return to Glenshee with the children for a short break, to see how they got on before heading out to Chiesa. It lived up to its expectations of being poor quality snow, poor quality equipment and several days we had thick fog and mist which made it very dangerous to ski. Even more importantly we were worried as we didn't know where the children were with their instructor. We have not been back since.

CHAPTER 21
FRIENDS SKI IN AUSTRIA

Scotland had been very useful as our second ski resort, to find something that would help fill in the long winter nights and the winter blues. We discussed whether it would be a great idea for a group of us to try to get together to take two weeks out and book a skiing holiday together. We needed a total number of ten as this would give us a good discount and would be a good number to take. Chris and Sue who had come with us for the short break to Glenshee jumped at the opportunity along with two other close friends, so we already had six. My ex-wife's two sons, agreed to join us, along with the wife so all we needed was another person to complete the ten. Chris had a work colleague who had mates travelling to the same resort. Sadly, they couldn't fit him in with their party as there were no more rooms available at the hotel, they were staying in. He therefore agreed that he would be happy to come along with us. This was on the condition that whilst he would be at our hotel he would probably spend most of the day time with his mates. As this gave us the ten people we need and thus the discount we needed this seemed to be a good deal. We all got together and agreed a two-week skiing holiday to the resort of Soll. It looked the perfect resort for beginners as well as second year skiers. We decided that we would all take the lessons offered in the package for the first week and the second week simply enjoy what we had learned and have a less strenuous week on the slopes. The holiday was booked, and we were due to fly from Luton, our nearest airport straight to Munich in Southern Germany and thereafter a transfer coach to the resort.

A couple of weeks before the holiday I received a phone call from the travel agent that there had been a terrible mistake. Not all the party could travel from the original departure airport of Luton, instead some had to travel from Stansted. I was totally gob smacked that such an error had occurred especially given the meticulous planning and double checking that we had given to the project. The answer was simply "no" this was not good enough. The only compromise open was that if we could not all travel from Luton then we would all have to travel from Stansted. As a token of goodwill, the tour company offered to lay on a coach to pick us all up from home and take us to and from the airport. The only problem with that was that the coach would have to pick us up at 2.45 am to arrive in Stansted for the first flights out at 7.00 am. It meant that everyone would have to gather at our home for 2.00 am ready for the pickup.

I left work a little early that day and drove the twenty miles home from the office to make sure all luggage and equipment was packed before I got my head down for a few hours sleep. On arrival home there was a message for me to ring this number and talk to the office manager's daughter. When I rang the number and spoke to this young girl she asked if her Dad was going to be late to pick the car up. I was not aware the car I drove which was a company car was being collected. She confirmed there had been an emergency and that the firm needed the car while I was away. I asked what time he was due to arrive, and she confirmed sometime between 7.00 pm and 8.00 pm and could I hang on to give him the keys. I was not planning on getting my head down much before this time but once eight o'clock passed nobody turned up so I retired and got a few hours sleep before our adventure started. When I woke, my wife then confirmed that nobody had in fact turned up and she had given up herself at nine o'clock and managed to get a few hours sleep herself. The story would unroll after we returned from holiday.

Everyone arrived at 2.00 am and sure enough this great big 42-seater luxury coach arrived to collect us at the allotted time and took us ten off down towards Stansted. We had the added luxury of coffee facilities on board, and it was all very splendid. Those that hadn't had the opportunity like us to sleep, got their heads down for a few hours. Arriving at Stansted I was really impressed just how relaxed and simple the airport was and how easy we sailed through luggage collection, passport control and into the departure lounge. It was still a very small airport and didn't have the international reputation it does today. It was so relaxed we were expecting someone to come up to us hand us the keys and ask us to lock up when we left. Our flight also was very relaxed and we duly arrived at Munich to be met by our transfer coach that took our party and others on towards our destinations at the various ski villages in and around Soll. In those days the borders were still closed, and it was necessary to stop and show passports to the border guards both on the German side and the Austrian side of the border. This wasn't a problem as those that had travelled into foreign countries were more than aware of this requirement. However, Steve, my then second wife`s son was standing on his own, away from the party and looking very sombre and deep in thought. I approached him thinking he was not feeling well and asked him if he was okay. He was virtually in tears. He then made me realise just how I had, over my years of travelling, taken for granted a lot of what I looked at but didn't actually see. He just simply uttered that this was probably the most beautiful place he had ever seen. I at that point looked round at the high mountains the trees and the snow-covered tops and realised that for the uninitiated eyes the beauty of the Alps is unsurpassed and indescribable to those not as lucky as us to experience such views. I was to experience something similar many years later with another friend of mine.

We arrived in Soll and found it to be a really pretty Austrian village with the typical chalet type houses bars and restaurants. We were taken to our pension called the Sonnenhof perched slightly on a rise above Soll away from the town and the main road which had views down onto the long open fields. Folks were now skiing back down from the mountains to the village at the end of the skiing day. It was just remarkable. We each had a lovely typical Tyrolean chalet room with wooden furniture, all with a balcony overlooking the valley and the ski areas beyond. Meals were provided with hearty breakfasts and a cooked evening meal cooked by our chalet member Raff an English lad assigned here for the season. When Raaf wasn't working in the chalet his time was spent as a ski "bum" on the mountains and wow was he a very competent hard skier. However with all fast skiers he too could fall short to mother nature and her hard lessons. One evening after getting back to the chalet a very battle scarred Raaf greeted us looking rather sorry for himself. He had a number of visible bruises and cuts to his head. Apparently, he had been doing one or two high jumps involving crossing his skis in mid air. The problem was he had run out of air when his skis were caught as he landed spinning him out of control and consciousness. When he awoke he was in hospital having treatment. He had been carried off the mountain by snow cat and transported via ambulance. That little exercise had cost him virtually what he would hope to earn in wages and tips for the month.

For our first morning we were to meet at the very bottom of the slopes and ski lift. Here we had to again take it in turns to ski down a short slope and thus get selected into our various ski groups. Eventually after a few hours we picked up our skis and poles and headed over to these very smart gondolas and headed up to the top of the mountain. The gondolas were so different to anything previously experienced. First of all, these containers moved slowly along while skis were put in the outside boxes. Once the skis were loaded we then stepped inside the gondola with seating for four people each side. As the gondola made its way to the end of the loading station so the doors closed automatically. The gondola then caught the main chain and cable and launched itself forward to climb upwards. Once we reached the top, the gondola left the main cable for a slower cable where the doors opened, we stepped outside picked up our skis and then headed for the door out into the open where three quite lengthy slopes awaited us. Here we would spend the next few days skiing down into the bottom of the three slopes. These were divided up to different degrees of ability. The one to our right was served by a two man chair lift and onto a relatively easy blue, the one in front a drag lift up to a not so easy red run finishing off blue and then finally the left hand left which was a four man chair lift leading to a red run. One of our members Lorraine, shuffled forward on her skis, and accompanied by a stranger sat down at the given point for the chair lift to then carry them up to the drop off area. She remarked to the stranger next to her that she didn't think it was very safe even though about fifteen feet off the ground. Her temporary travel companion also a novice agreed.

It wasn't till she was off the lift and caught us all up on the slope that she realised that there was in fact a safety bar above her. What she needed to do was to pull the bar down and then put her skis in the bar positioned at the bottom for this purpose. It was shaped like a large safety tray that fits onto a highchair. Without the safety tray the child could fall out, with it the child had something to hang on to and couldn't fall out. The same principal was supposed to be exercised on the chair lift. No wonder it didn't feel very safe. Another incident was when another member of our group was half way up the drag lift on the second slope, shifted his weight and immediately lost his balance and became a "casualty" in the deep snow. Lucky his fellow companion on the double tow lift was able to hang on, still laughing, till she reached the top and was able to compose herself for the ski back down. The four man chair lift was a different kettle of fish again. When the four man chair lift reaches the top of the lift area, it discharges its four occupants to a short flat area that has a sheer ice wall in front. To those that are reasonably efficient it gives them time to gather their thoughts and their equipment and skate off to the side. Those that are not so efficient happily then fall into each other and end up in a pile in front of the ice wall. However with only a few seconds to clear this means the next load of skiers on the next chair lift are then arriving to pile into them. Before you know it there is a pile of skiers some 12 or 16 deep which requires the lift to be stopped while everyone untangles, picks themselves up, clears the area before the lift can start again. This seemed to repeat itself several times during the course of each day taking away even more lack of confidence from the dear novice skiers. Amongst all this mayhem was an elderly lady, assumed to be a local, not wearing any of the "standard ski gear" but instead had a pair of jeans, a long black coat and a winged hat and she was having a wild time using her basic snow plough style (resembling more a gorilla holding a tray) and she skid everything that was in front of her without fear or favour. She was an absolute breath of fresh air to see her whizzing round the slopes, completely oblivious to fashion or style and just simply enjoying herself.

Now the ski lessons in Austria, are of a different standard to what we had been used to in Italy. First of all Italy was really just treated as fun while we learnt. Here we were actually specifically told by the ski instructor that we were not there to enjoy ourselves we were there to learn to ski. Also, our lessons were not just two hours a day and then the rest of the day to enjoy ourselves. The lessons were two hours in the morning, and two hours in the afternoon. By the end of each day, we were truly shattered. Our first morning was spent on the first ski slope with the two-man chair lift learning to move from snow plough to step turns. Each step turn would end up with a parallel traverse of the slope before the next step turn to go back the other way. It was daunting as the slope was a lot steeper than in Chiesa but by lunchtime we had more or less cracked it. The afternoon was a whole different kettle of fish. We met just outside the gondola station. Here the ski instructor directed us over to a T-bar lift. Now I should explain that most T-bar lifts have been replaced. They are awkward and difficult to ride. If the other person with you is taller or heavier then the balance is going to change, making the ride very difficult. What didn't help here was this T-bar was going to take us up the side of a very steep very long Red Run, and eventually had we stayed on it, finishing on a Black Run. We were advised we would go up to a certain height beyond the level of the four man chair lift further over to our right. Here we were to leave the T-bar and try to shuffle out onto the red run. This all sounds very easy in theory. However we were all more or less novices. My T-bar partner and I were just about to get off the bar without falling over and managed to shuffle over what looked like a snow kerb onto the run. The run was very steep and to my level of skiing very slippery. One girl and her husband were not able to get off the lift in time and were carried on up to the beginning of the black run. I can still hear her screams of sheer fear behind me. I couldn't stop to help her as I was having extreme difficulty myself. We would never see them again. We heard later that someone helped them to get their skis off. They then side stepped or slipped down off the mountain slope. They then headed for the gondola and never came back. As for me I had completely lost it. I could not remember how to traverse the slope, I had forgotten how to do step turns and every time the skis started to slip I fell over. Within the first 40 feet my confidence has completely gone. I was disorientated and didn't know where I was and there seemed to be nobody there to help me. I did catch up the instructor briefly whose only words were "well if you can't keep up we'll have to leave you" and indeed she did. By the time I reached the level where the four man lift ended I was a complete wreck. I was so emotional and indeed frightened I really decided I couldn't or indeed wanted to do this anymore. I saw my second wife in her group and she could see that I was in a hell of a state and suggested that I simply get down take my skis off and wait for them to finish their lesson. I did one better. I took my skis off, headed for the gondola and left the mountain. I just headed back into the village found a bar and had probably too many drinks to drown my humiliation, my frustration and my fear. I had never experience anything like it before or after. When my second wife caught up with me she had to spend some time calming me down as I was ready to catch the next plane home. What she suggested was that I dropped a class down to hers. She explained her teacher was so much different to the ogre that was in charge of our group. After a night's sleep I agreed to give it one more try.

The next day I went back up the mountain. We had a word with my second wife's instructor and she happily agreed for me to join them. Thank goodness. She took me back several steps and slowly, slowly over the next few days re-built my confidence. As for the ogre she looked at me with daggers as if how dare I leave her group that was going to reflect so badly on her. I settled down, learnt to do proper side steps, learnt to do proper traversing and my skiing went on to a new level and by the second week was really enjoying my skiing. In fact our lift pass whilst not covering the entire ski resort of some 200 miles did take us to the edges and give us some really good long runs to practice on. I would in several years to come return to the resort. My first task was to go straight to the T-bar. I rode the T-bar past the place where I had vacated those years before, on and to the top of the black run. Here I stepped out onto the slope. I donned my gloves and my ski poles and literally launched myself off. I came down that slope like a rocket. My turns were advanced weight shifting turns and before I knew I was back down. The adrenalin was totally pumping. But I had beaten my nemesis and felt really good to have done it.

One of our favourite places to have a rest was on the first slope where the two-man ski lift was. Halfway down were some benches on the side of the slope. Next to us were several Austrian chalets where folks would come and stay for a ski weekend or holiday. it turned out one of them was owned by the then famous Austrian Formula one driver. In Austria he was treated as an absolute hero. He even had his own Black and Gold Gondola kept reserved for when he travels the mountain to his chalet. One day we sat there, and someone had actually tried to drive up the narrow roadway got within a hundred yards of the chalets and wheels had started spinning. Some of the boys in the group went over to help out by pushing his sports car out of the snow and back onto something a bit firmer. It turned out to be the Formula One Racing Driver.

Sadly, my confidence had not returned sufficiently to be adventurous so when most of the group decided to try to tackle the long red run back to the village I declined. The route followed the gondola which I noted was very lumpy, full of moguls and looked like it was going to be very difficult and not enjoyable at all. So, we would ride the Gondola back each day to meet up with the lads back in the village and a suitable bar. However, one day we noticed a teacher with a group of nursery school children heading off down the back of one of the slopes and between a few wooden mountain huts. The yellow walking sign that they passed under indicated that the village was so many hours walk. We decided we would tag along but at the back. We followed these children down narrow tracks, through woods, across fields. Every so often the tired little legs of the children stopped for them to rest before carrying on. They kept staring at us as to why we were there what were we doing and all very confusing. After about three quarters of an hour we came to a small crossroads. The teacher and the children veered off to the left. We noticed the signpost showed the village was to the right. We waved to the children, and we were on our own. Luckily, we had a couple of hundred yards before the track turned again and dropped us back to the bottom of the Gondola. Here we could hold our ski sticks in one hand, put our skis parallel and ski the long and gentle slope across this huge three quarter mile field back the edge of the village. How our skiing had improved from that first day.

In the village we found a bar that we liked and so we would all meet up there after our days skiing. The bar was very lively full of youngsters and the beer flowed while the music played very loudly. The atmosphere was brilliant. We could stay till we were due to eat and then leave to walk the short distance back to our chalet for evening dinner. This particular evening were reporters milling around looking for some scandal to print. One of them asked me if there was any nude skiing or other antics going on. I just told the girl to go away in no uncertain terms. However, two lads apparently agreed that they would ski down nude. The following day it hit the headlines how debauched the resort was, how sex parties and all sorts of nonsense went on. I was very cross as it couldn't have been more further from the truth. The youngsters that were there in the bar were just out for good clean honest fun. And that was the most of it. Of course the daily newspaper that printed the story got more and more unprofessional as the years went on.

By now we had finished our first week and our lessons. We could now take it a lot easier getting up in the mornings going up the mountains and even finishing when we were ready. One day we decided to be a little bit later going up the mountain. It was a beautiful sunny morning, so we took our time wandering around a few of the shops before waiting for the bus to take us up to the Gondola. As I stood there, on the other side of the road waiting at the bus stop going in the opposite direction, was a group of skiers. One of the skiers looked very familiar. I shouted out "Simon" whereupon the person turned round with a huge grin in his face. It was indeed my first wife's brother. The group had been up early and had skied over to Soll from the next village and were waiting for the bus to take them back again. What a small world to find someone you knew two thousand miles away standing on the opposite side of the road in a small ski village.

Throughout the fortnight we were in Soll we had all undergone several mishaps. Most of us had fallen over. Steve was our star character though. Not only had he fallen over, he had managed to take with him some poor fella on the T-bar going up quite a steep slope on the second slope. In addition, he was out of control on another and did the unthinkable by knocking over a ski instructor. Luckily the instructor was not injured but Steve was not very popular. These instructors rely on staying fit and staying upright to be able to work. If they are injured and cannot teach, they don't get paid and as it is a relatively short season of the year this could prove rather financially difficult. One afternoon during our second week a couple of us were resting on the benches on the side of the first ski slope in our favourite location. As we sat there watching all the skiers working their way round the various slopes and lifts we heard the sound that everyone dreads. A helicopter was approaching us fast. Now when there are injuries there are three types of rescues. First of all, if it is minor but the skier cannot ski they are taken off the slope on the back of a skidoo. This is a motorised type of motorbike with a conveyer belt type propellant as opposed to wheels that would be stuck in the snow. If the accident is a little more serious and the skier cannot easily walk or leave the slope by his own means, then a stretcher is brought in. The skier is laid on the stretcher which itself is on skis. The medic then skis off pulling the stretcher behind him till he either gets to the Gondola where the injured is transferred and taken off the mountain. If it is not possible for the Gondola to be used then the medic has to ski all the way down the mountain for the ambulance to wait for him at the bottom Gondola station. The injured is strapped onto the stretcher but is basically facing backwards. This means he has the experience of coming off the mountain at the hands of these very skilful medics but travelling backwards. The third option is for the serious injuries. This is where the helicopter is called in. The helicopter can land close by the injured who get quickly transferred to the helicopter that can take off and head quickly to hospital. On this day the helicopter came in very quickly. It landed right in the middle of the general area between the three slopes and right in front of the restaurant come café where many skiers were sat with their refreshments. Now bearing in mind that any skiers of intermediate or advanced levels would have headed off into the 200 miles of ski slopes available at this resort. Those left behind would be the beginners and not so experienced. Seeing a serious injury and the need for a helicopter would mean creating quite a trauma for the spectators as well as the injured and any accompanying the person injured. As we had quite a large group and given the history through the week of the various accidents that had been experienced, I felt sick that this person may be one of our group. I suggested to my second wife that perhaps she should stay put and I would go and see if it was any of our group. I skied down really not looking forward to what I was going to find. Having reached the area I took my skis off and walked up hill to the area that the medics were. What I saw was absolutely awful. It was not anyone from our group but a young woman laying on her

138

back with medics trying to resuscitate her. She had turned deathly blue and had blood coming out of her ears. This was not a good sign at all. Having established it was not one of our group I didn't want to stand around gawping and left. I took myself back up to the chair lift and back to where we had sat. By this time the casualty had been loaded onto the helicopter and taken away from the scene. There were lots of members of the public standing around in tears and it was a very sad moment. Later we heard that the young woman had not survived. She had been an American ski instructor that had come over with a group to enjoy the Austrian ski scene. On her day off, she with others had built a lump of snow to be used as a ski jump. It was located at the bottom of the four-man red run and therefore was steep enough to get a good speed for this rather large lump of snow. All had gone really well and they were all having great fun. Sadly, the young American lady took her jump missed her landing and crashed over. She then started to slide rather rapidly towards one of the metal supports holding the four-man chair lift, full of skiers above. Seeing that she was in serious trouble she managed to alter the direction of her fall. Sadly, her direction changed from away from the metal girder but straight towards the large oak tree right in front of the restaurant. She apparently hit the tree sideways with such a force that her body was wrapped round the body of the tree before coming to a halt. The sheer force of impact was enough to damage her internal organs. She did not stand a chance. I think everyone that had experienced this accident became very aware of how easy it is and how quick it is for a fatal accident to take place. At all times when skiing it is so important not to go faster than one's ability be aware of all the dangers and be aware that this sport has that have to be taken seriously.

The holiday finally came to an end, and we headed for home. The flight back to Stansted was met by the luxury coach that took us all back to Milton Keynes. Back at home everyone said their goodbyes and disappeared home. As for us, we had the fortnight's washing and tidying up to do before Monday morning's return to work. On Monday morning I took the company car, that was still on the driveway despite rumours that it was going to be taken, and headed for the office. In the office there was a great deal of humour going on as to whether their joke had taken effect. It turned out that the whole exercise of the phone calls to me at home, the messages that the car was needed, that I should stay up to wait for John to call and collect the car was a set up. The conspirators thought it would be humorous to get me to stay up and be totally shattered with no sleep by the time I reached the snow slopes. With a dead pan face I sombrely pointed out that their joke had backfired. Carol had told me to go to bed to get some sleep she would stay up wait for John to arrive, give him the keys of the car and then join me. Of course, because John never arrived it meant Carol had stayed up all night. Because of her poor physical health and with all her spine problems and because she didn't get any sleep she was going to suffer badly. She ended up having to wear her dreaded neck brace. By the time we arrived at the hotel she had completely seized up and it meant she was unable to ski for days and in fact helped to ruin her holiday. Of course, this was all nonsense as Carol had given up within an hour of me going to bed and joined me. We both had a wonderful holiday and free from what I had described she had suffered. My double back on them worked though. She was sent flowers, phone calls from the senior partner and his deputy apologising for the terrible joke they had pulled and were so embarrassed. I never did tell them I had played their joke back on them.

CHAPTER 22

SKIING HOLIDAYS ABROAD BRINGING NOT NECESSARILY FOND MEMORIES

My work colleague Paul and I had decided to put caution to the wind and break away from working for other folks. We therefore set up a law practice in Milton Keynes where we would sink or swim by our own hard efforts. The office came into life in August. We had set aside funds for each other to survive by March. If by this time we were not making a profit and paying our own way, we were really doing something wrong.

My first month's drawing came in December. I was going to be able to draw the massive sum of £485. I was now on my own having gone through another divorce earlier in the year. As such, I decided a Christmas at home was not really ideal. As such I searched for a reasonable ski break which would take me to a ski resort I had not previously heard of in Cavalese in Italy. Standing alone on Milton Keynes station, with bags and skis was a very strange lonely experience. The thoughts of the possible adventure ahead gave me the confidence to climb aboard the train and depart. The train then actually ran from Milton Keynes through London and on to Gatwick. Here there was the flight awaiting me to take me to Milan in Italy.

Winter can always throw up problems travelling. Air travel is even more susceptible to problems especially when travelling to countries where snow and ice can be expected at any time. The first thing you notice when flying abroad in the winter is when once on board and before taking off the aeroplane is visited by what looks like a large tanker with a hose that extends large enough to reach the wings. One of the runway mechanics then walks along the wings of the aeroplane with the hose and sprays the entire wings both front and back with what looks like steam. What is actually happening is that anti freezing liquid is being introduced so that when the aircraft is travelling at thirty-one thousand feet the wings won't freeze up and drop off. This is of course an awakener at what conditions are like and the dangers faced with every flight.

The coaches were waiting for us at Milan to transport my fellow ski fanatics and myself on to the resort. I bumped into a couple from Thame that I had met in Chiesa some years before. They were also travelling to the village of Cavalese. After several hours heading into the mountains the coach pulled up and we were shuffled out to our various hotels. Sadly, it would turn out that I was in a hotel on my own. Various other members on the coach were spread out amongst the other several hotels in the resort. This was a bit of a blow as it would mean that mealtimes, evening drinks and breakfast would be spent on my own. My first night I got settled in my room and had a couple of drinks in the bar before retiring to my room for a well-deserved sleep. The weather the next day was just glorious. Although there was no snow in the village there was no shortage of the white stuff to ski on. We had a short walk to the ski lift station. The problem with Cavalese was that the ski slopes were all on the other side of the valley. Between us and the slopes there was a steep drop with a six-lane motorway running below us. The journey was carried out in a large cable car that held about 60 skiers with equipment. On the far side were further ski lifts taking skiers off to various slopes depending on the difficulty and capability of the skier. It was a lovely resort as was the skiing, but more suited for the beginner or early intermediate. It was not long before I had skied most of the slopes available and was looking for something a bit more testing. I had teamed up with the couple from Thame who like me were looking for something a little more interesting. The next day I took the ski-bus out of the village and down to the start of this huge ski area. The area divided Italy and Austria with a cross of cultures in both areas. I was sat at the café ready to go and explore the new region when my mobile phone rang. It was my friend Phil. He rang to wish me a lovely holiday etc. he asked me when I was leaving. I told him that I was already there and sat on a mountain talking to him on my mobile. We had all just started to enjoy the benefits of mobile phones and in particular the little Nokia. Phil was totally gobsmacked that I was talking to him from so far away and so high up and the signal was so clear. We swapped niceties and hung up. I skied the new area, and the next day took my friends with me to explore. I should explain that my skis were what was known then as Giant Slalom Skis. This means they were two metres ten in length. They had a narrow curve along the sides. This means they were designed to go fast. Once speed had been built up by leaning the weight either on the left and ski to turn right or the right had ski to turn left this was how control was made. I have to say it also took a lot of adrenalin to gain the speed and to rely upon these two planks strapped to your feet to go where you are hoping they would take you. Those first few days were marvellous. I even managed to show my male friend to do this large carving turn. His wife stuck to her normal turns but him and I travelled very fast and very radical. This was of course until the following day we arrived in heavy mist and fog. I should explain 'white out.' This is a phenomenon that is peculiar to the mountains. Because the ski slopes are white with snow, everything looks flat, and everything looks very confusing. Now with my eyes I cannot focus fully looking down the slope. Everything to me looks flat and even. Its only when you start to ski down that your legs are trying to go in a different direction to where your brain thinks they should be going. It is very unnerving. It was here that I learnt to have to ski with my feet and not my eyes. I couldn't see the dips, the moguls or even the depth of the slopes. The only way down for me was to ski behind my friend's wife. She stuck to her basic snow plough turns and I was right behind her copying everything she did. What a come down to the radical skiing I had done the day before. I didn't care at least I wasn't falling over or hurting myself. That evening after we left the slopes and was waiting for the bus back to the resort I noticed opposite these two huge ski slopes one slightly larger than the other. On each of these slopes were local lads practicing their ski jumping. It all looks very tame on the television but to see it live is terrifying. These guys were throwing themselves straight down this narrow slope launching themselves into the air and hurtling downwards till the ground met them. Here they then had to stop before the ski jump ran out of snow. I then noticed that worst of all these slopes were made up of artificial fabric. Now having skid on artificial slopes back in the UK I know they resemble plastic hairbrushes turned upside down. The bristles are absolutely lethal if you fell over and have many a nasty graze caused by catching my hands and arms after I have fallen. These guys were throwing themselves down these artificial slopes and what was worse landing on the artificial bristles at the bottom. They certainly had my vote.

After skiing each day and before evening dinner I would have a wander round this lovely village. This was a beautiful rustic village with old stone buildings all lit up with Christmas lights and lanterns. The shops were all open selling all the Christmas ware including chocolates, fruit and alcohol as well as all sorts of gifts. Wandering round the village were various men dressed up as Santa Claus. Each man had on his back a mountain wicker basket full of sweets. Every child younger than about 8 years old were stopped by Santa Claus and given a present of sweets etc., the children's faces were just perfect. However, I did think to myself that all year round we are teaching our children not to accept any sweets or gifts from strangers. Here they were taking sweets from men dressed up in Santa suits. Didn't seem quite right somehow. Anyway, what I did discover was just how warm and friendly these lovely people were from this village. Everyone was made to feel welcome. The smiles and waves from locals just made you feel you were part of the community. They welcomed us with such warm hearts and arms.

My evenings after dinner were pretty empty. I would have an odd drink in the bar then retire to my room. The fact I was so far from home and on Christmas eve then Christmas day did leave a rather empty feeling inside. I had only the one Christmas card that I had taken with me that sat very solitary and alone on my bedside table.

It was soon time to pack up and get ready to leave. As we left this lovely friendly village and headed back to the airport it was snowing lightly. It was still snowing when we arrived back at the airport. My friends from Thame were not travelling back to Gatwick but were taking a separate flight to Manchester. We learnt that because it was snowing heavily throughout the Alps that there flight had not even left Manchester. Our flight had arrived but was circling above us trying to find a clear slot to land. It got worse when we heard that all the airports across the northern belt of Italy were closing due to the bad weather. Turin had closed. This was followed by Verona and Venice. Milan had two airports and the other one from ours had closed. This had got very serious. Somehow our flight was able to land and the passengers disembark. This meant that they did not have to fly back to the UK. But what was going to happen to us? The flight from Manchester was cancelled all together. We stood wondering what would happen to us. We then got the message to make our way to the departure lounge. Here we were ushered out and onto the plane. It was still being fuelled and still being doused with the anti icing agent. The pilot then came on board and explained the serious situation we were in. However, he was not going to spend time in Italy and especially miss out on New Year's Eve that was the following day. He moved his way to the flight deck and over the radio explained that the next few minutes were crucial. Out of the windows we spotted the airport ploughs and vehicles with huge brushes go under our wings and head out along the runway trying to clear it sufficiently for a possible take off. The pilot then announced that take off was going to be very noisy and very bumpy. He then drew back the throttle and the engines roared and vibrated violently with the force. He then released the brakes and the plane lurched forward. As we cleared the distance between us and the end of the runway we spotted the snow clearance machines turn off out of the way of the aircraft. Suddenly the vibrations became less as the aircraft suddenly pointed upward and we were thrown around in our seats. We headed straight up until we reached a ceiling of thirty-eight thousand feet. It had been snowing up to thirty-one thousand feet. The journey home was uneventful thank goodness and we were able to land at Gatwick without further trauma. My journey home was on the Gatwick to London express that went on through London and on towards Bedford. I got off at a village close by Milton Keynes where my father met me along with my daughter and got me home. I changed and managed to get to the pub in time for the New Year celebrations. It turned out my friends heading for Manchester were not able to leave Milan for a further three days due to the weather closing in. Fate was clearly on my side that afternoon.

Several weeks later and my lovely memories of this wonderful friendly village turned to horror. I discovered that there had been two American military jets who were showing off to each other. They decided on approaching Cavalese that they would fly underneath the cable car wire that stretched across the valley. Sadly, one of the jets caught the cable with its tail and cut through the cable like cheese wire. This resulted in the cable falling the sixty or seventy feet onto the motorway below. What made this an absolute horror nightmare was that there was a cable car full of ski tourists, mostly Germans that were travelling over to the ski slopes. They didn't stand a chance. They were all killed including the village cable car operator. The thought of this tragedy haunts me to this day when I think how this entire village would have gone into mourning for the folks that were lost. I was furious to further learn that the two pilots were quickly spirited out of the Country by the American air force before the pilots could be brought to stand for what was a very serious criminal action. As far as I know they were never brought to justice.

A few years later I took my son skiing to the Dolomites in Northern Italy. We were both on our own and so again decided to celebrate New Year on the slopes. He was a good skier by now and I knew we would be good company together. The village we chose had some great ski slopes that we would enjoy with the experience we both now had. The first day we spent exploring the various slopes and tested our equipment. We had found some amazing long twisting slopes that tested our Giant Slalom abilities. One of the slopes was the famous Camel Bumps. On this slope was held the annual downhill racing attracting top skiers from around the world. The camel bumps were famous as great speed were needed to hit the top of the first bump and by taking off it was possible to pass over the next two bumps landing on the far side some hundred yards away. If the skiers got it wrong, then wipe outs were going to be quite nasty. We were able to hit these bumps but unable to fly across. Instead we were able to achieve a couple of turns in each drop pass over the top into the next etc. we were still travelling at great speed and learnt every respect for these skiers that were able to just fly across.

After three days of exceptional skiing I decided that it would perhaps be a good idea to try to slow proceedings down and have a simple day of skiing and perhaps take some photos stop for coffees and generally give our legs a rest. I should explain there is no other sport or exercise that can come close to the muscles used in skiing. Given that most of us back in Britain only ski for a week once a year means that we really needed to be aware not to take risks or ignore that our legs would get very tired. As such we took the skis up and did a couple of runs. We then decided to head over to the long camel bump run. I skied down about hundred yards and standing on my skis sideways to the steep slope took my camera out and took several photos. Having put my camera away back in my rucksack I was ready to catch my son up fifty feet away. Now there is a ski move where with the skis pointed parallel to the slope the body is twisted to face down the slope. Then slowly releasing the skis from their edges holding the slope the natural reaction was that the skis would unwind from this coiled stance and then follow round to head down hill where I could then ski downwards. Sadly I over balanced. Instead of the legs uncoiling I fell backwards. Because my skis were stationary, they did not release my boots from the bindings. Instead, I just fell over my skis with my legs still attached. I felt a pop from the back my right knee and straight away knew I had injured myself. I couldn't move. My son came up and helped me release my skis. I then tried to stand up but got this sharp searing pain that dropped me back to the floor. It was obvious I was going to need help. Everyone, even my son thought that as it was such a simple fall that it was going to be just a bruise or a sprain. Just below us some couple of hundred yards away was the café restaurant. We managed to call someone's attention and one of the rescue guys came up on a skidoo. He tried to help me stand up and climb aboard the skidoo as a passenger for him to take me back down. I nearly passed out with the pain. It was a case now of a hammock to be hitched up, brought up and set me on it. The skidoo then with me behind in the ski hammock zoomed downhill to the cable car to get me off the mountain. I was helped by a couple of rescue guys into the large cable car and eased down onto the plank seating that runs round the edge. It was here that the searing pain hit me again and I did indeed pass out. By the time I came round two guys were carrying me out of the gondola and onto a stretcher into an ambulance. The ambulance took me to the hospital where the numbers of injured skiers were incredible. I was particularly aware of the numbers of ski boarders that were injured. Most of them had broken wrists. In quite a few cases both arms had their wrists broken. I was questioned whilst on the stretcher as to what insurance I had. When I advised and produced my personal insurance this seemed to open up all sorts of doors. I was whisked off and away from the rest of the walking wounded. I was given some excellent personal treatment that involved X-rays etc. I was eventually plastered from my ankle to above my knee, given a pair of crutches and put into a taxi back to the hotel. I was told I would now have to rest. My skiing holiday was over. I was rather hoping that because I was injured the insurance would cover me to return back to the UK early. Sadly, this was not the case. I had to sit it out till the holiday was over and to travel home with everyone else. I spent a very boring week hobbling round on crutches with my leg extremely sore. The knee started to swell so badly that by the time the end of the holiday arrived the plaster, that had a slit along the front, had opened up wide enough for me to put my thumb in the gap. I was pig sick that New Years eve was spent in my dressing gown. At midnight, I was stood at the doorway of the hotel watching all the ski instructors and anyone good enough come skiing down the slope at the back of the hotel all holding red flares.

It was time to come home. My son did most of the packing and carrying it to the reception area of the hotel. We were going to be taken to the airport at Innsbruck by private ambulance. This huge ambulance arrived that looked more like the ghost buster's vehicle. What luxury. We arrived at Innsbruck where we were delivered at the arrivals and duly ushered through customs etc. I was helped onto the airplane and given priority seating where I could hold my leg out straight. The flight was pretty straight forward and arriving at Gatwick I along with other walking wounded were met by various golf buggy type transports. These golf buggies got us to the arrivals desk and we were whisked through again without any delay or fuss to meet the ambulance to get me home. My face then dropped. What on earth was this waiting for me and what a contrast from what dropped me off in Austria. This was an old National Health Service seventies type ambulance that had been re-commissioned to the private insurance company. The two ambulance men assured me that it was perfectly safe and able to get me home. I was loaded into the back while my son disappeared off with the ski gear and luggage to the car park. He was to follow us home independently in the car. We set off and all was going reasonably well until we were on the M25 and heading for the M1. At this point I asked whether the vehicle was in fact okay as there was a strange smell coming from below my seat. I was assured that yes all was well. I was laying in the bench facing backwards. I suggested that the driver looked at his reversing mirror out of the back window. We were leaving a huge grey cloud of smoke so thick you couldn't see the other cars behind us. The driver agreed yes there was a problem and headed for the next exit off the motorway and down towards the service road. Halfway, the driver gave a bit of a yelp and when I looked round there was now flames coming out of the dashboard. The driver immediately braked, stopped the ambulance and was out of the driver's door and gone. The guy in the back that was supposed to be looking after me, nearly as swiftly was out of the backdoors and away. I tried as best I could to get my crutches and hobble my way to the back door, drop down the steps and onto tarmac and hobble away from the distressed vehicle. The problem was that the only way I could see that was safe was back up hill towards the motorway. As if by magic, two policemen arrived in their patrol car. One announced to me that I was going the wrong way and couldn't go up towards the motorway. When I asked him to suggest an alternative he said I must make my way to the front of the vehicle. As this was now on fire, I said the only way this was going to happen is if he accompanied me. Like a couple of fellows in a three-legged race we positioned ourselves in front of the ambulance as quickly as we could and he sat me on the large wall where the slip road met the service road beneath. At this point it was now a beautifully sunny clear day. I was sat on the wall wearing my full ski suit as this was all that would fit me. I had my plastered leg protruding through the suit and there I was smoking a cigarette. Behind me was a police car, two policemen and two ambulance men. Folks driving past were just mystified by this strange and unique sight.

My mother was waiting back at home for us, so I thought I had better ring home before my son arrived to put her in the picture of what was happening and the reason the delay. When I told her where I was and what had happened, I heard this strange noise. When I asked if she was okay, she had collapsed on the floor in fits of laughter that she was trying to suppress. I did eventually reach home. My son had

149

been and gone leaving my mum with the car and the ski equipment. I had been advised by the Italian surgeon that I should take the set of X-ray photos to my local hospital as soon as I got back as there may be further medical attention needed. I didn't bother that afternoon, but the next day got someone to give me a lift and went into A&E in a wheelchair and with my X-rays. I eventually was seen by a doctor who looking at my Italian X-rays simply ripped them up and threw them into the bin. He announced they were defective and not good quality. He arranged for his own set of X-rays to be taken so he got a better story of what had happened. It certainly was not as drastic as the Italian doctor had announced with possible iron supports being worn for the rest of my life, probably not to walk again and even living in a wheelchair. The story wasn't good as I had seriously damaged my cruciate ligament. Ideally, I should have an operation to clean out the torn and damaged tendons which would help. The doctor asked whether I would like to go through the operation or perhaps wait to see how it repaired itself. He did offer the proviso that if the knee didn't successfully repair itself then I should contact my doctor and arrange to go in for the operation.

I tried everything I could within reason to walk and exercise and try to loosen up my knee. I even drove my friend to Switzerland thinking this would help. Alas, any reasonable strain left me limping and my knee very sore. As such I did after eighteen months contact the doctor and he in turn arranged for the hospital to take me in and undertake the necessary operation. I was admitted and set ready to go to the operation theatre. A couple of young trainee doctors came in and attempted to put the cannula into my hand to take the anaesthetic to send me out for the operation. A more senior lady nurse came into my room took one look at their efforts tut-tutted and removed the cannula, re-fitted it, then it was ready to insert the anaesthetic. Now they say a little knowledge is dangerous. This was the first time I had been in hospital since I was nine months old. All I had experienced was what I saw on the television. Now I always noted that when the needle went into the arm or in my instance the cannula, they always squirted a drop of fluid out of the syringe to get rid of the air. If air was to get into the veins this would cause seriously problems even death. To my horror the nurse simply put the needle into the cannula and squeezed. I felt this cold sensation entering my hand and up along my arm. All I had time to do was raise my free hand and try to say "hey" and just passed out. Somewhere off in the distance some time later a voice was calling me. "Allan wake up – wake up Allan!" and I opened my eyes. I was still alive and they hadn't injected air into my body. I was so relieved I launched myself forward and grabbed the nurse with both arms just grateful I was alive. Only problem was that this was not a nurse, but the theatre senior sister. What made it worse was she was the daughter of very good friends of mine. I have known Tracey since she was a little girl. I knew she was embarrassed at this very affectionate hug. I was so grateful to be alive I didn't care. Many years have passed, and I have been in and out of theatre for numerous operations. On most of them Tracey has seen my name, came out to talk to me and give me re-assurances and her parting words were "And when you wake up Allan you don't need to grab me and give me a hug". I have never lived it down.

CHAPTER 23
MY MATE'S FIRST TRIP ABROAD

By now I was living on my own as my marriage had broken up. A similar story had occurred to a very good friend of mine Phil, albeit that he had been split from his wife for nearly a year. I was unaware of his split, as I had lost touch with him due to pressures within the marriage for him to cut all ties with friends etc., When his wife left him, it was very suddenly one day while he was out at work. When he returned, he found his fishing chair, a small portable television a few bits of cutlery saucepans and basic cooking facilities but nothing else. She had cleaned him out of everything including all his photos, ornaments, the children's things, and even the pet dog. By the time I found him he was in a poor and sorry state both financially but also mentally and was very close to suicide. He was in debt and didn't know which way to turn. As a lawyer with my lawyer's hat, I advised him to sell the house and clear his debts. I was on my own rattling round in a four bed roomed house. I suggested that he take up one of the bedrooms for himself. This way I could look after him; keep an eye on him and bring him back to some form of normality and dignity. With any relationship you soon fall into a routine and Phil and I soon settled down to our own routine. We would go our own separate ways in the mornings to our own separate jobs. In the evenings I would normally be home first cook the meal then we would chill out telling each other some story or other or going over past tales.

I realised that Phil, from Manchester, had never been abroad whereas I had travelled extensively since I was young. He would latch on with great interest to stories I had to tell of my times abroad. A plan was beginning to hatch. Now the one country I have always loved and always want to re-visit even today is Switzerland. To me this is the most beautiful, breath-taking country I have ever visited. It is clean, it is efficient, it is majestic as well as beautiful and something you cannot fully describe to anyone who has not been. In previous years I had travelled to Scotland several times for a skiing holiday but found the journey very long. Motorways all the way had not been built. It was also very boring and I really didn't want to repeat that for a while. It was coming up to Easter. It looked like the weather was going to be favourable and so I made a suggestion to Phil. Instead of turning left on the motorway and heading north we should instead turn right and head for Switzerland. I could read his mind, "That's a million miles away". Now I have tried to explain to folks many times that from us to the Swiss border is closer for us than the highlands of Scotland and of course with easier and simpler road systems. I asked Phil to trust me and we left home around late morning heading for Dover. We caught the mid-afternoon boat to Calais and by early evening we were on the French motorways heading south. We hit the French Swiss border at eleven that evening. I was hoping that our first nights stop would be just over the Swiss border in Vallorbe. However, this was still a very sleepy town with very few hotels and by the time we arrived nothing was left open. We had to double back some 13 miles back over the Jura mountains into France and stay at one of the motels for the evening. As it was, it turned out the choice was wonderful as we had breakfast thrown in. We were able to return back over the Jura in full daylight with a splendid clear blue sunny sky.

By the time we reach Lausanne it was bordering on lunchtime. I suggested that rather than hit the motorway we would stop over in Montreux on the shores of Lake e Geneva for lunch. We parked the car, found this lovely little restaurant above the busy street adjoining the lake. Up some stairs to the first floor, the restaurant had an open balcony over-looking the lake. Having seated us at one of the tables close to the side overlooking the lake the waiter came over and asked us in perfect English whether we were ready to order and suggested a half bottle of Rose wine. Now my experience of rose wine ended with

Mateus Rose, back in the late sixties early seventies, which back then tasted like vinegar. The waiter must have read my expression as he offered a small glass as a taster. It was immediately love at first sight. We had our meal and our bottle of rose wine.

Phil just sat there in the sunshine completely blown away. The lake stretched out below us with little boats bobbing up and down. The paddle steamers travelled past, and of course the back drop of mountains topped with snow just completed the scene. It just could not have been ordered any more perfect. This was another example of taking this all for granted over the years and once again I looked to actually see what someone for the first time must have been blown away by; the sheer splendour and beauty of the place. Phil needless to say was away in his own spiritual heaven.

Sadly, all good things must come to an end so with great reluctance I had to drag him away. He was very disappointed that we had to leave and even more disappointed when our route took us away from the lake and its backdrop of mountains and headed in land towards the flatter plains of Switzerland. He even remarked that I had promised him mountains that were fast disappearing behind us. I said nothing. A couple of hours later and with Berne behind us we approached Lake Interlaken (or Lake Thun as the locals call it). Once again, the landscape changed dramatically. With every mile the hills grew larger and larger till white capped mountains seemed to be bearing down upon us. When we reached Interlaken itself we turned off the motorway and headed off up and into this wide gorge towards our destination. The little mountain train passed us as we drove along as if to challenge us on who would reach the end first. The gorge became narrower and narrower till we reached the top and what would be our destination, Grindelwald. This little Bernese piece of heaven sits nestled at the base of the Eiger the Jungfrau and other majestic high mountains. We stopped at the first hotel asking if they had rooms. They accommodated us in the top floor which was basic, but clean, comfortable and suitable for our needs. We had time to get into the town before evening had drawn in. Now there is a special place in Grindelwald that Phil and I still talk about today. Right in the middle of the town there is a large car park where all the Swiss local and postal buses meet and disperse to the various locations in and around

Grindelwald. The little railway station that brings passengers up from the main line station of Interlaken stands just across the street. On the other side of the square from the buses there are three little café type restaurants. In the front of one of these was a very low brick wall. Now at this time of the day that we arrived there is the hustle and bustle of the skiers returning from the mountains via the mountain train buses and even gondolas that all converge in Grindelwald. I should explain that there are two areas that are popular both with skiers in the winter and walkers in the summer. One is reached from the railway station that links Grindelwald with the mountain. This route goes up arriving at the base of the Eiger and then continues down the other side to Wengen. At the halfway station folks that are skiing can take countless ski lifts all spanning out in different directions. Alternatively, further along the high street in Grindelwald there is a bubble lift or gondola that travels up the other side of the high ridge to an area called 'First.' From the top of First it is possible to ski off in various directions taking various routes back down. Some take hang-gliders and paragliders up and launch themselves from the top. We have seen paragliders and hang gliders make their way slowly taking in the breathtaking scenery all the way back down the valley and gorge to Interlaken some fifteen miles away. Others climb the thermals to circumnavigate the Jungfrau or the Eiger.

The bars in the main square in Grindelwald were buzzing with returning skiers all anxious to share with their friends the days stories of the skiing adventures. We only had room to sit on the wall with a couple of beers whilst waiting for a table. This wall has become a Masonic sign for Phil and I. He was just transfixed to the spot. All he wanted to do was stare up at the three mountains that stretched before and high above him. To one side at the top it was possible to glimpse the massive Glacier that stretched from the edge of the Eiger some twenty eight miles into France. Again, I witnessed this spiritual inner peace come over Phil as he stared more or less in disbelief but also in wonderment. His expression changed and he was just simply taken over by the sheer scale and beauty of the place. I have travelled back to this area many times since. The one unwritten rule I have is that when I arrive I simply text Phil the words "greetings from the wall my friend". This is not to cause upset or mischief but simply to show him that I am thinking of him and that special day that we shared for that fleeting moment back on our magic weekend, me and him taking all this beauty in for the first time. We have vowed one day to return together, but unfortunately time, tide and personal fortunes have prevented.

The next morning, I realised we only had a few days and wanted to get the most of our visit. We both agreed that a whistle stop tour should be expedited. We bought our passes from the little station office that would cover all the trains lifts etc. We set off on the first leg from Grindelwald on the train to the halfway station called the Kleine Scheideg at the foot of the Eiger. We were ushered on board along with all the skiers and tourists and with a total of three little trains following each other. We went first to the lower village picked up some more passengers then slowly worked our way up to the halfway station. Here everyone disembarked either to disappear off on their skis to admire the views from the restaurant's cafes and souvenir shops. We had a quick beer at the station then took another connection on another little railway train that travels from the Kleine Scheidegg right up to the top of the Eiger.

It should be explained that the journey up to the Eiger is mostly in a tunnel cut out over a hundred years ago by workmen. At some points of the year, they would be stranded, and have to live in the tunnel due to severe weather outside. The train driver stops the train at two points inside the tunnels for passengers to get out for a brief few moments. This allows them to walk along a short but wide passage to the edge where there is a window that looks both down to the foot of the Eiger and upwards. These passages were in fact where the workman barrowed the spoil from the tunnel and dumped over the side. In those days it would have been open and exposed to the elements and very dangerous. The second passage higher up is even more intimidating with the sheer drop it exposes. It also contains a huge iron door to the right that is very securely locked and bolted. This is where the mountain rescuers can climb out onto the sheer face of the Eiger for mountain rescue purposes. When the train finally reaches the top, it literally looks like one of the London underground stations. There are lifts that carry you up and into the restaurant and observation tower built above. From here access can be gained to the outside plateau of ice and snow. This area looks down in one direction

156

at the glacier stretching out below and before us and bends off to the right in the distance for thirty miles off towards France. The day we were up there we could see manned sledges in the distance being pulled by huskies. These dogs are trained there on the mountains and shipped to various destinations around the world. The day was glorious sunshine with not a cloud in the sky and the views were just startling looking out for miles and miles between the peaks of the mountains. Up onto the small plateau and then the view back in the other direction first of all down to the Kleine Schiedegg below. Beyond this to the right the little dots that made up Grindelwald itself. To the left of where we were standing lay the village of Wengen. One felt literally on top of the world. This particular location is in fact the highest point in Europe, and it really feels that way. The air is very thin making breathing difficult. What it also does is it makes one feel emotional. Both Phil and I remarked how it left us both feeling really tearful. Strange phenomenon!

Our next part of the visit was the ice caves. Now what the Swiss have done is cut passages into the existing Glacier. So, in effect you are walking along a passage where the walls the ceiling and the floor is entirely made of ice. The passages are lit and handrails are provided for those not adequately kitted with the correct foot wear. What greeted us at the end of the passage was just amazing. The Swiss had cut out off the passage little grottos and in each were ice carvings. Some had statues in ice of Eskimos catching fish, there were polar bears, penguins and all manner of objects and figures. The most amazing was a sculpture carved out and paid for by the world peace organisation of the Angel of Peace. This sculpture must have been 8 feet tall. With wings spread out the Angel was looking down at her cupped hands. Perched on her hands was the Dove of Peace. The whole sculpture looked like polish glass and in it were the layers of ice that had formed millions of years ago. Sadly, this sculpture is no longer viewed by the public as the numbers of visitors have warmed the air causing it to melt.

We were on the Jungfrau at the top of the Eiger probably for about two hours but like all good things, it had to come to an end. We slowly worked our way back first of all to the restaurant then the lifts back down to the underground station where the train was waiting to ferry us back down the mountain. By the time we returned back to the halfway station of Kleine Scheidegg we felt we had returned from another world. A splendid fresh sublime world that is hard to describe.

We then boarded the second train that leaves the halfway station and works its way down the other side of the mountain to Wengen. Here we left the train station and stepped into total peace and quiet. Wengen is a very old rustic village that does not allow any form of petrol engine vehicles into its streets. Instead, they run what can only be described as electric station carts. These carts are for the benefit of those tourists staying at one of the many hotels in Wengen but only carry their luggage. The guests still have to walk. It should be pointed out that some of the Hotels are named "Regina" and "Grand" which truly live up to their names as being very majestic and I should imagine very expensive. Despite the costs guests still are expected to walk. We took a stroll into the village and ended up at a really small church. There is a viewing platform that overlooks the majestic valley cut out by a glacier millions of years ago. Below and off in the distance is where the village of Lauterbrunnen now stands. On the other side of the valley and above Lauterbrunnen is the famous waterfalls that drop hundreds of feet and is prominent on many of the Swiss tourist brochures. In fact, these days Base jumpers climb above the water fall and jump from this very spot for thrills and adventure. Again, the weather could not have been more perfect. The sun beat down on this wonderful tranquil spot and bathed us in total tranquillity and silence apart from the odd bird and the 'whish' sound of the train making its silent way down the mountain. Even I found it difficult to tear myself away from this spot even today. We had lunch in a little typical Swiss café complete with chequered tablecloths sampling the local wine and mountain bread.

Instead of returning the way we came by train we took the cable car located at the back end of the village. The cable car took us to the very top of the steep slopes straight above Wengen. Here we have to walk past the Heli station that waits to take heli skiers and tourists out onto the snow-capped mountains for powder skiing and viewing. Just past the Heli station is a gondola station that returns back down the mountain passing over this enormous snow field with hundreds of skiers working their way back down this particular section. The Gondola ride is in fact the longest in Europe and is so long that it has been split into two sections that allow skiers and walkers to disembark. This is designed in such a way because the snow melts quickly here at the end of the season. Having a middle station gives skiers the advantage of still skiing while the lower slopes have lost all their snow. The full gondola ride from top to bottom takes about 40 minutes. In this time you pass in what seems total silence over breathtaking views. The end of the Gondola is in fact in lower Grindelwald some 300 yards from the lower village railway station. We walked to the station and caught the returning train back up into Grindelwald and the hotel. That evening we had a well deserved evening meal and a few beers before two very tired and very contented chaps took to their beds having fulfilled one heck of a successful day.

The next day we agreed that we would do the return leg of the train journey to Wengen. Instead of getting off at Wengen however we continued on down on the train to Lauterbrunnen at the bottom of the valley. Here we took a funicular up the side of the valley to a plateau. Here a little single carriage train awaited. On the way up and to balance the cable pulling us up another funicular comes down the mountain in a single line rail that passes In the middle. At the front was a small cow sitting in the carriage normally reserved for skis and luggage. Phil made the quirky remark that "here comes the empties". When we reached the plateau the train was waiting for us to take us the three quarters of a mile to the little town of Murren. This is a very rustic village where no cars are allowed. All the houses are the little old Swiss chalet type properties with their overhanging roofs and amazing woodwork. At the end of the village is another cable car station. This cable car would take us halfway up the mountain to a single high rock mass. We had to disembark one cable car, walk around the gangway, where another cable car was waiting. This second cable car took us way beyond the tree line to one of the most famous mountain restaurants in the world. The old James Bond restaurant. So called because it featured in one of the James Bond films. It has a rotating restaurant where a diner can sit and eat his meal while the whole tower slowly turns revealing the majesty of the surrounding Alps mountains. We had travelled all day. Once at the restaurant we had just enough time to grab a meal, and a beer of course, before making our return journey. Each step was repeated in reverse and before we knew where the day had gone we had left Wengen, on the last train of the day. We reached the halfway station of Kleine Scheidegg and was being jostled with the late skiers returning back to Grindelwald. Once we were back in Grindelwald we returned to "the wall" where a well-deserved beer or three were ordered. We just sat and talked about the day's adventures and the wonderful places we had visited. Our evening meal was devoured by two very hungry and very tired lads who again slept very well that night. Unfortunately, the next day was to be our departure. We had soaked up our Easter in this wonderful place and paying our bill loaded the cases into the car and started back down towards Interlaken. Grindelwald had one more treat for us as if to say farewell and don't forget me. The evening before as we travelled back down from the mountain, the bottom half of the mountain was snow free. In fact, there were a few farmers now leading their cattle back out into the pastures adjoining the farm buildings. The next morning, we found that It had been snowing through the night. Those poor animals that were led out to the pastures were now being led back indoors again. Everything was crystal clear and bright white and glistened in the sunshine. What a beautiful picture to bring home with us.

Our journey home was via Lake Geneva again as I wanted to stop along the shoreline somewhere before our final drive back to the UK. We arrived at the pretty French influenced village of Rolle not many miles from Geneva itself. It is a pretty little village with its own harbour; a paved area in front and the rows of shops, houses, restaurants and hotels on the other side of the road overlooking the lake. It was an absolutely beautiful sunny spring afternoon when we pulled into a parking space along the front. I went into a little hotel that was run by a very elderly lady. The furniture and decorations were from a very forgotten era and was, I supposed quite spooky. When I asked in my broken French whether she had any rooms she led me up the stairs into this rather dingy Edwardian period bedroom with just one large old oak bed. When I pointed out that there were two of us, she intimated that we could double up in the one bed. I didn't think that was such a good idea. Phil is a good friend but not that good! I thanked her and left. Next was a very modern but small hotel a few doors down. Everything was modern marble with pure white linen curtains and drapes. It was beautiful. The man confirmed they had rooms, with two single beds, and so we booked in and dropped our bags off before wandering over the road to sit in the sunshine outside one of the harbour cafes taking in the late afternoon sun and downing a couple of well-earned beers. We decided we would eat in as neither of us could really be bothered exploring further for food especially given it was Easter and most restaurants shut early. We therefore cleaned ourselves up, showered shaved and came down to the restaurant for early evening. The dining room was very quiet and eventually the waiter came over asked us what we wanted. We both chose steaks and off he disappeared. He would appear shortly after to ask if we wanted any drinks. Having tried the wine on Lake Geneva on the inward journey we decided we would try some more of the rose wine. However. I made the mistake of asking for French wine. The waiter physically took a step back aghast! "You don't like Swiss wines" he indignantly asked me. I didn't even realise that Switzerland had much of a wine industry. I blurted out that I would be happy for him to recommend and off he huffed to fetch a bottle. I must confess it was very nice. So nice that we had finished the first bottle before our food even started to appear . In fact the second bottle was looking a little suspiciously empty before I called over a lady working in the hotel and asked where our food was. The waiter had completely forgot! So having slightly suggested to him that it would have been nice to actually eat our meal with our Swiss wine, making him feel very guilty, the food finally arrived. It was a steak to die for. An evening very well spent and not to be easily forgotten. We slept like kings that evening. The next day I got the bill and nearly fell over. Like an idiot I had divided the hotel tariff by the French denomination of francs to pounds rather than the Swiss francs to the pound. It was very expensive, but hey what the hell it was worth it. We had spent a wonderful weekend finished off by a remarkable last night on the shores of Lake Geneva and now we were going home with tales to tell the grandchildren so to speak. Our drive home was very leisurely as we had both taken the working day off as an extra day. This of course meant we could stop off at the warehouses in northern France close to the ports and stock up with a few cases of alcohol for the remainder of the summer and Phil could visit the local tabac to stock up on his cigarettes. We arrived home early evening and both felt we had been away for much longer than the actual five days since we had departed that Thursday lunchtime previous. What a great break without any problems or hitches but some wonderful memories.

MY MATE'S SECOND TRIP ABROAD

I have always loved camping and all the freedom that camping offers. However, I do find that like ski equipment the gear that is needed for a successful camping trip, seems to disappear by itself all over the house garage and shed. To try to keep it all together in one place has always been a nightmare. Even with the famous "Ainsworth" list for camping weekenders and camping weeks, items still seem hard to locate and pack. As a result of this continuous task of spending more time hunting out all the necessary gear coupled with the fact that once found it then has to be loaded onto and into the intended vehicle designated for the trip I decided that I would perhaps join the modern day camper. Very good friends of mine had been advising for some time to investigate the concept of a Folding Camper. Now to me a folding camper is the same as a trailer tent, something I wanted to avoid at all costs. My friends tried to educate me by describing the folding camper as being the same as a caravan, as wide as a caravan with hard sides like a caravan, but with canvas top walls and roof which when folded out was the same size as a decent caravan with two bedrooms and all the facilities. I did a bit of homework and discovered a couple selling a Pennine Pullman folding Camper only a mile from where I lived. Taking my friends with me for back up and to advise with a knowledgeable eye, we soon found what turned out to be a really lovely piece of equipment, very well looked after and very well stocked with all the equipment. The price being asked was very reasonable, so a deal was struck, and the item paid for and away the folding camper was towed. Now with any piece of equipment it is always best to have a "dry run" first. I recalled the hilarious outcome of my first trip with parents and new tent when we

162

discovered the tent pegs and mallet were missing. I decided to take the folding camper complete, to a small municipal camp site only six miles away for an overnight stay and try out. Having arrived at the site and finding a pitch I unhitched turned the trailer so it was facing the right way and unfolded the two sides to reveal this enormous unit complete with beds etc., It was wonderful. I thought that I would try my hand at putting up the awning. Now, this became a whole different ball game. When I took the poles out of the bag along with the awning, I discovered a whole array of poles of different sizes and shapes and really couldn't make head nor tail. Now every camper will agree that when you first arrive on a site every other camper has this gleeful hope that you are going to make a mess of things. They even gather their chairs and tables to actually sit and openly watch you. I was even more a celebrity as there were not many folding campers around at that time, and the monster that had grown out of the box was drawing a lot of attention. Aware that all eyes were on me I did try very hard not to make a complete fool of myself without much success. After about an hour of trying to fathom out this collection of poles and cloth of which nothing seemed to match the fog began to clear and I discovered to my amusement, as well as the onlookers, that in fact there were two sets of poles and two sets of awnings. One was a very simple set up for literally an overnight canopy with open sides and front and a small frame to hold it. The other was a more robust set up thicker poles, and thicker canvas with the sides and front separately stored. Once the realisation had reached me it was very quickly assembled to reveal what was to turn out to be a remarkable piece of equipment. All necessary items required for sleeping, cooking and eating were all stored on board. It had its own four burner cooker, its own sink and fridge and compared to the camping lifestyle I had been used to it was sheer luxury. The added beauty was that when closed up everything needed for camping remained on board and was easily towed and stored. When it was time to pack up and head for home I noticed that one of the spectators who had watched my every move when I first put my unit up was in fact now packing away himself. Wishing to learn from this expert I promptly sat on my chair to watch. The poor chap had a complete disaster on his hands. First of all, it was a trailer tent not a folding camper. The folding campers were a lot less forgiving for folding everything incorrectly. Even after five attempts my camping neighbour left the site without the unit being fully folded and secure. It turned out that he had been watching me to give him some ideas as it was his first trip too.

Having now become a seasoned folding camper expert from my one day and one night away it was time to plan a more adventurous holiday. Now, Phil my mate was still living with me. As we were both kicking our heels as to what to do for holidays, I suggested that we should take the folding camper to Italy. This was a location he had never been to and one I thought he would love. He was still pretty well run down from his recent marriage break up. What he needed was to be taken somewhere where food was plentiful and beers and wines flowed. Where else to cheer him up with all these categories but with the good old Italians? First, I had to prove to him that Switzerland was in fact two countries. When we had visited that Easter obviously the whole place was in winter mode. Everyone was in their winter clothes or ski gear. Everywhere was enjoying indoor life with log fires, candles and protection from the cold winter days and nights outside. Now it was summer and all folks would be enjoying life outside. All the houses would be adorned with flowers with the aroma of barbecues and outside cooking and living. We set off again for the continent. As we had done previously, we headed down the French motorway over the Jura mountains and arrived this time in daylight at one of my favourite little camp sites in Vallorbe. It was late Saturday afternoon and the first thing we needed to do after setting up camp was to think about food. The folding camper was true to its advertising and was completely setup with awning and all mod cons within less than an hour. That freed us up to organise something to eat. Now I remembered that upstream from the camp site was the little trout farm that a chap had set up years before that if was still there could provide us with our evening meal. We drove up the valley for about a mile pulled into the track and sure enough the fish were still there alive and well and waiting to be caught. Phil has always been an ardent and dedicated fisherman with all the right equipment to catch fish that I had only read about, let alone seen. He found it highly amusing when the owner gave us two bamboo canes with what was literally a piece of string tied to the ends of each and a rather large hook dangling from that. Armed with a small pot of boilie baits we launched ourselves off to the sides of the river that had been cordoned off to try our luck. The fish were plentiful but clearly not hungry or not interested in our efforts to invite them to join us and be the main part of our evening meal. Whether the owner felt sorry for us or was rather anxious to get home I am not sure but suddenly he appeared with a handful of these boilie pellets and threw them into the water just in front of us. The water absolutely bubbled with the fish going wild for the food. We quickly cast our hooks into the middle of this boiling water and within seconds both of us hooked a fish. That was our evening meal secure. Next stop the village and the local co-op. We had only just made it before it closed. We bought a bag of charcoal and went back to the camp site. The BBQ was lit and the fish gutted and prepared with butter and pepper inside. However, we could not find the tin foil to wrap it in. No worries, we will stick the fish onto the grill and go for it. While the fish simmered away on the fire, we then looked for something that we could add as an accompanying side dish. All we could find was a tin of baked beans. I had packed light with the intention of stocking up on arrival. No point carrying coals to Newcastle so to speak. Now anyone who has cooked fish will I am sure agree that the fish is all very well cooked on one side but when you try to turn it over on the actual grill it seems to have acquired its own natural glue to stick to the bars. We tried and made a bit of a pigs ear turning the poor things over to try to cook the other side. Once completed we decided that perhaps we would not try to remove the fish as further disasters and chaos would prevail. So we duly sat ourselves on the grass cross legged, in front of the camper. We were next to the fire both armed with our side plates, a fork and the BBQ grill. Propped up of the floor we proceeded to devour our evening meal accompanied by a saucepan of baked beans. I have to say looking back it was just a wonderful and memorable start to that fantastic holiday. We still laugh about it now and what the other more civilised campers must have thought.

The next day we packed up and left Vallorbe and headed down into Switzerland towards Interlaken. We had no particular camp sites in mind and literally drove with the hope that something would work out. We initially found this site that was huge. It had hundreds of foreign campers in caravans, tents, folding campers and camper vans. All their guy ropes were crossed over each other which really didn't seem at all appealing. What was worse the weather had taken a turn for the worse and it was absolutely pouring cats and dogs. Anyone that has been to the Alps in a down pour will understand that we really did not want to spend any time outside. Erecting any form of temporary shelter in that weather let alone a camp site that resembled a folk festival would have been horrendous. We drove on. Luckily Phil spotted a camping sign in East Interlaken. Following the sign over this quaint little bridge we passed over the river that divides the two lakes of Lake Brienz and Lake Thun. A sharp right-hand turn dropped us down onto the banks of the river where we discovered this intimate little rally site. It only had about thirty or forty camping spaces that had been taken up with probably twenty of us. The lady was so friendly and made us so welcome and showed us a really sheltered pitch. By this time, it had stopped raining and was just perfect. We decided we would stay here for a few days. This way I could show Phil the Switzerland he had experienced only a few months previously but this time in the summer months.

Our first evening we walked into Interlaken. We came across a group of Aussies who were staying at one of the adventure hotels. I would explain this part of the world is a Mecca for water adventures including kayaking, water rafting, canyoning as well as paragliding and all the water sports. These lads decided they would add abseiling to the list. They had climbed to the roof of the hotel and had thrown the ropes over the sides of the hotel down to sheer concrete and were launching themselves off the top straight down. Some had mastered the new art of abseiling front first (something the SAS and secret services called Rat Jumping and had perfected). It really was quite something to watch.

The next day after breakfast we crossed over the little bridge again where the train station was located. Here we caught the little electric train up to Grindelwald. Now Phil by this time had a game going in his head. He would check out the times of departure of Swiss public transport. He would then stare at the nearest clock to see what happened. It became an obsession of his to just for once announce that the mode of transport was late. He was always disappointed. As the minute hand reached the allotted time the train left with us in the back carriages. After about five miles the terrain changes into two very large valleys. The train stops, the guard unhitches the front four carriages. The front of the train then leaves to take the right-hand valley which eventually comes out at Lauterbrunnen. This is halfway before the James Bond Restaurant and for those tourists heading direct to Wengen. Our back four carriages then departed for the left-hand valley winding its way up to Grindelwald. At the top we arrive at the little station where another mountain train awaits to carry passengers up to the Kleine Scheidegg. Here the connection would take you over the other side to Wengen and on to Lauterbrunnen. At Lauterbrunnen the front half of the train from Interlaken would be waiting to take passengers back down the mountain to meet up with the back half of the train from Grindelwald to complete its final five miles back to Interlaken. The whole system was just amazing and worked like clockwork. No wonder Phil was taken up with his project and mind game at just once trying to secure a delay. In Grindelwald needless to say after a stroll round the small town we ended up back at "The Wall" for a customary beer. We then caught the mountain train to the Kleine Scheidegg. This time instead of catching the connection down to Wengen we went round the back of the little station and caught the train up the mountain to the top of the Eiger.

It is very difficult to describe an electric train that is full of passengers that travels up a mountain to a point that is the highest in Europe. Now the train is in the exact same form as the other mountain trains, it has a cog system that when it gets a little steep the cogs engage which help propel the whole train upwards. The only difference is that halfway up it becomes like a London tube train completing its journey in a tunnel. Halfway up the mountain there is a station where in winter the skiers would disembark for the last (and highest) run back down the mountain. It is also a station to serve the large house next door with what seems to be a whole run of stables. These stables are in fact dog kennels. It is here that the Swiss breed and train the famous mountain rescue dogs. It was chosen for its remoteness so that the dogs only come into contact with the handlers during training. From here they are taken up to the huge thirty odd mile glazier ice field which stretches all the way over to France for further training with sledges etc. The Husky type dogs themselves are magnificent and are very strong and well kept. Anyway, leaving this station behind the train disappears into the tunnel. Shortly after, it comes to a halt at an inner station. The purpose of this is so that the passengers of the train can disembark and walk down a short tunnel to some windows at the end. When the railway was being built this was one of the tunnels that the workers used to dispose of the debris, rock etc that was excavated. Looking through the windows there is a sheer drop for thousands of feet of the north face of the Eiger. It really does make you step back especially if you have a fear of heights. In the days when the tunnel was being dug out the men would be living in this service tunnel throughout the winter because the weather was so bad they would be snowed in for several months a year so all their provisions would be carried up and stored. Of course, there were no windows in those days, just the open end of the tunnel. We got back in the train and it set off but then a few minutes later it stops at another station. Same thing as before, out of the train down a narrow service tunnel to more windows and an even steeper drop. The purpose of this stop is two-fold. First of all, to show the passengers how steep the ascent is becoming but also for a more practical reason. Beyond the window and just out of reach actually fixed into the side of the Eiger is this huge metal circular ring. Now throughout various times of the year folks actually climb the north face of the Eiger and very often get into serious difficulties. To save the rescuers coming up from the bottom which would take hours and hours especially with survival equipment, to save time and in many cases lives, they crawl out of the doorway further along the passage out to this ring, so that they can go either up or in the other direction to the souls that are stuck and stranded to save them. Equally they can bring the survivors of such disasters back in through this gap and then on the train back down to safety. The Eiger has a very strange phenomenon that cannot be pre forecasted called "kettling". The cloud formations are so quick and fierce that sometimes coming across the ice flow from the other direction they are forced up to the top of the mountain. Here they quickly freeze and fall just like steam from a kettle. Sometimes this thick cloud is so bad that climbers cannot go up or down for fear of losing their grip so they have to stay still. Sometimes the cloud is so thick that they have to be rescued and helped back down as a result of hypothermia. This is why these facilities are so important to remain and be maintained to this very day. We finally reach the top and the station looks very much like a metropolitan city underground station with lifts and stairs that lead up to the three-storey giant restaurant and visitor centre above. We took the lift and instead of choosing the restaurant exit chose instead to go straight to the glacier caves. Now I should explain that this glacier is so vast they have built tunnels into the ice that form the floors the walls and the ceilings. The ice is polished smooth and with the artificial lighting gives a very weird and sombre atmosphere. It is obviously very cold and damp. We had toured this labyrinth of tunnels at our first visit. We had another opportunity of checking out the carved ice sculptures. It was lovely to see the carved Eskimos sitting round a pond fishing complete with rods line and fish all carved out of the ice. We saw the carved bears and other animals in another of the grottos and this continues all the way round. Of course, the ultimate was seeing again the special angel that had been carved. As previously explained, she had been carved out with donations from the world peace organisations. She stood nine feet tall with huge, expanded wings. Her hands were cupped in front of her, and she looked down at the dove of peace sitting in her hands holding a piece of laurel. It was beyond beautiful. The problem was that it was so famous visitors from around the world came to see her. The amounts of bodies and the heat generated by those bodies caused the ice sculpture to begin to melt and within a couple of years the damage was irreparable. I believe she is still there but in a shadow of her formal glory and locked away from public view and damage now. Phil and I have had the privilege to have seen her. The veins of the centuries of forming ice clearly making up her various levels of heights. Truly a spectacle to have had the privilege to have seen. From the ice caves and passages you then emerge into the daylight of the restaurant and its facilities. From here you climb up the open stairways to the doorway leading to the upper plateau. Here there are viewing areas very heavily roped off. If ever there is a real life re construction of what it must be like to sit on a cloud and look down at this beautiful world, here it is. This point is the highest point in the whole of Europe. Grindelwald and Wengen seem like mere spots on the landscape below. Even Kleine Scheidegg seems so far away and the trains like model railways. Even the clouds are below us and if anyone is religious or spiritual this is one place, I believe that they can find solace and be close to their god. The other direction is a slope that falls away to the actual glacier itself stretching out beyond the mountains in the distance that curve round to France. Several venture out on the glacier and if you are lucky and it is a clear day you can sometimes see the husky dogs and their sledges in the distance crossing this vast area in training for their lives in the remotest areas around the world. As for myself, I cannot explain whether it was the altitude, but it becomes hard to breathe quickly. Or it may have been the awe of the spectacle surrounding us that I had never experienced before in my life, but I was left feeling very emotional and it was a moving experience that I have never forgotten. Everyone should have this "must do once in my lifetime" on their bucket list to visit the Jungfraujoch which is what this plateau is called. I should explain before moving on that the area has a purpose. It is a weather station. However, it does not monitor the actual weather as we know it. Because it is so high it is immune from most of earth's pollution and therefore monitors the rays and discharge coming from the Sun. This way it can forecast changes in climate and earth reactions caused by the sun's activities. A very clever project.

We had one more day in Interlaken. We didn't want to waste it. Now, many years before I had visited Eastern Austria. Here, I had discovered a museum that had been built in the forest where numerous houses had been reconstructed from around Austria and were typical of the time they were built. The houses were stocked out with the clothes and furniture of the period. However, I only got to see inside two of those houses and always said one day I would return. I then heard that there was another museum but in Switzerland. It turned out to be behind Brienz on the lake Interlaken, some few miles from where we were camping. Brienz village is itself the wood carving centre of the world, many pupils come here to master the craft. From the water landing stage or railway station there is a bus that runs about three miles to Ballenberg Open Air Museum that I named the Silent Museum. Here in this vast area and mostly in the forest there are dozens and dozens of houses from the various canton areas of Switzerland. These houses represent the French, Italian and German influences that make up Switzerland. As you walk along the little paths leading between the various areas and hamlets making up the cantons the houses take on different shapes and sizes. There is a complete farmhouse with all its furniture and barns where meats are being smoked even today. The chemists house is complete with all its bottles and potions and medical equipment. There are 'music-box' houses that are complete with double size cot beds, furniture, clothes, plates, cutlery and cooking utensils. Even the gardens have vegetables growing in them, left as if the occupiers had gone off for the day. The whole museum is manned by volunteers, dressed in traditional costume. Some help out in the houses, others in the restaurants. There is a water driven sawmill where volunteers cut the huge logs brought there to be sawn. These are actually used for the continuing restoration and repair works within the museum. There is a foundry where other volunteer staff make all the nails and metal work needed on the houses and buildings. In one of the basements of one of the houses an old gentleman was making wicker work baskets and trays to sell towards the upkeep of the museum. He had just finished a backpack that the woodsmen used to carry on their backs into the woods to forage for sticks, mushrooms and other seasonal wonders. I asked him whether it was for sale, and he told me it was very expensive. It wasn't and I bought it and today it still stands in a place of pride in my hallway holding all the walking sticks that I have made and purchased over the years. We spent the whole day in this park, and Phil and I were both spell bound by the way life must have been so many years ago. The atmosphere is greatly helped with the enthusiasm of all the volunteers working in the park explaining life as it was and the era and canton they represented. What a wonderful day. I have been back several times and not been disappointed with each visit. The last time I called sadly the basket weaver who had sold me my backpack had died.

Reluctantly after a couple of days in Switzerland it was time to head off. Having packed our belongings away into the folding camper hitched up to the back of the car we said our goodbyes to all the various friends we had met and then headed off. The road took us down the side of the Lake Brienz then up into the mountains and a most beautiful windy pass up and over the range and down towards the southern tip of Lucerne and its magnificent lake. Here we picked up the motorway that would take us through the Gotthard Pass and on into Italy. The pass itself is a tunnel some twenty odd miles long. It is an experience like driving through the Blackwall Tunnel at rush hour with cars upon cars in two long lines driving through. The windows could not be lowered because of the amount of exhaust fumes and the heat had to be borne until we reached daylight. Once out of the tunnel it was a twenty five mile downhill run into Italy and the northern tip of Lake Maggiore, our destination. We passed along the western shore of the lake through lovely typical villages where the local material of stone had replaced the wood used on the other side of the mountain. These stone-built buildings were common right along the Italian side of the Alps. We knew we had reached Italy by the evidence of the buoy in the middle of the lake with an Italian flag depicting the boarder which made us smile. We went down to the more popular area of the lake passing through Stresa with its huge expensive five star hotels, passed the three famous islands and on to Arona towards the southern end of the lake. We pulled into a camp site close to where I had stayed as a youngster and fingers crossed, they had spaces for us. We had left it a bit late in the season and the Dutch and Germans had long since arrived. Also, the Italians head for camp sites within driving distance from home to set up the caravans for the summer complete with rugs and budgies. There was space and in fact it was a very close distance from the shore of the lake.

The site was primarily full of local Italians who maintained the custom of bringing their caravans and belongings to the site at the beginning of the season and remaining all summer. So, they all knew each other and any newcomers got the inquisitive look treatment. We familiarised ourselves with the location of our camper and the site itself and decided that as it was getting late in the afternoon, we would follow the Italian camper custom of finding a supermarket now the heat of the day was starting to disappear. We didn't have far to look as about a mile back towards the town was a rather large well stocked supermarket. A trolley and half hour later and we were stocked with the customary barbeque meat salad and of course the alcoholic refreshers as well. When we arrived back at the camp site, we had some visitors now camped next to us. A couple of lads had turned up with rucksacks and small tent and had set themselves up. We said hello but really wanted to get on and have our food washed down with the two litres of white wine. This followed afterwards with the two litres of red wine. Now the two lads turned out to be from Israel. Whilst their homeland made wine it apparently is so expensive that their drinking is very limited to special occasions such as a birthday, wedding or such other celebration. To see us down a bottle of large wine with our meal and another for after meal was mind blowing and quickly, we established ourselves with a reputation.

The next day after a long rest by the shoreline taking in the sun and the surroundings, I suggested to Phil that I would make us a spaghetti. Now having been travelling to Italy since I was a youngster I do pride myself on making a reasonable standard spaghetti. The onions were peeled and fried added to the mince meat bought from the supermarket that simmered and finally added the chopped tinned tomatoes garlic etc. whilst the spaghetti itself was bubbling in the pot. I did notice an Italian woman staring over at me. I think by this time they had established that Phil and I were perhaps a gay couple albeit that this was still way too early to be accepted as part of the norm as it is these days. As an exercise, as I served up I put a small plate to one side on a tray with a glass of wine and took this over to the lady that had been watching me intensely and asked her in my Italian if she would do me the honour of trying this as she was clearly the maestro coming from Italy. Her face lit up and away she went having her free meal and her glass of wine. When she returned the tray and empty dish later she would simply compliment me with the simple words "Perfetto" now that was the biggest compliment I could have wished for. Meanwhile we had another two sets of eyes watching us. The two boys from Israel. These poor fellas were sat cross legged on the dirt with a single burner cooker trying to conjure up some muck in a pan that I could not even describe let alone try to consume with all the will in the world. Feeling rather sorry for these two I suggested to Phil that we share our rather substantial shares and so two loaded plates of freshly cooked spaghetti Bolognese became four plates. I think these lads had not eaten property for about a week by the speed our offerings were consumed, washed down of course with the wine we have bought that night. They then opened up to us by confessing this was their first trip to mainland Europe. Before they left they had asked their friends and family to check their camping list to ensure that they had all the necessary equipment on board. Yes, their list was fine, everything they needed nothing extra necessary. When they arrived on their first camp site, prior to arriving at ours they were absolutely mortified to discover that everyone in Europe that went camping actually had a tent. Secondly that with such a tent they would have a sleeping bag. They had left Israel minus such basic facilities. You see they were used to wandering off and sleeping under the stars in the desert so things like tents and sleeping bags would have been no use whatsoever. Secondly, they realised that they could not just start an open fire but really should purchase a stove and something to cook in. This was very basic cooking.

The next day when I got up and looked out of the curtains of the awning one of the lads had taken the empty jar of Dolmio out of the carrier bag hanging on the tree, ready to go out for the rubbish. Having added some water he was swilling it round to pour into his metal mug cooking pot to try to heat up a meal for them. I quickly intervened, offered them breakfast which was full English including bacon and sausages. They "forgot" they were Jewish and devoured the lot. After that I was to feed them for the remaining six days we were there. In fact, in the mornings, I kept the curtains closed for a while to get started as they were literally sitting like a pair of hungry wolves waiting for me to "open up shop."

At that time when Phil and I had travelled to Italy it was not very common for same sex pairs to go unless they were gay. Eyes started to peer at us and expressions on the Italians faces started to unfold the realisation that maybe they thought Phil and I were somehow romantically connected. Now I don't personally have any prejudices against gays but as long as nobody assumes I might be gay myself. Speaking a bit of Italian, I soon put that right talking as loud as I could about my son and about my daughter and about my family. I think they got the message.

Knowing this area very well and in particular, Arona I volunteered for the Israeli boys to come with us when we went into town. Here we parked up and walked along the water's edge and the old rustic shops and houses divided by typical coffee bars and small cafes. The Israeli boys had never had proper Italian coffee so we found a bar suitably located with tables and chairs outside on the pathway with a full view of the lake and ordered our coffees. Of course, espresso was a must for our first round. The two boys sat there like they had died and gone to heaven. Sun glasses on admiring the scenery sipping their coffees and not wanting to reach the end even though each cup is no more than a mouthful. We needless to say had to drink several coffees before I could drag them away. We visited the famous statue of Saint Carlo one of the famous saints in the Catholic religion that overlooks the lake. I had taken my children up inside the statue several years before to stare out of the eyes and nostrils inside its head. Once we had finished our walk round the little town of Arona we headed back via the supermarket. Here we stocked up on the evenings meal that was going to be a barbeque along with several bottles of both red and white wine. Once we were back I got the barbeque lit and we all enjoyed the most marvellous meal together sharing stories and jokes and of course a litre bottle of red followed by a litre bottle of white. The boys were blown away as they can only afford one bottle of wine a year normally in Israel and then to celebrate a special event. They were really blown away when we finished, washed and cleared away, then went to the camp site café for late evening aperitifs of whisky and brandy.

This particular area is very pretty with its tree covered foothills rolling down from the majestic Alps bordering Switzerland. The area has many hidden gems to include lakes, villages and places of interest to go and visit. One of such places is Lago D`Orta or Lake D`Orta, located some miles behind Stresa. I had again visited this area some years before with my parents friend, Paolo. To reach the lake one has to drive up winding, twisting, tree lined roads with hair pin bends and steep drops to concentrate the mind. On route we passed the Umbrella Museum showing the early creations up to modern times. When we arrived at Lago D`Orta we had to again park at the top of the village and walk our way down the medieval streets. Eventually I was back in the huge piazza or square lined with street cafes and the aroma of freshly ground Italian coffee. We sat facing the Convent built on the island a short distance from the shore. As we sat in one of the street cafes watching people in their leisurely strolls photo taking and general admiration of such a beautiful location, we noticed a gentleman, on his own, approach from the left. As we watched him pass by, very smartly dressed in his freshly ironed pink shirt, cream flannel trousers and light canvas shoes with his cardigan slung round his shoulders a certain familiarity came to mind as to who he resembled. As we studied this well dressed but slightly elderly loner smiling at those he passed, we suddenly both came to the same conclusion – it was Lionel Blair the famous English dancer. He looked very debonair and certainly very fit and upright for his age. Eventually we had to leave this wonderful place, retrace our steps back along the narrow streets, up the stone steps back to the car park and take one last look back before heading back to camp.

The next day saw Phil and I drive round to the other side of the lake. This area is not so full of tourists and in fact is far more rural and flatter than the side we were camped. We drove for several miles passing the castle on the hill that overlooks the lake and can be seen for miles along the lake especially at night when it is all lit up. The road tried to take us off to the right, and inland but I found a narrow country lane to bring us back to the shore line. Here, parking up in a small car park we crossed over the small road to a set of steps that led us down the side of what literally is a rock face down towards the water's edge. Halfway down a medieval pathway cut into the side of the cliff, took us first of all to what looked like someone`s house albeit very, old again built into the side of the rock face. This turned out to be the Keepers Lodge. Passing through a covered passage again continuing along the stony path it led us to the smallest church built again into the side of the rock above the water's edge but still with the cliff edge towering above us. I should add that in the thirteenth century or thereabouts there was a very rich merchant on board a boat on the lake which hit a tempest of a storm in which he feared for the worst and believed he would drown. As a result, he prayed to God that if he was saved he would build a church as a thank you for being spared. Needless to say he was spared and the church was built. Not being content with just building the small church the merchant slowly became more and more of a recluse and indeed more of a hermit. He dedicated his last years to the worship of God and eventually when he died, he was buried inside the church itself. However, the grave was not one of usual status i.e. underground. This final resting place was a glass case with him laying on a small slab fully dressed. He had been mummified and had lain here for seven hundred years. To preserve the body the light inside the church was very dim, but there he was, in his fine splendour dressed as he would have been as a merchant quietly laying there as if asleep with all of us completely mesmerised at the excellent condition and preservation he was in. His small hands were showing his finger nails and his face was as if in a deep contented slumber.

After leaving the church we travelled on to where there is a car ferry to return us over the lake. The ferry is a flat-bottomed boat with the captains cab set to one side providing ample room for cars. The ferry took three to four cars wide and some 10 in length so it certainly was not a small vessel. Before we caught the ferry back over there was one more delight I had in store. Having parked the car in the back streets we walked to the entrance of a rather basic cable lift that took us up some 3,000 feet or so to a mountain restaurant. I say basic because the actual vessel to transport us resembled something more like the basket they give you to put your clothes in at a swimming pool which you hand in with your shoes turned upside down in the bottom section. This basket, however, was just deep enough for two people to stand one in front of the other, and hanging on we shot out of the cable station going straight up and over several houses. Talk about a baptism of fire. False confidence is then regained as it drops back down to some twelve feet above the grassy slope and slowly works its way up hill between the trees until the car ferry looks more like a little dinky toy. For the last hundred yards it then leaves the trees and is fully exposed to just rock and a sheer drop where hope that the day that it fails is not in fact today. As it reaches the top a huge two storey restaurant opens up in front of us with several viewing platforms to stand and admire the majority of the lake stretching below. In front are the majestic high Alps as far as the eye can see. Below to the left are the three islands beyond the shoreline of Stresa and off to the right where the lake leaves Italy and stretches into Switzerland. On a clear day it is a must to go up for the view. The food and wine is also very good. For those brave enough, situated to the side of one of the viewing platforms are some metal steps that transcend the safety rail that leads to what looks like a feeble sloped platform suspended out and over the sheer drop below. Here those with hang gliders, carried up on the side of the swimming pool basket, and those with paragliders would walk up and launch themselves off into mid air. I had 'butterflies' in my stomach every time we watched someone take off.

Sadly, all good things eventually must come to an end. The Israeli boys had already gone heading for one of their parents time shares in Switzerland. It was also time for us to leave. Packing the folding camper and hitching up we headed back along the lakeside towards Switzerland. We followed the shoreline down as far as the train station that many years ago had brought myself and my parents through the mountains. Disappointment was an understatement to describe my feelings that the station had long since closed and the service cancelled due to a fire in the tunnels years before. There was no alternative we would have to go back down to the lake up round the Gotthard and home the long way. I did however recall someone saying that there was a new tunnel and motorway that had been built further up. I first of all needed petrol so we found a remote village further along the way, and fully fuelled decided to climb till we found the motorway. We climbed and climbed, went round hair pin bends, more climbing, the car was beginning to struggle with the gears and the weight of the camper behind it. Suddenly that wave of fear that my father must have felt all those years ago passed over me. I realised we were well and truly on the climb up the dreaded Simplon pass. The pass that we had only crossed over once with its sheer drops and feared and avoided at all costs. There was no alternative, I had to press on. There were cars behind me vehicles coming down and there was no way I could stop turn and go back down. My hands and brow started to sweat. The fear was not the sheer drops that were now protected by large steal barriers, but the fact that this little car with its 1600 engine was struggling in second and first to climb these steep gradients and would I blow up the engine boil over, what was I going to do if I broke down. No AA recovery man was going to retrieve us from this nightmare location. Slowly we climbed and I became more and more worried. Phil became more and more supportive although giving me a running commentary of a scenery that I really didn't want to look at. Finally, after thirteen gruelling and painful miles we reached the top. My relief was very short lived because now we had to go down the other side. All the memories of the vehicle with the brakes failing in Austria came flooding back. I crept down the other side, using gears and minimal breaking till eventually to my huge relief we reached valley level and the car was still in one piece and had not let us down. However, we were on the wrong side of the next set of mountains from where we wanted to be camping for the night. My memory and research was half right though. The train that came from the side I wanted to be on, through the mountains to our side then through the second tunnel to Italy still run although now it was just simply through to the Interlaken side. We followed the motorway signs for about 25 miles then turned off onto the side road towards the train station and the shuttle service that would take us through the mountain. At this point I looked up and spotted a trail of cars way up high looking like matchbox cars. I commented, jokingly that I hoped we didn't have to follow that lot. Sadly, my humour turned to reality. We started climbing again. Up and up round hair pin bends again, back to second and first gears. My hands became sticky again holding the steering wheel like I would drown if I let go. Finally, we reached the little station and the queue for the train. My heart was in my mouth that this poor little car really was being subjected to torture and at some not-too-distant point it was going to die a death and fail on us. It didn't, it kept going. We reached Interlaken and our little camp site once more with the adventures of the past week and a half behind us. We were only going to stay one night. It was here that we met a wonderful German couple, both teachers who had travelled all the way down from Germany in a split screen Volkswagen camper. He was besotted with steam railways and had persuaded his long-suffering wife that it would be a wonderful holiday exploring the narrow-gauge railways of Switzerland especially the ones still running steam. Apparently, there was a very good one at Brienz where the open museum was located but that would have to wait for another time. We had a lovely evening with this middle-aged couple who spoke very good English. They also spoke very good French. We said how embarrassed we were that as English we expected everyone to speak our language but as a nation were too arrogant or lazy to learn another's language. The next morning we left, and I placed one of my business cards with phone number and address on our campers arm as he was laying snoring in his camper with the door wide open to the world. We never did hear from them again but always wonder if he got to see all the wonderful sites the Swiss narrow-gauge railways had to offer.

We were due to stay a couple of days but having had such an amazing adventure we both came to the decision to "leave the party which we were enjoying ourselves" and so made plans to head home the next day.

We drove our way back to the French side of Switzerland passed swiftly and without pause through Vallorbe over the Jura to France.

Turned onto the motorway and settled in to our long journey back to the French port. Phil was navigating and at this particular junction which I seemed to remember was a major junction for us to head north from our current journey from east to west. I asked him to check the map and he quickly advised I should take the next exit. I asked him if he was sure and he confirmed yes that was the one. After we turned off and had been heading on the new motorway for about twenty minutes, I pointed out to Phil that my instincts were that we were definitely going in the wrong direction. He adamantly insisted we weren't. So I had to use my Boy Scouts method of persuasion. "where is the sun" I asked Phil. In front of us he said. "what time of the day is it mate" eleven o'clock he said. Right what does that tell you. No answer. Well if the sun is in front of us and it is eleven o'clock in the morning then we must be heading south. Silence. We were lucky as only a couple of more miles was the pay station where we were able to turn round and head for home in the right direction without having to suffer financially only the embarrassment of driving 35 miles in the wrong direction and of course the 35 miles back to the start point. Unfortunately this was not going to be our only detour on our way home. We got about a third of way up the French motorway when suddenly we started heading west towards Paris. I asked Phil if he could check the map and whilst we had come off the actual route we should be on the motorway was taking us towards Paris but there was a motorway dissecting that would take us north. We approached nearer and nearer to Paris. Now I was beginning to live my other fear, beyond anything that the Simplon can throw at me and that is the infamous peripherique around Inner Paris. It is very difficult to describe this road of pure terror. If one can image the M25 on a Friday night being absolutely packed with cars, caravans, vans, lorries and juggernauts of every nationality and description in a traffic queue that is actually moving at over seventy miles per hour leaving little space for manoeuvrability or mistake, that is probably coming close. I hated it. The last time I have ventured round this beast was when we took the car, two children and the boat on its trailer on the way to Italy many years ago at three in the morning. It was terrifying then. As we came closer and closer my hands started sweating more and more. Luckily just before we reached the infamous highway of hell, we spotted an outer ring road which we leapt on and safely rounded the capital without fear or danger and soon was heading north towards the port. Now the custom had been set from our Easter trip that we really did need to divert to the port warehouses for some cases of wine, and of course to the tabac for some tobacco. These supplies if we were careful should last us nearly to Christmas. After our short detour and additional weight being added to the vehicle we completed our leg to the port to catch our boat home. While we were waiting to board our ferry, the incoming traffic disembarked to reveal line after line after line of MGF sports cars with all sorts of extras in the way of lights, carriers, some with hard tops, some with soft tops crossing over for their weekend tour of northern France. It was Friday night and was a lovely spectacle to see all these British enthusiasts coming over to enjoy themselves. As for us we got back to home in the early hours of Saturday morning. We had the weekend to recover and to reflect before both being back to work on the Monday morning. What a fantastic adventure we had both had. Even to this day we still talk about the wonderful places we had visited, the wonderful people we had met and the good times spent on what turned out to be the perfect holiday.

CHAPTER 24
THE FIRST CARAVAN TRIP TO THE LOIRE

The advent of what I like to call my "Age Advancement" had arrived. I had grown a little too old for crawling in an out of tents and from cold folding campers and so I made a change from my folding camper to a caravan The problem with my particular folding camper was that it was now getting dated. When I opened it up I had to rest the folding half on my back while trying to locate the support bars and this was beginning to prove heavy and difficult. I had inspected the latest models that had a cable to ease this function, but I had also taken a closer look at the modern caravans too. Now after my nightmare journey to and from the north coast of Devon during the Fastnet disaster weekend, I swore I would never entertain a caravan again. However, the model that was really catching my eye and interest first of all had an electric mover. This would ease getting the unit in and out of the driveway and in and out of position on site. The caravan also had an anti-snaking tow hitch which also had its own braking system. This meant that when heavy lorries, buses etc passed by, their wind wash would not push the caravan all over the place which can be very unnerving. The caravan also had on board a fixed bed, a toilet, heating etc. It had no comparison on the original caravan and it was really a no brainer to now up grade away from canvas.

The first choice to experiment with the new caravan was to take it abroad. As I had travelled most of my adventure life abroad this would not prove daunting and if anything would at least guarantee good weather and an enjoyable holiday. Despite previous bad experiences of camping in France with its basic camping facilities I was nonetheless persuaded that a camp site in mid France would be ideal and the facilities suitable. As such the booking was made for ferry crossings etc.

As I was still employed in full time work it meant that I could only leave for holiday at the end of the working day when we could set off for the Dover and the channel crossing that early evening. The caravan had been previously packed so we were on our way in less than an hour. Being a Friday night the M1 followed by the M25 were both naturally busy with Friday evening traffic. At least it was flowing and as we had a late evening sailing in any case there was no rush. Everything seemed to be going well till we reached halfway round the M25. Suddenly all lanes came to a grinding halt. Nothing was going to move for at least forty-five minutes. Eventually, the first lane gently moved forward but only as far as the slip road where we were directed off and down the slip road at Braintree towards the A14. When I wound the window down to enquire of the police officer directing traffic he advised that there was a "jumper on the bridge" i.e. the Dartford Crossing bridge and despite best efforts was not being persuaded to come down. As such if we were to come off onto the A14 travel south as far as the Southend Road and head into London, the police officer advised we could cross the Thames at Rotherhithe and once on the other side continue towards Dover and our sailing. This all sounded very acceptable except that when we reached Rotherhithe the tunnel was closed. Even had it been open it certainly wasn't able to accommodate a car and caravan. Instead we had to continue to the next crossing being the Tower of London. Bearing in mind I am new to this caravan towing experience I was becoming somewhat nervous. This did not help the situation arriving at the Tower of London bridge at midnight with Friday night London traffic all pushing to reach the south side. By the time we did eventually judge distances widths and speeds and ventured over the bridge I was beginning to feel that maybe we had made a big mistake after all. Obviously we couldn't turn back so soldiered on through Elephant and Castle and on through South East London eventually picking up the motorway and arriving in Dover at around three in the morning some five hours after our scheduled departure. The check in reception were very sympathetic and advised that they had checked through hundreds of people in similar circumstances and all had ended up catching later boats. We were put on the next available sailing and arrived in the early hours of the morning in France. I drove then till late morning to arrive at the predestined campsite that had been recommended to us. I was not surprised but extremely disappointed at how bad it was. The site was miles from nowhere. It was sandy, dirty, dusty and the facilities as poor as I had remembered them in the nineteen-sixties. Having worked all year for my holiday I was not prepared to spend my fortnight holiday in this awful place. We simply drove round the site and out again and headed east back towards Switzerland. We were located south and to the west of Le Mans. We passed through the Loire and in the guide book a site came up south of Saumur. We took a deviation to the site as it was now late morning early afternoon. My heart sank when we arrived, as this was again no better than the first even though it was run by an English couple. Bearing in mind I had been working all the previous day in the office driven through the night including London and now the French motorways I was getting very frustrated and irritated. Even more now I just wanted to return to familiar ground i.e. either Switzerland or Italy. I was persuaded to get a couple of hours sleep before I set up. In the meantime a bit of research was done while I slept and another site found just down the road. The camp site was advertised as being on the banks of the river and just below the medieval town of Montreuil-Bellay. In desperation we left the caravan and drove down for an inspection and oh what a huge relief. It was such a lovely campsite. We returned back to the caravan, apologised to the owner explaining his site was too remote for us and left. The campsite at Montreuil-Bellay was just beautiful. Tranquil, well laid out, next to the river and was just perfect. Unfortunately, my bad luck had not quite finished. I must have been so tired that after detaching the caravan I backed the car away and crunch. I had driven into the tree behind me. What made matters worse was that I had the bicycles on the back on a bike rack. Unsurprisingly it was my bike right at the back that now sported a very twisted wheel and tyre. I just couldn't believe that this could have happened.

Our first night and next day were spent really just resting and regaining our enthusiasm. After that we then first of all explored the medieval town that sat above us on the rocks and ramparts/walls of the medieval castle. The narrow streets were full of little coffee shops and other wonderful French shops. A place I would fall in love with and return several times for its peace tranquillity cleanliness and location.

My first job however, was to try to get my wheel on my bike fixed. We headed the 13 miles into Saumur and if by luck as we came down towards the town on the right-hand side was a retail park. On the outside of the park and facing us a small bicycle shop. We drove round took the bike off the rack and the chap inside was very sympathetic and although his English was about as basic as my French the wheel was changed and a new tyre fitted. As I left the shop there in the window was this most beautiful Spanish racing bike. It was just a lovely bike. I had been doing a lot of cycling back in England but used a very old rather rickety Austrian Puch bike. It had ten gears operated by two levers on the frame and basic brakes. It still gave me a lot of pleasure and clocked up a lot of miles. Maybe it was time to treat myself. Throughout the week I was to re visit the shop numerous times trying to convince myself to buy the bike, then talked myself out of it. Finally on the last day I drove down walked in and said to the owner that I would buy the bike. I was earning good money and the amount of cycling I did justified the purchase. He took this wonder machine out of the window, and I handed over my credit card. At this point he looked at me shook his head and said that he did not have a credit card machine. Oh Lordy what could I do. Did I have cash he asked? No, the banks were shut and I was therefore out of luck. He then said in his broken English to give him a cheque. I had to ask him a couple of times as I thought I had misheard him. No, he was happy to accept an English cheque. He rang his bank and asked the person on the other end what the exchange sum was, and I duly wrote the cheque out and handed it to him. However, I was so worried to ensure that my honesty and integrity was maintained I made him take my passport my driving license my camping card and photocopy them. I gave him a business card and confirmed by address. I was more stressed that he was. I assured him that I was honest and upright, and the cheque would clear and he just nodded and waved me off. I rang him from England a week after arriving home to make sure the cheque had cleared, and it had and he was very grateful for my concern. I went back a year later and got told off when I produced the bike for a service. He told me off that I had not looked after it properly. He serviced the bike and made me promise that I would take better care of this wonder machine.

A little history about Montruil Belay, as it is relevant to where I live in Milton Keynes. The chateau was owned by the Longville family who themselves had several eccentric relations. One in particular back in the 17th century was the daughter of the household and decided to ride her horse up the spiral staircase of the turret on one of the corners of the chateau till the horse had nearly reached the top panicked and refused to go any further. After great struggles to get the horse down, in the end it had to be blind folded and several servants had to coax the poor terrified animal backwards down the winding stone steps and back to ground level. Another member of the family became a monk and having travelled to Britain helped establish a monastery not far from where I live and that the village of Newton Longville bears part of his name. These days the chateau has its own vineyards and produces a very delicate but fruity white wine. Along with the paid tourist visits this helps to pay for maintaining the building.

Most of the chateaux in the Loire are made out of a soft white stone. This stone is quarried along the Loire valley. Once the stone is extracted it leaves large pits or even caves. Now these pits are wind proof and were secure against marauding wild animals and thieves and made ideal shelters. Just outside Montreuil-Bellay lays two Troglodyte settlements utilising these pits. One is a simple property at the bottom of the pit accessed by way of stone staircase. On the outside it resembles a stone cottage with windows front door etc. when you go inside it is literally walking into a very cosy warm dry cave with a large room with fireplace, tables, sideboards, beds etc., it is a fully functional working home. When there was an extra member of the family born the head of the family would simply dig out another room and extend the cave accordingly. This method proved so successful in the Loire that whole communities evolved. Many can still be seen along the high banks of the Loire to the east of Saumur. In a village again not far from Montreuil-Bellay a complete community had utilised a particularly large pit to house over twenty families. This community was complete with chickens, pigs and pens for sheep etc.

each house was completely furnished and faced into the centre of the pit. It was a thriving community with the last person, a lady, dying in the late nineteen-sixties. Now everything is preserved as a museum of former rural life. Around the village are photos of the inhabitants and reflecting their way of life. Nowadays the troglodyte properties and villages are selling for huge sums especially to the Parisians who travel down for weekends and holidays to use as second homes.

The other evidence of the mined stone is in huge caves. A short drive from the campsite you pass an unassuming farmyard. When you drive into the forecourt there is a door off to the right. With permission from the owner of the farm we were led inside through the doorway. Here a series of passages opened up, these themselves lead down into the bowels of the earth and round in a huge circle back to the start. Inside these lit passages are various chambers off the main causeway. Here mushrooms in their various stages of spawning are being cultivated and are sold to the local restaurants, cafes and hotels. Also the owner keeps a lot of the original cutting tools and other equipment down there to show how first the stone was cut and removed and later harvests sown and grown. A most fascinating place to visit. Down on the actual Loire river itself travelling west out of Saumur on the southern shore, there are various caves turned to another use of storing wine and champagne. Here the wines and champagne are stored for the maturity and onward selling. However, we came across another cave along the banks of the Loire on the outside of Saumur that had yet another use. Pulling into the car park there was a façade of what looked like the outside wall of a normal café built into the cliff. Above the doorway was advertising for a café. Opening the door and entering you are met with a long well lit passage that extends downwards and off to an angle. After a couple of hundred yards in eerie silence voices can be heard. As you get closer to the voices there are first of all several grottos selling various wines. Then there is a counter where you are greeted and led to a clothed table amongst dozens of others set out in three huge connecting caves. A set menu is served consisting of three courses including wine. Needless to say on both occasions we visited, coach loads of visitors had arrived, mostly elderly retired folks, to enjoy a lunchtime meal. It is so quirky and different it is very hard to describe. After the meal which takes about an hour and a half you are left to wander back outside into the sunlight which is quite blinding after being down in the caves.

On the way to Eastern Saumur it is well worth visiting the convent at Fontevraud. Here a huge collection of stones similar to those that built the chateaus with high walls can be visited and which used to be a convent. In the main church of the convent which itself is huge lays the remains of Richard the Lionheart, his sister and his parents. The place has a chequered history. It started off in the medieval days as a convent. During and after the French revolution it became a state prison holding political prisoners then ordinary prisoners that was active till just before the second world war. The whole building has a magnificence about it yet so tranquil and pretty.

The chateaux that run along the sides of the Loire are magnificent but again take on various guises and themes and well worth a visit. One that is now a museum holds a collection of various weather veins. These used to be displayed on the tops of the barges that frequented up and down the river. Apparently, they are quite political and meaningful. As you wander round this particular chateau there is a huge room that seems to have numerous simple stone statues. They are very crudely formed with what is a basic head on top of a torso with no arms or legs or indeed any particular shape. However at a given time the lights in the room dim, music starts to play and video players cast colours and shapes onto these statues. The figures suddenly become alive with medieval costumes and with music merriment as if there is a medieval party banquet being acted out in the large room. After a short while that image disappears, and another appears of a different era different costumes music and merriment. It is all quite eerie as a spectator.

Quite a few of the chateaux have their own wine cellars and vineyards to supply and sell such wines. The one in Montreuil-Bellay produces a particularly good white wine although the red wine is not as gentle. Another chateau about ten miles away has the most delicious red wine. This means of course that a visit to the various chateaux is a must to stock up first of all on the holiday wine then the wine to be brought home.

One aspect of the medieval town of Montreuil-Bellay that is not quite so wonderful involves the monument outside the town hall. I noticed a name written on of an elderly lady in her seventies that after her name simply said "died in Auschwitz". A fellow camper from England who has visited the camp site for many years explained that at the bottom of the hill of the town lays an old railway marshalling yard. Here the local Jews were collected, housed in basic camp like huts, guarded until they could be put aboard cattle trucks, into Saumur and then on to Germany and then various concentration camps. He took me down to the site. All that remains is a large triangular piece of ground which has a collection of stone steps that looked like at one time they gave access to chicken coups. They were not for chickens but for the Jewish prisoners of war. After a suitable number were collected, off they were taken and would never be seen again. The strange thing is that on the triangular piece of ground not one animal existed no birds were singing. It was as if the area had been condemned as evil and nothing wanted to pass on or over it.

Anybody visiting this campsite and town is highly recommended to take their bicycles as it is a great area to explore on bikes having miles and miles of little narrow country lanes that cross through the countryside with very little hills to climb and is so typically French as you would expect from the literature and posters. We were making our way back from the Convent one day and met an elderly English group that were making their way back to the village and the campsite. As I knew what was ahead I asked them if they wanted me to lift their bikes up onto my four bike rack and give them a lift at least to the edge of the village. They were very polite but declined my offer. I was surprised to see their return to the camp site so quickly. When I asked one of them if they were okay on the steep hill he announced that yes they were fine as they all had the new electric powered bicycles.

I have been back to this camp site several times but unfortunately some not as straight forward as my first visit. Our second year we booked a ferry from Portsmouth across to le Havre on the basis that we could have a simple drive down to the coast, put ourselves on board, have a nice meal then a gentle long nights sleep before arriving fresh and ready for the final few hours' drive once in France. This worked splendidly going out. We had a large ship got on board found a suitable cabin for our needs and sat in the restaurant having waitress service as we chugged out of Portsmouth and on to our destination . Unfortunately the return journey was not quite so easy. When we arrived at the port the ticket collector remarked "Oh, you have a caravan". Strange but yes that is what I am towing. Over the course of the next hour I noticed other cars, vans, motorcycles etc., but not a single other vehicle as much as towing a trailer or caravan. We were the only ones. I then soon realised why as the Catamaran came steaming round the corner. Now anyone who knows about the seafaring Catamarans will tell you boarding is carried out from the same opening and departure. Each vehicle drives down one side, turns and comes back down the other. They are packed in like sardines. There is a certain restricted amount of space at the front where the odd larger vehicle or trailered vehicle can be carried. The only problem is that the vehicle has to be turned round, and actually backed down the hundred feet or so boarding platform on board. Now this is my second trip. Reversing has not been something I have particularly practiced since acquisition of the caravan especially a hundred feet backwards down a sloping narrow gang plank blind with only my side mirrors to help. Needless to say after about the 7th attempt I was beginning to fluster. This did not help when the second in command came alongside the driver's door shouting through the window that everyone was on board the boat was scheduled to leave and if I wasn't able to get myself on board I would have to be left behind. I assured him in simple English that given the fact they had booked me that event was not going to happen. Luckily an English sailor took pity on me stood next to me and the driver's window and directed left turn, right turn, slowly back etc., till I was safely aboard with caravan and car. The first two hours of the voyage I was a physical and nervous wreck. I do remember however that the vessel travelled so fast that we caught up a bird flying across the channel and actually over took it.

CHAPTER 25
TRIP TO JORDAN

I have known Jenny and John for many years. In particular Jenny as she and I go back to the Milton Keynes Development Corporation days. John was a professor at the department of Egyptology at the Durham University and such a highly respected man. They met, and were married and both lived in Durham where John worked at Durham University. His work took him mostly to Egypt but also to Syria, Iran, Jordan and other Arab states where he was highly regarded. In recent years and given his amazing knowledge they began to organise field trips for themselves and a selected group of close friends. Various locations were chosen within the Middle East. One year, Jenny contacted me and asked if I would be interested in accompanying them in a small group to fly to Jordan for a field trip. This would involve overland transport the length and breadth of the country. Naturally, I jumped at this once in a lifetime experience. I should add that John is a typical academic. He was such an intelligent informed man and what he forgot I would never have the privilege of experiencing. However, he was not a people person and could certainly not be able to organise folks on a tour anywhere. Jenny on the other hand was the ideal person for organising. She is very dynamic very confident and very good with dealing with problems that may crop up during such trips.

Our trip started from Heathrow. From here we flew on to Amman for our first forty-eight hour stop over. The hotel was in the middle of Amman. It was not the best but clean and adequate for our stay. After we had unpacked and got ourselves sorted we were taken off in a mini coach to our first destination just outside Amman to what was called the "Turkish Village". Here a group of Turkish refugees had built a small compound comprising houses, small commercial units and a restaurant with dance floor. We were able to buy a few curios from the shops including the Arab head scarves which would prove invaluable later in the desert. We then went down to the restaurant where a huge spread of Turkish food had been prepared for what can only be described as a feast. I must confess I love Turkish food and all its spices, so I went to bed that night with a very contented tummy.

Now nobody from the Christian world warns you that the Muslims start their prayers before dawn. This is to enable the Muslims to not waste daylight hours praying when they could be at work. The first Minaret started off at around five thirty. This is a long tall building domed at the top with bright flood lights, mostly green. From here, the morning prayers are blasted out by loudspeaker to the congregation below. It is definitely a morning wake up. It seems to go on for eternity. Eventually it stops and so you can settle down for a couple of more hours before starting the day. Well, this is what I thought before the second Minaret started up a few minutes later. We had to endure about four of them in the end.

Our first day was spent visiting the old ruins of the Old Testament citadel or castle in the centre of Amman. A formidable building that towers above Amman itself. it is a wonderful viewpoint from the top that looks out over the city of Amman and also the seven hills forming its boundaries. The first thing that hits you is the poverty below. Most of what you can see and as far as you can see is made up of shanty buildings of breeze block, cardboard and corrugated iron. Here over a million people have lived since the first war with Israel. This shanty area has slowly grown with Palestinians, Syrians, Iraqis and even Egyptian refugees some not having seen their homeland for fifty years. It is a godsend that Jordan's king is so charitable to allow them to settle given that Jordan itself is not the richest of countries.

At the top of the old ruined castle that is referred to in the Old Testament of the Bible is a building housing part of the museum. Here we were greeted by staff who at first sight of John were virtually bowing and scraping to him as if he was royalty. Such was the recognition and high regard for a man that is known throughout the middle east. Whilst John and the staff caught up on the gossip of events we went to inspect many artefacts found throughout the region and Jordan to include part of the dead sea scrolls. These were in incredibly good condition given their age of several thousand years old. The building was full of pottery and day to day living tools and utensils but thousands of years old.

From the castle we crossed over the road to a fully working Roman amphitheatre that looked like it had been used only yesterday with its wooden staging etc., some of us climbed to the top of the very back stone steps while others were on the stage and even at a virtual whisper we could hear their chatter which was incredible.

The minibus which would prove to be our companion for the next ten days picked us up and we drove to the Tombs of the Seven Sleepers. Here we found an array of caves where coffins had rested for two thousand years. What intrigued me was that he whole site was protected, even revered by the Muslim priests given that to my knowledge, these were Christian deceased and not of the same faith. It was explained to me that the Old Testament is part of the Muslim religion as well as Christian and Jewish religions of which the three religions hold in great esteem. The story goes that a group trying to escape persecution from practising early Christianity took shelter in the caves but fell into a coma type sleep. After awakening from their sleep a thousand years later they tried to find sustenance only to then quickly return back to their coma like state and perish. I found the whole area very moving and haunting with piped music, candles and even flowers to remember those that had perished.

The next day we were up bright and early and hit the main highway heading north towards the Syrian border. First we stopped at Kerak, a large medieval fort built by the Crusaders to protect them from the marauding Moors who they were fighting during the Christian Crusades. What an amazing and massive fortification. The views from the top looked down this long wide valley towards the sea. This was the route the crusaders would have first taken once landing into the Holy Land on their way to fight. It was here at Kerak that Raynald de Chatillon a rather vicious and evil count, was cornered and eventually captured by notorious Moor leader Sal-a-din. Chatillon was beheaded for his atrocious crimes against the innocent Arabs and camel trains in particular. Before he was beheaded, the Arab leader Sal-a-din had offered water to an English lord who, once he had drunk passed to vessel to de Chatillon who then drank. Sal-a-din knocked the vessel from Chatillon's hands shouting "It was not me that offered you this drink" as it was a custom that had he done so he would not have been able to execute him. It was then Sal-a-din that then executed Chatillon.

Our next day we were back on the road and headed for Jerash. What an amazing city of ruins destroyed by various earthquakes over the centuries. Built by the Greeks and inhabited by the Romans it was a vast network of stone roads, shops, temples, archways and amphitheatres all destroyed by various earthquakes over the centuries. In one of the amphitheatres we experienced Jordanian soldiers dressed up in kilts playing bagpipes for the audience which was rather bizarre. It was at the north of the city where there was a stone trough catching water and which Jesus was supposed to have taken a pitcher of water and turned it into wine. Behind on the hill a short way away was the ruins of a temple with its huge columns still standing. John asked me if I had my Swiss army knife with me to draw the blade and poke it into one of the gaps between the thirty feet high stone columns. As if by magic the knife then began to rock up and down on its axis. It was of course the movement of the column that whilst not visible to the human eye was shown through the movement of the pen knife. Several onlookers quietly moved away I suppose thinking this was magic. In the centre of Jerash was a huge roundabout where the grooves of where the chariots had passed over the centuries still showed. Also, along the sides and down the side streets lay the shop fronts. A most fascinating city to visit. At the beginning of Jerash where we had parked was a huge stone archway which all traffic would have passed under. The huge archway was built to honour Hadrian the Roman emperor for his visit to Jerash. Sadly, Hadrian never did come to the city.

From Jerash our journey took us north to the extreme border of the country at a small abandoned settlement called Um-Qais. It was here the Bible tells us that Jesus encountered a mad man and putting his hands on the man extracted the madness and transferred it to a herd of pigs that ran down the hill into the Sea of Galilee. Whether this is believed depends on your depth of religious conviction given that the sea of Galilee lay below us about five miles across rocky terrain. What was encountered was the degree of security and barbed wire that divided us from the Israeli side across a deep and wide ravine. Opposite this was again more barbed wire and a steep climb up to a plateau that over looked the sea of Galilee. It was obvious why the Israelis invaded this area as it is the Golan Heights where Syrians and others bombarded Israel across the sea with rockets and shells. Um-Qais now is a ruin of Roman structures, buildings and large columns that must have been a very wealthy location in its heyday. The small café at the top of the hill overlooking the ravine offered welcome shade from the very hot sun and gave us a chance for a coffee and a break before setting off again.

Our journey then took us from Um-Qais and down from the desert like conditions of the internal Jordan countryside and down into the very lush Jordan valley. This is sometimes called the garden of Jordan producing much of the salad products exported to the rest of Europe. On our journey now heading south and before stopping for the evening we were able to fit in a stop to Mount Nebo. This is located up on the high plateau overlooking the Jordan Valley with what is now Israel and the promised land in the distance. It was here that Moses stood and looked down and across to the promised land that he had spent 30 years leading his people from the chains of slavery in Egypt to their final destination and freedom. Sadly of course, he was not allowed to go across to the promised land but instead remained on the mount and ended his days as a hermit. He was supposed to have lived till he was a hundred and thirty years old but again this is taken with a pinch of salt. At the top there is a visitor centre that celebrates the religious side of the Mount and holds a huge metal statue of the staff that Moses carried during his wonderings in the desert.

Leaving Mount Nebo we made our way to the only town in Jordan that holds a Christian church. It was dark when we arrived at Madaba, meaning Tree of Life. After dumping our cases at the small two star hotel went to a local restaurant for a Jordanian meal and then to bed. The next morning, we were up quite bright and early. Looking from our window was a view of the Christian church across the road. Climbing onto the roof was a church member making his way over to the two large church bells which he then proceeded to ring. This was a strange procedure and there was clearly no way to ring from ground level. After a typical Jordanian breakfast of coffee, fruits and flat breads etc., we wandered over to the church. Not a particularly outstanding building or internally any different to many churches I had visited apart from a cordoned off section at the back of the church surrounded by numerous tourists of various nationalities. When we were able to reach this area it exposed part of the floor that had been dug away. There at the bottom of the excavation some eighteen inches deep was the most beautiful mosaic. This mosaic turned out to come from the seventh century and had been buried for well over a thousand years and was only revealed with recent repair work. The mosaic showed an ancient map of the Dead Sea the river Jordan leading into the sea with a fish swimming away from the sea depicting that the sea was toxic to fish life. The other side of the river was a complete street map of Jerusalem. The detailing and the quality were just exquisite. Jenny took me to one side and we wandered off down some of the back streets of Madaba. Eventually we came to this courtyard where a co-operative of women were busy working in their workshop. Apparently, the proprietor wanted to create a co-operative whereby women who mostly did not work throughout Jordan could come together learn a trade and earn money. In particular he took on disabled women. They were all taught ceramics and in particular the mosaic plates and plaques that many tourists bring back from their visits. Unlike the tacky poor quality mosaics you could buy from street corner vendors, these were very high quality. The women were all jovial and enthusiastic and full of life and very proud of their co-operative and the standards of work they achieved. I did indeed buy a very special circular mosaic that depicts the Tree of Life and now have it proudly placed on the wall in my hall. The mosaic is still intact and in very good condition.

Our day had only just begun and climbing back into our minibus we headed south along the very dusty Highway of the Sun towards Aqaba. This highway is notorious for road accidents especially involving continental lorries racing each other for the port from

Syria, Iraq even Turkey to deposit their contents onto ships heading off from the Red Sea Port. The situation was really bad with lorries having to wait days at Aqaba for the authorities to check their papers before being allowed to proceed. Lorries therefore would race to try to get as close the front of the queue as they could. This resulted in some horrendous crashes and loss of lives. When we travelled the route, the road had been widened and the road into the port divided into two, one for the tourists and one for the lorry drivers. However, they were required to report to a city many miles back from Aqaba for clearance before proceeding. This made the final journey much safer. We would however stop off at another deserted medieval castle that had in fact been built by the Moors. This was an extraordinary structure as it was the only one built by the Moors, who preferred a hit and run regime rather than a substantial fortification. The old castle was surprisingly in good condition given its age and was still inhabited along with a small village at its foot by several families, one being headed by a retired teacher who would give us a guided tour. After having an in depth visit with lots of information gained we left for our final journey that day to the hotel at the edge of Petra.

The hotel at Petra looked so out of place. Here we were in pure desert conditions with large rocks and dry arid sand and desert as far as you could see and sat in it was this plush five star hotel built with gleaming glass and steel and very expensive cars and coaches dropping off and picking up wealthy customers. We all felt a bit out of place in our desert fatigues covered in dust. The hotel was to be our home for next three days and given some of the accommodation we had experienced we all felt like royalty. The dining area, the selection of food, the beautiful air-conditioned rooms were all just wonderful. We all had a wonderful shower and wash and after evening dinner we each had an early night ready for our adventure into the Petra area itself. Another facility I had never experienced before was the laundry. Gathering up all our dirty and dusty laundry accumulated since arriving on our adventure, we handed it to the hotel reception in a rather large black bin bag. The following day a knock on the hotel room door and this package of little plastic bags, all sealed, contained socks handkerchiefs shirts pants etc, what a lovely experience to re-pack clean clothes.

Early next morning we had to be up washed, dressed, fed and ready to meet outside to walk the three quarters of a mile down this very stony, dusty track into the cracks into the high cliff like rocks that formed the famous Petra entrance. The locals who are all descendants of the Nabataeans who have lived in this area for thousands of years, were trying to entice us into hiring donkeys or carts pulled with donkeys to ease our walk down, with comments like "four by four air conditioning" and "she will love you forever", but we just smiled and waved them off with "No Shoran" or no thank you. I didn't realise why we had to leave so early in the morning till we go to the far entrance of the tunnel of cliffs. First of all, nothing can prepare you for the sheer magnificence of the Treasury as it grew in front of you. Then stepping out in front of the Treasury so that slowly the morning sun came across the rocks and shone down onto the Treasury and revealed it in even more splendour is a memory that I will take with me for the rest of my life. What was fascinating was all these tourists that came rushing down stood took several photos of themselves and the Treasury and then went rushing back to their coaches and off to their next destinations. What they clearly didn't realise was round the corner it opened up to some fifty square miles of historic antiquities in the shapes of five high places and another building similar to the Treasury. There were burial chambers, the Roman soldiers' grave caves, derelict Grecian church and abandoned cave dwellings where the original Nabataeans lived before they were evicted first by the Romans and later by the Jordanians themselves when early tourism arrived. At the end of each commercial day and after the tourists have vacated, the local Nabataeans are then ordered to leave the valley floor where their ancestors lived and died, for them to return to the new town built for them on the hill above Petra. We would spend three days exploring this amazing area and still didn't get to see more than half. We were able to walk up three of the five high places. Given the dryness of the desert conditions and the heat the walks were quite testing. We had to walk up stone steps and passages leading to the top of each. One high place revealed large carved slabs where ancient sacrifices were carried out to appease the gods. The second climbed up and past a similar structure as the Treasury itself below and also carved out of the rock on the side of the mountain. At the top there are remarkable views across the adjoining mountains. One of the high places which we didn't manage to climb would have taken a whole day travelling by donkey and would have arrived at the burial place where Moses brother, Aaron, is buried. The temple looks amazing especially given the height it is and it is at all times protected by Muslim priests.

On the last day we travelled the short distance away to where we were shown what was referred to as Little Petra where very few tourists go. Here there is the separation of the cliffs to reveal a walk through to a far smaller area than Petra itself. What was more fascinating was the archaeological dig that had discovered a small settlement by humans during their first move from hunter gatherer to settling to become farmers. Man had wandered northwards from central Africa passed across the Red Sea into what we now recognise as Arabia and ended up in the Jordan area where farming and settlements were started before migrating further into northern Europe and beyond. Here we were privileged to see one of the first such settlements with areas set aside for planting and growing etc.

To say that my stay in Petra was wonderful is an understatement. I would say my visit was a life changing experience that I will cherish for the rest of my life.

Sadly, our time had arrived to leave and so back aboard our minibus and back onto the Kings Highway this time heading for Aqaba on the edge of the Red Sea. I was a little disappointed having heard the romantic stories and descriptions of this city. What we found was basically an ancient rather sad looking sea port located along the furthest eastern edge of the Red Sea. The city is still greatly influenced in design culture by the Turkish Empire that occupied the region for many years. Here you could buy spices and all the wonders of the orient. There were some magnificent modern hotels overlooking the sea but further round the shoreline there was a barbed wire fence the other side of which Israel with one of the Israeli cities, Eilat, within waving distance. In fact, we could watch the planes land and take off from its airport and watch the lights of the nights' traffic driving through its streets. Because of the troubles experienced, the Israelis are very protective of the water border with armed military boats constantly patrolling against any illegal entry. Jenny joined me on my trip down into the town and ushered me away from the normal shops to a little arcade in the back streets and in particular this little tourist shop where we went in. Whilst the shop was itself full of cheap tourist tack it also had a collection of old photos showing the proprietor of the shop and Omar Sharif. It turns out that they are very good friends and have been so since the making of the film "Lawrence of Arabia" where the shop proprietor stood in for Omar Sharif as his double and stunt man. In fact the opening sequence is where Peter O`Toole is stood in the desert by a well. An Arab comes riding out of the desert haze on a camel and shoots the Arab companion of Peter O`Toole. This Arab on the camel was not in fact Omar Sharif but our friend now standing in front of us, now running a gift shop in the back streets of Aqaba. It seemed so surreal.

After an evening's visit to the old town and a night's rest we were up relatively early and headed back up the Kings Highway. At a resting place we changed vehicles for the back of several four by four pickups. We were then taken by Arab guides off the main road and way out into the desert. Here the scarves bought at the Turkish village on our first night came in very helpful. They kept the sand and wind tearing at our faces and throats. We would end up at Wadi Rum a vast desert of pink sand and tall pink rocks that was very hot and very empty. We stopped at one spot next to this tall bare rock where there was rock art on the side of part of it. The rock art showed camels and humans and were purported to have been drawn by the exiled Nabataeans after they had been evicted from Petra by the Romans. It was as if the art was saying: "we were here please don't forget us." Next stop was by a derelict simple building where Lawrence of Arabia had stayed temporarily after his epic journey across the desert. This is where with the Arab tribes they attacked the Turks at the Fort in Aqaba before evicting them finally out of Jordan. The enormity of the desert and the vastness is really appreciated here. Way out across the vastness you can see Saudi Arabia way off across the desert in the distance. We finally reached the destination where the driver had been heading. It was a huge pebble shaped rock that offered shelter and shade against possible wind or the burning sun where we set up for our lunch. Hidden in the sand was a barrel about the size of an oil drum that was serving as an oven the driver had set up some hours earlier and had a lamb carcass cooking for some hours inside. Having brushed away the sand and lifted the lid revealed this amazing smell of cooked meat. I always carry with me my survival kit to include a small fold out army stainless steel stove. This holds a fire lighter and is big enough to heat a small one cup kettle. This was lit and a deserved cup of tea accompanied our lunch. Our driver worked on me for the remainder of our trip to glean this small folding cooker from me with the kettle which he had never seen before. After lunch and a short rest in the Bedouin Tent erected more for show for us tourists, we drove off heading back towards the drop off area. However, the trip wasn't over yet. We stopped and took up our positions sitting in the late afternoon sun. We were going to experience the sunset in the desert. As we sat chatting and waiting a local Bedouin in full gown came wandering over. He was carrying his metal tea pot and small whiskey type glasses and asked if he could join us. After sitting down he offered the four of us sat together a drink. This is basically a very sweet black tea or affectionately called "Bedouin Whiskey". We all thanked him and took a glass or two each. It turned out he was not selling anything didn't want anything apart from our company to be able to talk to and share the English he had learned. After what was the most remarkable romantic sunset I have experienced our little Arab friend quietly disappeared never to be seen again. As for us we rocked and shook our way back out of the desert in the dark back to our minibus to return to our hotel all looking like Indiana Jones, full of dust and sand from our days experience.

The next day it was the day we had to depart. Cases were collected and bodies loaded and we were off to the small airport of Aqaba. The cases were taken off and we boarded the small internal jet plane for the short hop back to Amman. We wouldn't see our cases again until we got back to Heathrow as they were transferred automatically at Amman onto our ongoing flight on a larger intercontinental plane back the UK. Thank goodness the aeroplane was a lot bigger than the tiny plane that had transferred us up from the Red Sea as it was going to be six hours before our arrival back in the UK. What a fantastic holiday we had experienced and thank goodness for both Jenny and John who were both a mine of information who shared so much of their knowledge and experience. They took us to places that the normal tourists would never see and shared their own happy memories with us.

CHAPTER 26

TRIP TO EGYPT FOR SCUBA DIVING

I had worked quite hard studying and taking both my written and practical Padi diving exam to enable me to carry a Padi diving card. This would enable me to travel around the world where many diving schools were located. My Padi card enabled me to hire their equipment and accompany their divers on organised dives. I had dived various locations in Britain and had travelled to Cyprus and dived at several locations there. However, everyone in the diving fraternity kept saying how the Red Sea was a Mecca for the scuba diver.

A holiday was booked, and bags packed to fly to Sharm-el-Sheikh. This is a purpose-built town on the southern coast of Egypt carved out of the barren desert for the tourist industry and diving. The flight was the longest I had taken to date. After nearly six hours we landed at the airport again built right out in the desert specifically for the tourist trade and located on the outskirts of Sharm-el-Sheikh. A coach took us to our four star hotel further along the coast. Now a four star hotel in most places in Europe would have been a rather luxurious stay with bedrooms, dining rooms etc being of a high standard. Unfortunately, the Egyptian scoring was lot higher than ours and I would say was more in the level of a two or three star. We arrived in the early evening just at the end of the evening dinner but was offered a table to eat. Now like many hotels in tourist locations they try to put on food that they believe the tourist wants rather than offer traditional food which they are more experienced to make. The chicken and chips that we were served were quite disgusting.

Horribly lukewarm and greasy. However, we were so hungry we just got the food down our throats just to fill ourselves up.

Our room was adequate for just sleeping in and the next day refreshed and after breakfast asked the hotel rep to recommend a diving school. We walked the short distance from the hotel to the diving school and registered to go off for several dives for the week we would be staying. We had to run the gauntlet of the Egyptian shops and vendors who all think they are our friends and trying to entice us into their shops to buy their wares at exorbitant prices. Having already been to Jordan I was rather familiar with the custom and the Arabic word "no-shakran" or no thank you was very useful.

Our second night at the resort found us being served with equally inedible canteen food which really was not to the standard that either of us wanted to eat. For this reason on the third night we decided that we would try to find a local restaurant that the Egyptians used and have local traditional food. We asked the doorman if he could organise a taxi for us and he quickly offered to phone "a cousin" of his. Most people we met had relations that they could recommend to serve most needs so this didn't surprise us. The taxi arrived and he explained to his "cousin" that we wanted to be taken to a local restaurant that he could recommend in town. This was no problem and off we set. The taxi driver was very friendly and chatty and took us down to the old town of Sharm el-Sheikh. The town was really lively and bustled full of locals shopping and eating. The taxi driver literally stopped his taxi in the middle of the road ushered us along the pavement leaving his car still with the engine running. We went into this restaurant with tables and chairs on the pavement and full of locals all eating what smelt like delicious local food. He explained to the proprietor what we wanted and left us in the owners hands saying that when we had finished the owner would ring him and he would come and pick us up. The owner then showed us to our table and asked us what we would like to eat. I suggested that as I was not familiar with Egyptian food could we leave it to him to recommend a three-course meal. He was thrilled. We had waiters jumping around setting up the cutlery, glasses of water etc., I have to say the banquet we were presented with was absolutely divine and certainly a whole different level to the food the evening before. We were made to feel so welcome and complete strangers were so friendly and chatted to us about where we were from etc., the price of the meal was so ridiculously cheap as well, so we really felt we had succeeded in finding a great night out in the old town. The taxi driver was true to his word and after a call from the restaurant owner was there to pick us up very quickly to return us to our hotel. While we were walking to the taxi suddenly these two boys arrived coming up the road on the back of their camel amongst all the other traffic. They suddenly stopped the camel climbed off, tied the animal to one of the side posts and wandered off into the evening crowd. It looked like a western but instead of the cowboy riding his horse into the town and tying it up outside the saloon it was the camel tied up along the main walkway. Just so surreal and amazing.

A strange practice that the hotel had was the way they dealt with bugs and flies etc. Now I wouldn't have thought that being built out of the desert surrounded on all three sides by desert that the resort would be infested with much of a problem. However, every other evening just as it was getting dark members of staff appeared armed with what look like giant paraffin cans. The difference was these cans were omitting heavy thick and putrid oily smoke. It smelt like an old diesel lorry or bus was parked in the grounds revving its engines. It smelt like they were burning old oil and then walked round spraying it into the bushes and landscaped gardens spread throughout the grounds of the hotel. Wherever you sat you could not escape this horrible vile smell or smoke which left you coughing and spluttering even away from the ground staff. How on earth their lungs coped with emitting this awful concoction every other evening I have no idea. I have certainly not seen this practice in any other location I have visited prior to this holiday or since. However, it certain achieved its goal as we were not bitten or troubled with any insect bites during our whole stay at the hotel.

For our first couple of dives, we were taken out to a very smart launch which then took us out into the Red sea. Here we anchored, got ourselves kitted up and over the side looking like the divers you see on the films. We all had our Padi training and so followed the procedure not only to enter the water but to deflate and submerge. The water was so incredibly warm that all I need was a shorty or half suit without fear of getting cold. As we submerged, we saw the bottom some ten metres below us. It was like diving into an aquarium at one of the garden centres but much larger. The first thing you notice is how white and clean the sand on the bottom is. Then how clear the water is with the visibility being much, much further than say in the Mediterranean. As we swam along in our group and with our "buddy" nominated to make sure you were looked after and vice versa we came across various rock formations. Swimming all around these formations were the most brightly coloured fish of all shapes and designs. They completely ignored us as clearly they see many divers over the weeks and months. To be amongst these incredible coloured fish was just magical. And as we left one rock formation to another, so the fish disappeared with another shoal reappearing at the next cluster. Clearly, they were safe from larger predators keeping close to the rocks.

Now I was always led to believe that once you went under water you couldn't hear anything. However, one of the young divers had round his neck what looked like a metal single cigar case. Each time he wanted our attention so he would shake the case and it was surprising how far you could hear him. He was able to point out all sorts of interesting things under water. We had a shoal of barracuda swimming across and above us that seemed quite strange. Another time he was close to me and shook his tin and pointed down to this rock that had a little hole at the front of it. He pointed down and beckoned for me to go closer. When I did I saw this huge head that looked about the size of Mike Tyson's fist and it was attached to what could have been a body of up to five feet behind it. It was a rather menacing, aggravated looking Moray eel rocking his head from side to side looking very agitated that we were in his space. Despite offers to go closer from the guide I declined as those teeth looked very sharp and very menacing. I felt that it could get from its position to mine rather quicker than I could move to get out of its way.

Being underwater you have to not only keep an eye on the amount of air you use and signal to the guide if you are getting low. You must also keep an eye on the time that you spend under water. Strapped to the air vest is a block with dials. These dials have details of how much air you have, the time, and other bits of useful information. There is a chart that the Padi course teaches you to work out how long each dive should take. At the most the air in the tanks lasts for about 35 minutes which is actually a good length to dive as it can be quite tiring. Once we return to the surface if we are to change tanks and return to the water then we first have to calculate from the chart given to us with our Padi course how long that second dive can be safely performed. The reason for this is that air enters the blood stream and after a certain time can prove very dangerous. A situation can be created what many people recognise as "the bends". This can prove very painful and indeed fatal if not taken seriously and cautiously. This was a good afternoon and would probably enable up to three dives with each dive getting shorter than the previous one.

One afternoon on another visit to the bay we were offered what they call drift diving. This is where you enter the water and allow the current to take you along. From the swimming point of view, it saves a lot of energy. However, I was very reluctant having talked to drift divers in the sound off Islay in Scotland. Here they enter the race of water at one end and are shunted along in a very strong current which only expert divers would ever try. Having had the fears put into me I was very hesitant. The young guides were very good and very assuring that no tragedy would happen to me. In fact, I would hardly notice the drifting at all. The only requirement was in fact that our boat would have to come to us as there was no way we could swim back to it. So, I reluctantly and nervously agreed to join the group and down we went. I was really surprised how gently the current took us along. Now one of the tricks of diving is being able to inflate or deflate the vest worn that enables you either to sink or rise to the surface. Get this right and you can literally float what appears to be in mid air not going up or down. One of the young guides took this one step even further. He got his balance just perfect that he could cross him arms cross his legs like he was sitting on a stool and allow himself to be carried along. It looked amazing and so funny.

Not all our dives were taken off the back of a boat. We did a beach dive one afternoon that required us to haul our gear from the beach along a really long and not particularly stable pontoon out into the sea. The colour of the sea where most swimmers were located was this lovely light blue colour. However, where we were heading the colour turned to a very dark blue indicating a deep drop. I was correct. As we

207

dropped off the pontoon and into the water I found that the start of the long line of dark blue was in fact hiding a very deep drop into the abyss. We navigated parallel from the pontoon along the edge of this deep ravine. I am only qualified to dive down to twenty metres but as such is quite deep enough. The sea life was still very full and interesting with a lot of fish hovering along the cliff face. It was rather a strange experience that I had not been previously aware of when I went to look out and down into what was basically emptiness. With nothing for the eyes and brain to register on I felt a strange phenomenon coming over me of being slightly dizzy and like I was about to pass out. The guide with me saw my reaction and with two fingers pointed to my eyes and then to the cliff face and shook his hand not to look down. He was obviously aware of this reaction to some divers looking into nothing. It made me think how space explorers coped with looking out into open space and nothing for them to register the brain on and whether they had the same experience. I had gone through a similar situation when diving off Cyprus. We were diving in what the guide called the Theatre. It looked like a large curved amphitheatre but under water. As we came up and over the back wall we were faced with this emptiness and at that time I felt a dizziness where I felt I was going to pass out. That dive I grabbed the arm of the "buddy" allocated to me on that dive and hand signalled my problem. He got hold of me turned me slightly so I could focus my vision on something till it passed. Shortly after that we returned to the surface and confessed I found the experience then rather worrying.

The only point of the dive when the guide actually suggested me looking elsewhere from the cliff face was at one point when he pointed down into the deep. Plucking up the courage of looking down I spotted way, way below us at least another twenty metres a group of divers carrying different types of tanks to us. These guys were definitely very experienced divers and made my efforts and depth of dive very intermediate. Once the dive came to an end and it was time to climb out of the water. It was obvious first of all just how heavy these air tanks are. Having to navigate the ladder attached to the pontoon with fins in one hand and free hand on the other was difficult enough. To then try to climb up out of the water onto a contraption that was in fact rocking from side to side in the waves after a 40-minute dive was far than easy. I was shattered by the time we wobbled back to the beach. However, the experience was well worth it.

It was the last day that I would be able to dive. Another rule when going on a holiday where diving is going to take place is that you cannot dive on the day of arrival if flying. Likewise, you cannot dive on the day of the return flight. Ideally at least a good twenty four hours must pass between the dive and the flight. This is because the aeroplane is pressured to be able to reach its flying height. This can affect the human body the same as staying under water for too long with oxygen bubbles building up in the blood stream causing the bends. This can at the minimum be very painful and at the other extreme fatal. So, we went off in the boat for our last afternoon dive. We dropped over and enjoyed the same dive and sights as we had during the week. We had plenty of time left so the diving guide wanted to give me the best experience before it was over. However, after thirty minutes under water I noticed my air supply had got low which means we must now return to the surface. The diving guide had other ideas. Now, one of the procedures that has to be practiced and mastered to obtain the Padi certificate is to remove the mouthpiece under water. Once the mouthpiece has been removed you then place it back in your mouth making sure you blow before breathing to stop any water going into the lungs. The final part of this exercise is that you drop your own mouthpiece out of your mouth reach across to the spare mouthpiece carried by your "buddy" and again blowing out the water you can then continue to breath but using his spare lung mouthpiece which he has attached to him and connected to his tank. So, this manoeuvre was suggested with the appropriate hand signals, my mouthpiece dropped down to my side and positioned his spare into my mouth. This enabled us to swim side by side to extend the dive even further. Being sensible though the dive wasn't prolonged to a point when it would have proved dangerous and so reluctantly, we rose to the surface. By this time the light was fading, and we were now into early evening. The boat was some yards from us, so it was a case of swimming for it. I can say I have never felt so exhausted trying to swim on the surface complete with heavy tank to the boat. Front crawl was pointless and even breaststroke was really difficult. Despite having fins again, it seemed I wasn't getting anywhere. There was no point putting the breathing lung back into my mouth and swimming under the surface as my air had gone. I thought I was never going to reach the boat and they were reluctant to up anchor and come to us with such a short distance. How I managed to climb out of the water even with rescuing arms on board taking my fins and holding my arms and helping to pull me aboard. I was totally exhausted but exhilarated by this last dive. The story was not yet over. We reached the port disembarked from the boat and into the pickup to take us back to the centre close to the hotel. However, we suddenly came to a standstill with a complete grid lock. The roads were blocked in every direction on every road in Sham el-Sheikh by military jeeps and vehicles with blue lights flashing. Everyone dutifully sat there for what must have been twenty minutes and then eventually the military vehicles cleared and opened up the roads so we could complete our return. It turned out later that the king of Egypt had come to Sharm el-Sheikh for a conference. After the conference he left by cavalcade, but he insisted that all traffic would come to a halt as he was very much in fear of his life and being attacked by rebels. Egypt was becoming very unstable with unrest which would ultimately spread through the middle east. Whilst Sharm el-Sheikh was a very quiet non political area he was not going to take any chances.

Two days later we were packed, ushered back down the coast road through the desert and put on our plane back to the UK. We were rather expecting a quiet uneventful flight back. However six Irish lads that had clearly been away for a stag week were rather lively, fuelled with alcohol had different ideas. Jovial loud banter soon increased to a more colourful behaviour to the point that the other passengers were getting a little insecure in their seats. I noticed on the plane and standing on each of the two isles two rather tall men dressed in suits that had positioned themselves to watch our merry party. Another came from the back of the plane and positioned himself slightly to their rear. As the merriment was increasing one of these rather well-dressed gentlemen stretched over and had a word with a couple of the lads. The reaction seemed to be positive, and they quietened down. However, there is always the one that is going to be rather braver and less compliant than the others who carried on his own party atmosphere. Another word was had by the well-dressed gentleman with the other two moving a little closer. From the bulges on the side of their chests inside their jackets it was clear they were carrying side arms. These chaps must have been sky marshals on board to detract any threats to passengers. As the final straw was reached our lively friend and his mate who also decided to rejoin the party were physically lifted out of their seats. They were accompanied rather securely towards the front of the plane. Here they were re seated between two of the sky marshals and the other standing close by. This seemed to dampen what could have turned into a messy situation. The remainder of the flight was relatively uneventful until we reached home where several of our own police force boarded the plane and escorted the stag party off the plane and off into police custody. Such a pointless end to their stag break.

Although this break in Egypt was only for a short weeks holiday it was a memory that I will cherish. The views and wildlife I had experienced close hand, was just exceptional. Because of the unrest and political problems that were to manifest during the ensuing years after our visit, it will be very doubtful if I would ever be able to return to ever dive here again.

CHAPTER 27
FIRST TRIP TO MOROCCO

I was approaching my 60th birthday. My current Land Rover Discovery that had served me well was now very high mileage and was beginning to rust in the usual places. I knew it was time to change it and I was particularly keen to revert to a series III or Defender style Land Rover. I had found a fantastic vehicle from a couple living in the Wirral. Apparently, they were only selling the vehicle as they were emigrating to Australia to run an outward bound school and had this vehicle been equipped with air conditioning would not have been sold. The vehicle had already been modified by what I call the pretty accessories. Side bars, nylon nudge bar, huge fog lights, the snorkel etc., Rostile wheels and really looked the part. That July we took the vehicle and ourselves for a day out to the annual Land Rover show at the then famous Billing Aquadrome. Here we spent the day wandering round all the parts stalls, the dealers along with the various clubs, off road vehicles etc. What I had not noticed the previous years was that there were several firms offering overland trips to various corners of the earth. I did chat to one guy who organised trips into North Africa and Europe but I didn't think I could particularly spend several weeks with him in extreme conditions. I then stopped and chatted to Atlas Overland a small company run by Peter who seemed to have some interesting trips. Peter is a retired teacher and was very approachable and very interesting. He told us precise details of his trips and what actually happened and what to expect. He made the trips very enticing to the point where we took his brochure, said we would talk about it once we got home and then back to him. Having poured over the leaflets and information handed to us I thought what a lovely memorable present it would be to celebrate and remember my 60th birthday with an overland trip to Morocco.

I got back in contact with Peter paid a deposit and arranged to be added to the Classic Tour of Morocco that was scheduled for the coming November. Peter in the meantime suggested we got together to discuss more details of the trip, the requirements and expectations and that he would give us a fuller picture of what was about to take place. In actual fact what he was doing, and he admitted it in later years, was that he was also coming down to interview us. He needed to satisfy himself that we would fit in with the group he was putting together. After all we would all be living together, travelling together and going through some rather severe and sometimes difficult terrain and climate. He really needed to be satisfied that we would be able to get on with other members in the group in such conditions. I had of course been camping most of my life and discussed with Peter what we needed by way of equipment. He wisely advised that we do not spend a fortune on having the vehicle kitted out any more than it was now. He also suggested that we buy plastic boxes with lids to put our various provisions and store inside. This way if the trip turned out not to be for us we had not wasted money on a vehicle conversion. This I found very good advice and so eight large heavy duty plastic boxes were purchased and slowly loaded. We had one for spares, one for medical, one for clothes and personal needs etc., etc.

As it came closer to the time we were to depart, various members of the family must have thought we were about to disappear off to the edge of the world. As a compromise we invited them to pop over to wave us off as we were not due to depart till lunchtime on the Friday. At least they could then see us off and give us a bit of moral support for what lay ahead. Our trip was to start with a leisurely drive to Portsmouth. There we would be loaded on board the ferry for a later afternoon departure. We had a cabin booked on board the ship and we could have a nice evening meal and watch the lights of the UK disappear. Then it would be heads down till we reached northern Spain the following evening. My daughter was going to keep an eye on the house while we were away. I popped over to my daughters house the evening before to give her a key and say cheerio before our departure. On the drive back home I received a very strange text on my phone that simply read "Sailing cancelled please make your way to Dover where P&O ferries will take you to Calais for you to continue your journey from there". Given my past experience my immediate thoughts were that some friend was playing a practical joke on us. I text back "Ho ho very good but not funny" I didn't get an answer so when I got home I didn't recognise the sender of the message so contacted the web site. To my horror the ferries had indeed been cancelled due to industrial unrest. Britannia owners had got fed up with wild strikes and go slows from the staff. They announced without warning they were shutting down the entire operation. Everyone was out of work till they could sort themselves out and return to work without any further disruptions. I rang the help number and felt very sorry for the voice on the other end as he sounded like he had dealt with a lot of very angry customers. He advised me that indeed P&O ferries were being commissioned to take all Britannia customers on their existing tickets. All we had to do was turn up at Dover and they would take over getting us over to France. This was all very well but the idea of what started off to be a relaxing cruise to northern Spain now turned into a nightmare. First of all we had a dash ahead across France and then into Northern Spain before I caught up on the planned itinerary. We were now facing a very arduous two day drive overland in a Land Rover. I made various phone calls round friends and family to advise them of the change of plans. I then loaded the eight boxes into the land rover that had been waiting in the hall for the next day. We then got our heads down for a few hours sleep before we started our epic journey.

With a few hours sleep under our belts we left home at three thirty am and drove through the remainder of the night The weather was awful and raining. Having arrived in Dover with the dawn still not coming up we were at least pleasantly surprised to see that they were indeed geared up for us. We were ushered through the P&O booking in booth, through customs and on to the dock side and queued for the next boat to France. We arrived in France as dawn was breaking again in rainy weather and headed south. Now a Land Rover Defender whilst very robust is not the speediest vehicle to choose. We lumbered on down the motorway heading for what I hoped would be Bordeaux for our first overnight stop. It was clear that even with limited comfort breaks and fuel stops we were no way going to make the distance I was hoping to. In fact we arrived in the Loire again in horrible weather as the early evening was setting in. Experience has shown me that we really need to be on a camp site by late afternoon otherwise we would end up struggling in the dark. We of course had no idea where we would find a campsite. Suddenly we were driving down a road very familiar to me. We were on the outskirts of the small medieval town of Montreuil-Bellay where I had camped several times with the caravan. A snap decision and I turned off the main highway and headed into town and to the camp site I was familiar with. Now I was really not looking forward to erecting the roof tent in the rain and in the failing light but it was the best option I had. The lady camp owner recognised us and welcomed us to the site. I suddenly thought I wonder if any of the little chalets they had on site were available. The camping season was coming to an end and felt sure that most of the summer campers had gone home. We were in luck, and she showed us to this very clean very warm chalet that had hot running water and a very comfortable looking bed. This means we didn't have to unload any boxes apart from our toiletries and spare clothes for the morning. We even managed to get a meal cooked and served in the camp restaurant. Finally, I thought maybe our luck was changing. The next day the weather had cleared, and we would be able to set off in sunnier conditions.

After a full day driving again with limited comfort stops, fuel stops, etc we managed to reach northern Spain. In fact, we were able to catch up the time lost with a couple of hours to spare. Peter had recommended a camp site at Bergos which is about eighty-five miles inland from Santander. We found the site, put ourselves onto a camp plot, opened up the roof tent for a first proper nights camping. Again, the camp site had a restaurant but sadly the quality of the food was not as good as the one the night before. However, it was food, we were hungry, so best just get it down our throats and get ourselves bedded down. We slept very well that night albeit in the roof tent for the first time. Next day we were up reasonably sharply as we needed to get packed up and on our way. The itinerary Peter had originally set us was to allow two days from Santander to the southern point where we would all meet up. The second camp site was about two thirds of the country down. The drive down was rather mediocre as we would take the lorry route down the motorway straight through the middle of Spain. The countryside was quite boring, and the lorry stop services rather basic. We stuck to our regime of making sure we had a comfort stop every three hours and refuelling while we had stopped. The second camp site in Spain was rather basic but like in the Loire had chalets that we could hire. We had a rather lovely sleep after a visit to their onsite restaurant where the food was a lot more palatable than the first.

Our third day found us driving in a lot hotter climate as we descended from the central plains of Spain down towards the coast. We were due to meet at a camp site at the Atlantic facing resort of Tarifa. This seems to be a spot visited by a lot of students in their dormobiles armed with surf boards, and the Atlantic waves seemed superb coupled with ideal warm weather. Tarifa itself is a small town but unknown to us had a medieval quarter behind a castle type wall which sadly we failed to visit. We drove into the campsite and the camp director beckoned us to follow him into the site and to the area where Peter and a couple of others from the group had already arrived. We chose our plot and set up camp. One of the other campers that had arrived before us was driving what can only be described as the ultimate land rover defender off road vehicle. It turned out that it had originally been commissioned along with others by Ranulph Fiennes for one of his expeditions with no expense spared. Sadly due to ill health he cancelled the tour and the vehicles were sold. This one had twenty four volts, and every conceivable extra and toy that could be fitted. Water tanks, external sockets, winches and all the onboard needs. Sadly, the owner was sat on the lifting roof armed with duct tape. He had visited a local supermarket and miscalculated the barrier on the way out and took part of the roof off. This did not go down well with his wife who turned out to be a bit of a dragon and embarrassed by this mishap. His vehicle though was superb, and we all secretly guessed it must have cost between forty and fifty thousand pounds. That evening after everyone had arrived and set up camp, we were invited by Peter to go into the campsite restaurant for pizza and chips and a group bonding. It was a lovely evening. I particularly liked the adjoining room containing wall to wall cabinets suitably fronted with metal grills containing what must be a selection of every single malt whiskey in the world. Sadly we were not invited to sample any of the private collection.

Next morning after we ate, washed and broke camp, we were allowed an hour to drive to the new town of Tarifa to the supermarket. Here we could stock up with supplies enough to at least see us for our first week. On board the land rover I had fitted an South African twelve volt Engel freezer/fridge that would if required take food down to minus five. This was ideal to buy packs of meat from the supermarket ready for our tour. After we had loaded with supplies including lots of bottled water we returned to the camp to then follow Peter and the convoy down to Algeciras being the main port from Spain across the Gibraltar Straits to Tangier in Northern Africa. The loading was pretty smooth and straight forward and soon we were heading out to sea past Gibraltar and heading for North Africa in the distance. Sadly our arrival was not going to prove as speedy as our departure. The Morocco officials really have not got a clue. Peter pre warned us to keep our cool, don't raise our voices and just smile. It could take a couple of hours. Little men in ill fitting suits were running about with pieces of paper to make officialdom an art. We had to have an entry form for our vehicles, one each for ourselves plus another three pieces of paper that I never did understand. While we were waiting for these different pieces of paper to duly pass hands in both directions several times, a second ship arrived from Italy. Now sadly the Italians are not as patient and understanding as us British. Very soon they were sounding off their horns making their feelings known with hand and arm gestures while they were shouting at anyone in a uniform. The whole situation reduced itself to a circus. We just watched on in total bemusement. The more they shouted the slower the officials went. Eventually they decided they would get rid of us lot first at least to minimise the chaos that was now reigning. We were therefore duly waved through to drive to the far end of the quay. Here the money changers were, waiting to take our European money and transfer it into Moroccan. You are not allowed to bring their currency either into the country or take it out. Once everyone was through customs armed with currency we followed Peter out of the Port up onto the main motorway and away from Tangier. To say it was an eye opener experience is an understatement.

Peter directed us along the main highway for a few miles then over the VHF radio that we all had on board he advised us we would be turning off the main road and into the Atlas Mountains. Here we were reduced to tracks across rough terrain which slowly meandered up and into the hills and mountains beyond. We climbed for what seemed hours till we were high up looking down on a windswept natural treeless terrain. Our first comfort stop was to pull off the side of the track and brew up. Now I was proudly armed with my little one cup kettle and my foldout cooker with its single fire lighter which I lit and boiled my kettle. By the time I had got even close I noticed that everyone else had made and finished their drinks and stood around talking. Goodness what on earth did they have I didn't? I then noticed on the inside of most of their back doors was a shelf that dropped down revealing a camp cooker. On the cooker was what turned out to be a fold down kettle. What a brilliant piece of kit. That went on the list for when I got home. Another disaster then hit us. When we checked the fridge freezer it was in fact not working. As part of the preparations for the trip I had been recommended to what later turned out to be a rather infamous firm in Peterborough. Their "speciality" was preparing vehicles for overland adventure trips. I had taken my vehicle to them for numerous jobs to be carried out. I needed a full-size roof tent to be fitted on the existing roof rack. I also needed a roll out side awning to be fitted. In addition, there were other jobs such as fitting a double battery electric system to run both vehicle and leisure facilities and double jerry can fuel tanks to fitted. All these jobs cost me a couple of thousand pounds to be done. So when we checked the wiring on the new twelve volt fridge system I was far from impressed to find out it was defective. It had been wired up incorrectly. The infamous firm I had employed back in the UK had yet again excelled themselves with another cock up, this was not the first that I noticed. They had chopped my roof rack so badly that within a couple of years it had completely rusted. Other errors and omissions were yet to surface. I was told later that this firm were very good until they picked up a screwdriver or spanner. I was fast learning what that meant that they were pretty useless. Peter was amazing. From our remote high position in the Riff mountains Peter actually rang his mate in Peterborough from his satellite phone and explained the problem. His mate then dictated to Peter instructions on how to disconnect the wiring where to reconnect and get us going again. Peter carried out the instructions while on the phone and was able to fix the problem and the fridge came back into life. I was so impressed. However sadly the food we had bought the day before had thawed. This meant that we had to dump the lot for fear of eating contaminated meat. To say I was less than amused is an understatement.

Eventually we came down the steep narrow mountain tracks and back onto tarmac. Our next stop was a car park outside McDonalds in part of modern Fez. Now this seemed so unreal sat at a table with the Moroccans eating hamburgers, chips and drinking coca cola while dressed in their traditional clothes and head gear. My imagination would never have thought they would be into this modern American fast food. When we had finished our meals we left our vehicles in the car park of McDonalds climbed into several taxis and headed into the old town of Fez. Parking up outside one of the famous gateways leading into the walled city our guide, a friend of Peter, was there to meet us to lead up in and hopefully out of this ancient city. I should explain that Fez is a very ancient city that was once the spiritual and capital city. It is a closed city with high thick walls that surround it. Inside there is a labyrinth of narrow streets and passages most of them covered over. In places you could outstretch your arms and touch the walls on each side. We were warned that we must be aware of the donkeys being herded down these narrow streets as some were very bad tempered. I was not surprised with the amounts laden on their backs. Most wore muzzles so as not to bite passers- by. I was just amazed by the density of this amazing place. The smells, colours and diversity of goods being sold such as spices, textiles, leather goods, copper and aluminium pots and pans and meat stalls with severed camels heads hanging from a hook at the entrance. I understood very quickly why we needed a guide. To get lost in this maze of endless passages would have proved a nightmare. They all looked the same and being covered couldn't rely on finding the sun for direction. We ended up more or less in the middle of Fez and as we approached the doorway of a terraced property an old man handed us sprigs of mint. Strange custom but we didn't argue. As we entered the building it was clearly a leather shop with the ground floor covered in shoes and slippers. Each of the three floors offered a variety of different leather goods, jackets, bags cases etc. but on each floor so we noticed this pungent smell getting worse and worse. By the time we reached the fourth floor which opened up onto a covered terrace we knew why we had been given the sprigs of mint. Each of us held our sprigs very close to our noses. Walking over to the edge of the terrace we looked down on what seemed to be dozens of huge round stone vats. In each vat men dressed in T shirts, shorts and no shoes were jumping up and down on various leather hides. Each vat seemed to have its own colour, yellow, red, blue and each man treading down the leather hides had their bottom halves covered in this dye. The leathers were of course either cow hides or camel hides. There were several vats that seemed to contain a creamy coloured fluid. None of the men were standing in this. It turned out that this was level one of the process and the fluid was in fact watered pigeon dung which reeked of ammonia and burnt human skin should it come into contact. It was doing a fair job of my nostrils too. Apparently the men who worked here in this vast collection of vats did not reach old age with their lungs burnt out by the constant smell and intake of ammonia. I found the whole place fascinating given its history went back hundreds of years but at the same time was rather glad to get back into the fresh air.

Being guided out of Fez we were taken by taxi back to our vehicles and so we left this ancient medieval city to continue our journey. Our track took us once again into the hills covered in forest and on past Morocco's only ski resort. It looked ridiculous all set up with hotel, ski huts, slopes and ski lifts in what was at that time sun burnt terrain in the middle of this forest. Apparently, it had been commissioned by the king of Morocco and mostly for his personal use. We were not alone on the hills. The upper forest is inhabited with groups of wild baboon type monkeys. They lead a very solitary and secretive life and seldom allow themselves be observed by humans. We were very lucky to spot a family of adults and youngsters scurrying off into the trees as we first arrived.

Leaving the high forest hills we descended down onto a main highway and turned off at Zeida and in particular into what resembled a Spanish type villa or farm with whitewashed outer perimeter walls and Spanish style white washed buildings inside. There were some pretty impressive medieval ships cannons on duty in the yard. Apart from two couples the rest chose to hire one of the very simple but suitably decorated rooms for the night. A good night's sleep was enjoyed by all.

Next day we were back on the road, and it was not long before Peter directed us off the tarmac and back onto a dirt track. The track weaved its way towards the high Atlas mountains which proved extremely steep with bends and dips that would test our driving. On one of our comfort stops I noticed what looked like a goat track up the side of this steep mountain to the top and over. I asked Peter what it was and he quietly replied that this was our route up and over to tackle shortly. After I gulped and took a deep breath we set off and climbed. The time had arrived when my novice experience of a green field, stony lane, off road driver was about to change. Now I was about to learn to become a more experienced off road driver. I would now have to learn by trial and error about low ratio gearing. I would have to put into fruition working the turbo to keep up my revs for steep climbs and descents. The track we were now on snaked up steep inclines, disappeared round sharp bends, dropped down steep declines and all the time hugging the sides of the mountains on loose stony tracks. Our route would take us up and around one mountain, down and round another and pass over numerous ranges. On one side of the track there were sharp volcanic rocks that would tear your tyres should you get too close, the other side, whilst not a sheer drop, would have given a very long vehicle roll and leave a mess of the vehicle once it stopped. Our attention was definitely focused. We learnt to not go too close to the vehicle in front in case it stalled as reversing was not an ideal option and loosing the turbo boost to get forward again would prove very difficult. At one point it was so narrow and steep I had to lift myself up out of my seat and whilst still steering looked over the front of the bonnet just to make sure I was in the middle of the track. One of our group did get a little too close to the cliff side of the track caught his tyre and when we finally stopped and inspected his damage you could fit part of the front of your finger In the gouge. The tyres we were all running on though were designed to be tough and thick enough to withstand this torture. Finally we started to descend off the mountains towards the plains. However having climbed and dropped four of the five peaks I noticed that Peter looked a bit worried and when I asked what was wrong he said he was a bit worried out the wind. It turns out that ahead of us and the final ascent was a huge natural rock bowl hundreds of yards wide and as steep carved into the mountain. A previous group lead by Peter were unable to complete this last peak as it had become thick with snow carried by the wind. This particular trip though there was no snow, in fact it was quite warm. Peter simply said that wind also carried sand and this was a natural bowl to collect any heavy sand. When we arrived at the bowl his fears were confirmed. The bowl was covered in a thick layer of deep sand that was difficult to walk on let alone drive on. The alternative now was a side drive which would have taken us an extra eighty miles or four hours plus. This had already been a long day. We could see tyre tracks where previous vehicles had attempted to drive and reached about two hundred yards and had to slowly reverse as they would get stuck trying to go further. Peter hesitated then in the end said we should all stay put and he would see how bad it was. Now he was in a six litre very powerful Toyota with very little on board. He revved up, dropped his gear box into low ratio and stormed off driving on the left-hand side of the bowl with his vehicle at a precarious angle. He screamed his vehicle forward a third of the way up he turned into the bowl climbing the other side heading upward then two thirds turned again and across and up and onto the crest of the hill. We all had our hearts in our mouths. Then came the crackle on the radio. "Next!" When Peter had given us basic advice and instructions over the radio it was time for us to try the ascent. Intermediate turned into advanced driving requirements and I was next. My adrenalin was now well and truly pumping. Into low ratio 2nd gear working the turbo and screaming forward changing quickly into 3rd gear I kept more or less in Peter's route but outside his tracks. First third successful, second third successful, turned, screamed across the side of the bowl, turned and launched myself up and onto the top. My hands were shaking with the adrenalin. We cheered each of our members up and onto the rim. This simply left Karak, Peters number two, at the base of the bowl. He always stayed back in case a member of the group had a breakdown or problems. Peter just muttered to me "watch this". Now Karak was driving one of the new land rover defenders that had all the buttons and whistles. We heard him start up and launch himself forward. Instead of weaving from side to side he literally made a straight line up and over. The electronics of this amazing vehicle took over and showed what this machine was capable of. All he had to do was keep his foot well on the accelerator and his hands steering in a straight line. The vehicle literally did the rest. We came off the mountain and headed to our next night stop. Unfortunately the weather below was awful with heavy rains etc., the track we took run alongside a very fast flowing river that was flooding due to the water coming off the hills. Part of the banks of the track we were on had water pouring down across our paths and into the river. Indeed, parts of the bank had started to collapse. The convoy edged its way forward for another fifteen miles until we came across an open back lorry coming the other way who flagged Peter down. After a short discussion Peter announced we had to all turn round and head back. The track ahead had been completely washed away and it was not safe even for the lorry to try to cross. So, we still had to carry out a diversion to our final nights destination where we arrived after dark.

Our next night was spent next to a lodge with wooded grounds at Lake Tislit. We were all grateful for the hot meal that the proprietor cooked for us. Peter always tries whenever he can to stop here at some point as the proprietors wife, Malika, helped run an orphanage for the local children and was always grateful for pens, pencils, paper and any educational tools that Peter could carry. What a lovely lady she was. We had been warned back in Spain that we would come across children from time-to-time begging. We were asked not to give anything to them. The problem is that in many cases the parents send them down to the tracks to wait for the convoys to see what they can beg from them. These items are handed to the parents who then try to sell them. This of course means that the children are kept away from school. As painful as it was to drive past these little smiling faces with their hands out waiting for items to be thrown to them we had to drive past.

Another day and another part of the adventure. This time we passed over the next set of mountains and ended up at Todra Gorge sometimes known as Dades Gorge. It had a fast-running river running through the gorge with a dirt road twisting itself alongside it. Peter confirmed that in a previous tour the road had been washed away and the only way forward was to navigate into the river and drive along its bed till the road re appeared in front. At the Gorge there was a really lovely camp site which was painted in what would become a familiar orange pink wash. Again pitching up we went into the lovely restaurant where a Moroccan meal was provided and was delicious. Peter suggested if we had time, to walk down the road and into the gorge road. We took a stroll down the road but not really knowing where we were didn't venture far and turned round back to the camp site. What a shame as the next day we drove down where we had walked and at the end of the gorge the road suddenly turned into a steep set of hair pin bends. These twists and turns worked their way down like an alpine pass. It turned out we were driving down one of Morocco's icons that appears in many brochures and literature on Morocco.

Leaving the next morning we had one more mountain range with its narrow tracks to pass over being the Jebel Saghro range. These were magnificent mountains that looked like huge chocolate cakes that had risen out of the ground and spilled over. You could see all the layers of rocks in different colours of brown and with cascades that had reset themselves millions of years ago. The colour from the sunlight was just magnificent. As we left the mountains, we then descended into Draa Valley. We had now left the arable land behind us. No clouds or rain could penetrate over the various mountain ranges we had passed over. The scenery therefore turned to parched barren desert like conditions, it was very dusty and spread for miles before us and to the left and right of us. The one bonus for the sudden increase in heat and dust was that we were now on tarmac with windows opened, remember this vehicle did not have air conditioning. We then drove into Zagora the most southerly town before stepping into the mighty Sahara itself. Any travellers heading further south would use Zagora for a final rest, restock water and supplies, make sure vehicles were in tip top condition as this was the last opportunity to make sure you had got it right. It was here that Michael Palin stopped over when making his programme "Sahara". In the middle of town is a replica of his famous sign that says "Timbuktu 52 days" with Michael standing in front pointing at it. The original sign has been taken down and now sits in the museum but a replica has been erected and we all took it in turn to have our photos taken at this now iconic sign.

In Zagora we had a choice of a very nice hotel or a very dusty camp site behind an even dustier outer security wall. There was no competition. We would not regret it. We would spend three nights here to rest and recharge after our rather pressured trip so far. First of all, I asked the hotel if they offered a laundry service and when confirmed a black sack of smalls and dusty shirts and trousers etc., were handed over. The hotel had the most amazing gardens. As you stepped out from the hotel at the back and into its gardens you were met by large palm trees beautiful blooming shrubs and plants, narrow paths working their way round the foliage. Just inside the garden were large lounger areas with deep coloured sofas and cushions, beautiful coloured mats and rugs and typical Moroccan arches and beams. On the other side of the garden was this long bar with stools serving cool drinks to grateful guests. Beyond this garden the area opened up into a beautiful large swimming pool again surrounded by palm trees but giving adequate view of the sky which would prove to be magnificent after dark. The next day we were invited up one at a time into the town to a garage mechanic known to Peter. The garage took each vehicle in, put it onto a ramp and literally shook it and rocked it. They went over each vehicle with a fine tooth comb to make sure the vehicle was fit and capable for what was coming up with four days in the rough barren Sahara Desert. One vehicle turned out to have a broken spring so that was repaired, and we were all ready for the next part of our adventure. Now, I had taken my guitar with me which I played whenever I could. I tried not to disturb folks so at the hotel in Zagora I planted myself next to the pool later in the evening and played away. The feeling of sheer peace and tranquillity sitting under this myriad of stars above not spoilt by light pollution cannot be described well enough. The only audience was a couple of waiters that came out in curiosity. One of the songs I played at that time was Rod Stewart's "Sailing". Next morning at breakfast the waiter came out into the dining room spotted me and at the top his voice started singing" I am sailing I am sailing" laughing and pointing at me. I was so embarrassed. One regret I have always held since my stay at Zagora was after we wandered across the road to a little co-operative shop with a young man sat on the boardwalk strumming his guitar. He noticed me watching him and in very poor English this young fifteen year old asked if I played. When I said I did he invited me to get my guitar so we could play together. I never went back. I thought afterwards what a shame that two people from two different nationalities and ages did not share the one language that is understood, music, for a mutually appreciated time free from responsibility. This opportunity would not come my way again.

After our three days rest and relaxation we packed our boxes once more back into the land rover and headed off. We used our break to take the boxes out and with the dustpan and brush removed a pile of sand and dust that had come in through the open windows. This was going to prove a nightly task from now on till we got back to the coast. We were soon leaving civilisation behind us. The tarmac eventually also disappeared, and we were back onto dusty, narrow, stony tracks. We crossed this long valley and up and over the mountain range on the far side. Once through we were now well and truly into the desert. We drove south to as close to the Algerian border as we dare go. The Algerians have fallen out with the Moroccans in fact they seem to have fallen out with everyone. As such the borders are closed and they patrol very jealously any intrusions into their territory. At the furthest point we would want to travel we came across a military check point with a large coloured pole across the track and manned by military personnel complete with guns etc., after checking we were not smugglers or terrorists we were waved through. We were advised that the border was only less than 15 miles away and try to avoid going near it. They were even more persuasive when they explained to Peter that a Saudi Prince had travelled down to the region to hunt with his hawks. Apparently while out hunting he mistakenly entered Algerian desert space and an Algerian sniper shot him dead. The relationship between Algeria and Saudi Arabia sunk to a very deep low after this incident.

We now turned east running parallel to the Algerian Border. Part of the route passed over what we know as the Paris Dakar race. Now I should explain that whilst the desert looked flat and smooth it was for some miles going to be suffering from corrugation. In the snow slopes where the skiers passed from side to side they would form large moguls that needed experience to ski. Here in the desert with the cars from the race hitting this area at high speeds the wheels would bounce up and down and again would form inundations in the sand with each vehicle adding his own contribution. This meant that you had what looked like corrugated iron sheets laid sideways. Driving over it the vehicles were shook and bounced around so much so that my confidence disappeared and my speed got down to eleven miles an hour. Everyone else was now miles in front of us. Peter drew alongside and tried to persuade me to go faster saying that it would be okay and to trust my vehicle. All I kept thinking about was shaking this vehicle to bits and being stuck five thousand miles from home. Eventually Peter convinced me that if I could just accelerate to say twenty-five miles an hour I would realise what this vehicle was built for. I gritted my teeth, tightened my grip on the steering wheel and pumped adrenalin as well as the accelerator pedal and launched forward. The vehicle shook and rattled crazily till I got to twenty-five miles an hour. It was like turning a switch off. Suddenly everything went still. The vehicle was accelerating forward and I knew the shocks and springs were going crazy but they were taking all the punishment. I couldn't believe the transformation. So much so I was now driving at thirty-five miles an hour and quickly caught the group up. I apologised to Peter when we had stopped but he just explained it was something most people go through and just have to trust him and their vehicles and enjoy what they can do.

Further on we were to hit another anomaly that took us by surprise. This area must have been some forty to fifty miles minimum of very, very soft sand. The Moroccans have a special word for this as it resembles talcum powder when disturbed. Driving through it was just a nightmare. First of all it was low ratio gears and working the turbo to rev the engine, and to get the wheels to cut through this dust without sinking took full concentration. The other problem each driver had was that we had to keep the vehicle in front in view which with this dense cloud of sand was difficult. We had to be careful not to lag behind because once out of view you were lost. Driving too fast meant you caught the vehicle in front up and had to slow down thus fearing stalling and sinking into the dust. As we were having our problems so was the vehicle in front of us and the vehicle behind us. The final problems was keeping your thumbs outside the steering wheel because if it suddenly hit a rut or some other obstacle it would kick out and you could break your thumbs. Also the heat meant that shutting the windows was no option but keeping them open the dust came inside the vehicle like smoke. We couldn't win. After what seemed to be ages we came to a standstill. The super land rover or 'golden land rover' as it looked that was kitted out for Ranulph Fiennes had got stuck in the sand. Now Peter throughout the trip was to show us various tips on how to successfully drive off road and how to get the best out of the vehicle. This was all part of the plan knowing someone would get stuck. He now got us all out of our vehicles and together digging and clearing laying sand ladders we persuaded the vehicle from its un elegant parking in the deep sand back onto the top. However, as it was now a hundred and thirty degrees and very dry, Peter wanted to avoid that happening again so gave us a seeing is believing exercise. We were all asked to reduce our tyre pressures to just one bar. Now this is so low the tyre is virtually trying to come off the rim. However what it did achieve was that the tyre rather than sitting with just a half inch touching what would normally be the tarmac, now spread itself out across the sand with the same principal as a ski on snow. Wow what a difference. We literally felt we were floating over the sand till we got out of this very difficult area.

As we passed through the desert, we came across what was once a village built by the French when they occupied Morocco. This village was a mining village extracting minerals from the surrounding hills. The village was now deserted as the French had been expelled from Morocco years before. However, there were a few local Moroccans that had now moved into the deserted houses. We parked up and had a look along the village, saw the ruin of what was the cinema with some of the seats still in situ and where the projectors must have stood. The village was fed through the middle with a rather fast running river. Peter was beginning to look a little concerned at the speed of the water. When I asked him if there was a problem he explained that in previous years the bridge up in front had been washed away. He just hoped that we would find a bridge now when we got to it. We drove the short distance through the deserted village to where we were hoping to cross this rather angry river. Yes, there was a framework still standing forming a bridge which was the good news. The bad news was that on top of the framework, the Moroccans had laid a collection of poles, planks, logs and tree branches all loose and each moving when walked on. We were about to try to drive two ton fully loaded vehicles over them. Peter chose to go first and sheepishly steered his vehicle onto the first planks. Slowly he moved over these moving bouncing logs and with a huge sigh reached the other side. Walking back, he gave each of us the advice and instructions to get over. Each of us slowly took it in turns to move forward and cross over. You don't really see the true problem and scale of difficulty till you are behind the vehicle that has now moved off to cross. You actually see the planks lifting and moving under each wheel as progress is made. Then of course comes the moment when it is my turn with all eyes on me. The baptism of fire began. I moved forward slowly and indeed felt each log as it moved but not daring to stop and not daring to go too fast. After what seemed to be an eternity we finally reached the other side to loud applause and clapping. Again, another story to tell the grandchildren as the saying goes.

Next, we arrived at some very high and very impressive sand dunes. Here Peter had us all in a large semi circle and demonstrated first of all how sand dunes formed. He explained that there would always be a slow incline where the wind had driven the sand. However, at its peak there would be a sheer steep drop the other side. He demonstrated that the correct way to drive the dunes was to approach the slow incline as before in low ratio heavy acceleration to keep the turbo working and the revs up. When you approached the top of the dune to slam the foot on the clutch but leave the brake alone and not use the brake at all. This way the tyres would stop in the soft sand above the drop on the other side. Here the idea was to survey the slope and the direction it was taking and then slowly drive over the top and keep the vehicle on the slope, rather than at the side, to avoid the vehicle falling over sideways remembering the sand was very soft. If the vehicle started to veer off to one side, we would need to steer into the side slip to correct the line and not as Peter had advised he had seen in the past stick your arm out of the window to catch the vehicle as it fell over sideways. This sounds absolutely straight forward and simple till we put into practice what we had been shown. Without exception we all hit the top of the slope and hit the brakes instead of the clutch which is a very strong instinct. We all sunk the front wheels into the sand. We each required the benefit of Peter's winch to drag us forward. In my instance I managed to do this three times before I finally left my instinct of hitting the brakes behind and relied on the clutch and I was astounded how well it worked. Unfortunately, our friend in the 'golden land rover' got into hot water with his wife because he got stuck. She was a Kiwi and had told us how much experience she had of adventure travelling and how we all did not have a clue. She stomped off in a huff sulking that her husband had now humiliated her and shown himself up. She stormed off into the desert and the desert heat. Where she thought she was going to end up we had no idea as we were now several days from the nearest civilisation in vehicles. Lord knows how long it would have taken her on foot. The husband drove out to talk to her and persuaded her to return. However, the next day they announced that this was not the tour for them, and they were leaving the group to return home. Peter directed them to the track they must stay on and when reaching tarmac what to head for to get them back to Tangier several days away. The place was then nicknamed by Peter as "Kiwi Corner" to remember this woman and her tantrum. We did hear that they had reached the coast after several days and had indeed caught a boat back to Europe. Nobody saw or heard from them again.

That night we pulled up in a spaced-out group in the sand dunes and set up camp. After cooking something to eat we then all sat round the group fire fuelled by a collection of logs that Peter had collected on route. I played my guitar and the whole experience was pure magical. We sat on the roof for quite before climbing into the roof tent just staring at the stars above us. Nobody can explain to someone who has not experienced it just how humbling it is to sit below a sky that is so full of stars that you cannot pinpoint a spot where a star was not twinkling. The only irritation was actually the moon that was rising behind us causing its own light pollution. It was an experience that would remain with me for the rest of my life.

The next day we were up, hand washed, cleaned our teeth had our breakfast and cups of tea ready for the off. Needless, to say water was precious so wasting it was not an option. We took with us a dry hair wash that came in an aerosol can. I thought it was a toy but was so desperate with all the sand and dust that had come through the window I thought I would have a go. It is brilliant. Spray it on, wait for it to dry and then brush it all out. When I had finished it felt like I had washed my hair under a shower I felt so exhilarated. There are other little tricks that help save water like taking your metal drinking mug put half a cup of water in it and by wetting the toothbrush clean your teeth using the contents of the cup to sluice out your mouth using that last mouthful to gargle with. However, there was one couple who had had an additional feature added to their vehicle. By running the engine and turning the heater button to hot it fed a supply of hot water from the additional on tank supply through pipe work through the engine giving a hot shower at the back of the vehicle. We were invited to use it but would need eleven litres of water. We stuck to our dry hair wash and standing over a bucket for a face wash.

We finally reached what first looked like a French fort stuck in the middle of the desert and sand dunes. It was a purpose-built hotel made out of literally breeze block covered with a rendering of sand mud and straw. This was at Erg Chebbi and had the most amazing views of the Dunes D'or out of the back of it. This area had been used many times for all sorts of films made where Lawrence of Arabia style dunes were needed. We would spend a couple of days here to wash out the sand, clean the inside of the vehicles and get ourselves ready for the final leg northwards and back to the coast. This place was just truly wonderful. The long cool passage that led from the parking at the front again was covered in Persian rugs, Moroccan lamps large sofas and cushions and led out into a large inner court with a bar tables and chairs and its own swimming pool. The passage led off down two rows of rooms with a central garden area. The doors for the rooms were off this central garden area and the back of the rooms led onto a small terrace with views straight up into the sand dunes. Now as we were going to sleep on proper beds in an actual room it was necessary for me to retrieve the pillows and sleeping bags from the roof tent. The Land Rover was now parked at the back so climbing up and opening the roof tent, it was quite easy to pull the pillows out. In the distance I could hear a rumbling which sounded like a steam train approaching. Looking up I could see this dark grey smoky cloud some fifty feet in the air approaching us at rapid speed. It was a sand storm. I had never experienced one before. Realising what was about to hit us I had just enough time to roughly close the roof tent, jump off the land rover and armed with pillows head for the apartment door. By the time I had reached the door this thick swirling cloud was upon us. Now we were probably about four or five apartments from the end of the block. Each apartment had a small patio surrounded by a three feet high wall. A couple of apartments down was a small bird balancing itself and preparing for the sand storm to arrive. By the time it had caught up with us I couldn't even see the wall that the bird was sitting on let alone what had happened to the bird. I remember this hot swirling mass of sand hitting the side of my face. I can understand now why anyone caught in the desert gets as low as they can and cover their faces and heads. This stuff really stung and could have proved quite painful. It was a case of get indoors close the door and wait for it to pass. It wasn't long before everything went still and quiet again. Looking outside apart from a lot of dust and sand on everything there was total calm and peace.

We ate typical Moroccan food in the spacious dining room again with rugs, large sofas and art work. Breakfast was a selection of fruits, nuts. unleavened bread, honey and meats and they really spoilt us. Evening meal was tagines of lamb, couscous and again fruits. We really had such a wonderful stay. Our fellow traveller decided it would be a good idea at this stage to change his tyre that had lasted all this time from the arduous mountain passes when he had clipped one of the volcanic rocks and sliced into it. On the second day of our stay, we were taken to a co- operative some miles away that contained a series of workshops making rugs, lanterns, ceramics even the long tunic gowns the men wear. A couple of our group bought some rugs to bring home with them . However, space was a premium and we decided there was nothing that we really needed apart from the spices we had bought earlier when we were in Zagora.

Sadly, our time at Erg Chebbi came to an end and after saying our goodbyes we all climbed aboard our vehicles, followed Peter out onto the barren desert surroundings and bounced our way for some miles till we hit tarmac. This took us further east to the next town where we could turn left and start heading north and back to the Coast. Peter had one more surprise for us before we concentrated on our final drive back to the docks. Half way between the town where we had turned left and the mountains looming up in front of us appeared what seemed to be a series of mole hills set out slightly away from the highway. We pulled in and Peter went over to the hut that had been erected and the young man sitting there waiting to greet visitors. He explained to us the history of the place over a glass of what we call Bedouin tea i.e. a glass of tea heavily sugared but no milk. It turned out that these mole hills were in fact exposed wells. Below them ran a deep long gully from the mountains to the lush fields of the town back some thirteen miles away. During the rainy season these gullies would fill up with fresh water. Each family in the area were allotted a time over a twenty-four hour period where they would have to come down with vessels to collect water during their allotted time. This ritual had been practiced for over a thousand years and was quite extraordinary. Our young guide asked several of us to follow him to what looked like an entrance to a toilet with an iron door. This led to steps that took us down about fifteen feet to what was then the dry gully. Walking along this gully we could look up several of the wells. Apparently, they run tours from this spot back to the town but as this was thirteen miles and you could never tell what or when the water would arrive and with no other form of escape I put that idea completely out of my mind..

Back on the road we were now heading north back to the mountainous areas and finally back to Tangier and our boat back to Europe. Now one trick we had some difficulty getting used to but by this time had mastered was that of overtaking. We didn't have the problem in the desert but now we were on a main highway with bends hills and lots of slow-moving lorries and commercial vehicles. The convoy was up to half a mile long so it was not going to be possible to get every vehicle past any obstacle at one go. Peter would head off when it was safe to overtake. He would then continuously keep us posted as to when the road was clear. This meant the next vehicle could safely over take without fear of another vehicle coming the other way. The trust had to be built up when approaching blind hills and hair pin bends. If a vehicle did approach Peter would give warning, the next vehicle to overtake would wait for the oncoming vehicle to pass before having the confidence in Peter to then overtake. You can imagine the reactions of some of the other drivers we were overtaking. They honked their horns flashed their lights waved fists and I am sure we were called all the colourful words that would be internationally recognised. However we all got through without incident. I did get one German off road vehicle who was fed up being overtaken and was going to make it difficult for me to pass. Each time I accelerated to overtake he was there before me and was going to be as awkward as he could. However, there came the point in the road where he was not going to test his nerve as it was a steep hill on a bend. Peter gave me the nod that all was clear so dropping down a gear I started to overtake the German. He must have thought I had taken my brains out. He was tooting waving his fist demonstrating that I had no brain and flashing his lights. Little did he know the secret we were all sharing.

Finally, we arrived back at Tangier port. Getting out of the country was a lot easier than arriving. Each vehicle was checked for their paperwork passports etc., and each vehicle was taken onto a ramp and into a machine where it was x-rayed. We were checked for weapons drugs and any contraband. Needless to say, we were all clean and cleared. We then drove onto the dock side to await the boat. We had a couple of hours to kill before the ship arrived, and then the incoming passengers disembarked, and we were ushered on. Soon the ship pulled away from the port and sadly the shoreline of Morocco and north Africa disappeared into the distance. Before we knew it we were back past Gibraltar and into Europe. Leaving the port in Spain again proved no problem. We were now all free to make our own way northwards back to Santander where we heard the ships were now back to taking passengers back to the UK. We chose to take a leisurely drive up the coastal motorway. We drove till it had got dark and looked out for what we were hoping to be a suitable hotel for the night. Suddenly we saw what looked like a very splendid tall very posh hotel. Turning off the motorway taking the side road back we arrived at this very posh, very clean and polished building. The pristine forecourt with its expensive cars and very clean marble blocks next to international flag poles looked like a good place to park with my very dusty, dirty land rover. I wandered into the squeaky-clean reception where a young lady that looked like one of the Virgin airline stewardesses greeted me. I, of course looked like Indiana Jones. I was still dressed in my desert gear that was of course very dusty along with my desert boots. She didn't turn a hair. She confirmed she had rooms available and invited me to bring in my luggage. I explained we were carrying plastic boxes. One of the hotel staff followed me out to the land rover, loaded the two plastic boxes we needed for the night and led us back through the foyer to the lifts. We arrived at the floor we were staying on and entered what looked like an apartment as opposed to a hotel room. We had a balcony round two sides of the building, a bathroom that you could hold a party in and a bed that I could hibernate in for the remainder of the year. This was going to cost a fortune but who cared. We had been roughing it for a fortnight now and this was a bit of luxury we were entitled to. The "game" in Morocco was whenever we booked into accommodation we would take bets what would not work. If the hot water run the cold didn't, the toilet flushed but not terribly effectively, doors sort of opened and the electricity was very iffy. Here we were surrounded by sheer luxury. We showered, changed, and headed for the restaurant for something to eat before getting our heads down. The food I seem to remember was just exquisite. The next morning, we woke up and discovered that we backed onto the lushest golf course with a purpose-built village for the use of the golf course. The hotel was patronised by golfers popping over for the weekend as the airport was only a short drive away. After breakfast I waited with anticipation for the bill and was really surprised. This little piece of heaven cost us sixty pounds for the night inclusive of breakfast.

We were now back on the splendid motorway that the Spanish had now finally finished that runs from the south all along the coast up to the Spanish and French border. We passed over, through and past towns and villages made up of countless white washed houses and villas. We had glorious sunshine, clear skies and blue seas to our right. If we had chosen we could have continued on the motorway right up through France and back to the UK. We drove as far as Valencia and at this point had to leave the coast and head inland towards the north coast. We pulled off the motorway and onto a small, deserted side road. We had purposely filled our two five gallon jerry cans in Morocco as fuel had been so cheap. We filled the vehicle up again re-located the jerry cans and set off again. Our fuel stop would give us enough fuel to get us back to the coast where one more fill would get us home and give us a week's running around. Our last night's stay would be at Zaragoza, an ancient city in the middle of Spain. It was very busy and very commercialised and trying to find a hotel was going to prove testing. We spotted one on this block which we had to go round a couple of times to be able to find a parking space. Now if I thought the last place was posh this took the biscuit. There was a doorman with full long tailed suit and top hat on the door. Inside it was all pink marble flooring with a grand piano sitting in a sunken floor next to the dining area. The reception was this beautiful black marble with immaculate booking in staff. They confirmed they had a room and suggested I park the land rover in their underground car park. I explained that with the roof rack and roof tent I would not fit in and therefore was asked to park in the back road leading down into the car park. I was assured that they had cameras positioned that would give utmost security. I was asked if I needed help with the suitcases. I advised again we had plastic boxes. By the time we arrived at the overnight parking a very smart young man in white shirt and dickie bow was there to meet us with his trolley. We loaded the two boxes on top and once again as in the previous hotel the young man did not bat an eyelid. He directed us back to the front of the hotel. We retraced our steps through the entrance up the lift to our room. When we entered the room the boxes were there stacked and ready for us. Again, we enjoyed a wonderful shower and clean up. We got dressed and went down for what was the most amazing meal. I had this delicious steak with trimmings. Next morning we were surprised to find our bill for bed and breakfast was going to be seventy pounds. We had paid for our meal separately. Our boxes were taken back to the land rover where the young man waited for me to unlock and helped me load and we were on our way. A gentle drive now back through the centre of Spain up and finally back to the Port. We dutifully reported to the passport office and was ushered onto the parking bay. Here we caught up with the other members of the trip and eventually got on board where we found our cabins, unloaded our belongings for the night and settled down for our thirty-six hour trip back to the UK. Once back in the UK we all said our goodbyes and headed off for the last journey home.

We had been away nearly three weeks with all the travelling and it was a holiday that I could never have anticipated. There were times when we would be tested, times when things went wrong but all in all my knowledge of what this vehicle could do and was capable of was just so amazing. I had taken stock of lots of ideas that other fellow travellers had adopted on their vehicles and I was determined that I would incorporate and upgrade my vehicle. I was definitely hooked to do another trip not necessarily to Morocco but off-roading. I found the experience was exciting, exhilarating, worrying but an adrenalin rush from start to finish and was beyond anything I had experienced before. Thank you especially to Peter and Jo for leading us on a truly professional tour that would certainly change my life.

CHAPTER 28
WINTER TRIP TO ITALY

Having returned to the UK from Morocco, I now set to in adopting and adapting many of the ideas and designs I had noted on that trip. I first of all took the land rover to the engineer in Peterborough that Peter had contacted on the mountain to sort out the wiring mess on the fridge freezer. They did a wonderful job fitting a double battery system and other updates and upgrades. I then found a local fabricator who I discussed various modifications. I designed a large box to replace the spare wheel on the back door. The spare wheel was relocated onto the roof rack while the rear box was used for storing the folding toilet chemicals. Inside, the rear seats were removed and a plate fitted along with a drawer. Side lockers were fabricated and fitted along with the inside rear door panel being replaced with a plate and a fold down cabinet containing a cooker. It took me three and a half years all in all getting the land rover updated and prepared more comprehensively for Adventure Travel. The vehicle is to this day ready and waiting at moment's notice to set off for further adventures. All that is needed are clothes to wear and any food necessary for the trip. As a test run we decided to drive rather than fly to a winter resort for a week's skiing. We decided to drive down through France into Switzerland and on to the Northern Italian Alps and in particular the Monta Rosa mountains.

Because it was winter and the concern about heavy snow fall etc.,

I chose to rather than take the Jura Mountain route from Pontarlier and down to Vallorbe and Lausanne another well known, well used route during previous summer excursions. I thought it would be quicker and safer to carry on down the motorway to Lyon then over the mountains to Geneva. It turned out to be a bad decision. We had arrived in the southern section of France as it had got dark. The trip via Lyon and Geneva took us at least another hundred miles out of our way. By the time we had cleared Lake Geneva or Lac Lemon as it is known in Switzerland it was now late evening and we had another ninety miles to drive before we would reach the train station at Brig. Having had a long drive all the way down from Calais we were pretty tired by the time Brig was reached at eleven pm. The ground was covered with thick snow and minus degree conditions made it very cold. The trains run one an hour and we had just missed one. This meant a wait till midnight before we could board the train and get through the mountain to Northern Italy. It was a long cold hour but eventually we drove onto an open bogey carriage along with other vehicles waiting to cross and the train pulled out into the twenty-six mile tunnel through the Simplon pass. We had already phoned the hotel and apologised for being hopelessly late but was assured they would be open when we arrived. From Domodossola the small town on the Italian side of the Simplon tunnel we had a drive off the mountain. We then took a right-hand turn and drove back up another pass for yet another twenty-six miles. We finally reached Macugnaga the ski resort that was going to be home for a week. By this time, it was past one-thirty am in the morning. The hotel owner was indeed still awake and waiting for us although the booking in ceremony was rather swift as we all now just wanted to get into our beds.

The next day we brought the remainder of our luggage into the hotel and up to our room. Because we were travelling by road and in particular the land rover, we were able to take rather more luggage than normal which included skis, ski equipment and even my guitar. The hotel itself was a small two-star hotel run by a family. The two sons were the chefs and prepared all the meals, the father ran the bar and the mother organised the reception and the booking in and out. The wives helped out with the domestic side of the dining room and the bedrooms. All in all it all worked really well and a wonderful friendly atmosphere was enjoyed. Now one of the advantages of the location of the hotel was that it was right at the top of the village and coming out of the front lobby it was less than a hundred feet from the start of the beginners slope and the chair lift to the rest of the resort's skiing facility. Macugnaga was tucked into this huge crescent shaped valley topped by very tall mountains. Unfortunately, the crescent was so high it meant that most of the day during winter it was in the shadows as the sun could not rise above the height of the mountains. This drastically affected the temperatures which most days never climbed higher than minus twenty and always felt very cold.

The village formed part of a very old village with mountain chalets that themselves dated back to the seventeenth century. many of the ancient houses were still lived in and they were in amazing condition. The roofs were covered in huge boulders from the mountains that protected the roof and held the snow back when fallen. The front steps were thick planks standing on rock which apparently prevented vermin from getting into the properties for warmth during the long cold winter months. In the village there were antique shops, taverns, hotels and cafes, and it was quite a lively little resort. We discovered quite quickly that this was a little gem jealously guarded by the Italians and not publicised and I didn't blame them. It was only a couple of hours drive from Milan which opened the resort up to weekend skiers and therefore not needing advertising and tourists from further afield. One of the hotels at the bottom of the village was run again by a family with the son being one of the ski instructors while his wife an English girl helps run the hotel and in particular the reception helping translate for the English visitors and the mother who works with her could not speak a word of English. What was impressive was that this English lady had the previous season came back from a visit to England by overland driving a second-hand London taxi that they had bought for the use of guests from the hotel up and back to the slopes each morning. It did rather stand out from the normal I have to admit.

Each morning we would make sure we were adequately dressed in thermal underwear plus top garments and topped with our ski suits. It was so cold all these layers of clothes really paid off to try to stay warm. We did the skier walk which is not very elegant. It comprises heel then toe on one foot then heel toe on the other foot and waddle forward carrying our skis to the beginner's slope. Here we spent the first half hour warming up riding up the rolling carpet to the top of the slope and back again. We then took the two-man chair lift to the top of the next slope and took several runs back down what was basically a simple blue run. We weren't able to maintain a too longer time on the slopes as it really was very cold. The rest of the afternoon was spent in the hotel lounge chatting to other guests and the owners sons who were very interesting. It turns out that the father who was well into his retirement is a mountain guide. In fact in the summer he still takes guests over the Monte Rosa mountains on the two day walk over to Switzerland staying in a lodge high up on the mountain. He certainly looked a very fit man.

I decided that I should take a trip up the mountain myself and see what other slopes were available. My skiing had reached a reasonable level by this time. I took the rickety two-man chair lift up and then onto the second chair lift directly in front. Now this took a much steeper ride up and over the immediate mountain in front of me. When I finally reached the top I guessed this was going to be a particularly long run back. Skiing away from the chair lift I headed to the start of the piste. There were some elderly ladies in their fur coats who were not skiing but were merely visiting on foot. Two of them were linking arms with one peering over the edge where I was hoping to ski. Gulp this was a steep drop down and round following a line of trees. Over the years I have mastered the side slip and clearly this came in very handy here, as it was too steep and slippery to confidently make ski turns. Having reached the bottom of this section I was able then to regain my dignity and ski along the piste for quite a while tackling some not so steep slopes till finally, I came out into a clearing that looked down to the village below. Now this was the final drop and the slope was as steep if not steeper than the introduction section. Of course, it was a lot longer and more exposed. I must have looked a complete beginner using side slip, the occasional ski turn, falling over, picking myself up and eventually reaching the bottom with great relief. I then skied the simple blue run back to the hotel and called it a day and went back to the hotel. The sons were interested in where their guests had gone that day and I explained I had gone up to the top of the second chair lift and took a very slow rather sloppy descent on what I considered to actually be a difficult slope. They both looked at me in surprise and both said "you have skied the wall". Now I know this had been a difficult steep run.

Because of the height of the land rover sadly it couldn't be parked in the underground car park located opposite to the hotel. However, there was enough room to park outside the hotel itself and being a sturdy four wheel vehicle was fine sitting in the snow. The next morning to my epic downhill adventure the father asked if I could help him. Going outside I saw that several men had gathered at the bottom of the slope to the car park where a mini was now parked half on the slope down half on the footpath but part of it against the concrete bollard. Whatever they tried to do drive forward drive backwards push pull they were not going to move the car due to the fresh snow that had fallen. Climbing aboard the land rover and positioning it to the top of the car park slope I connected several tow ropes down to tie to the car. Very slowly and in four-wheel drive I slowly drove forward dragging the mini up the slope behind me. The problem is that the land rover is such a powerful vehicle that you just don't notice having another payload tied to the back. I had to take it very, very slowly and keep my eyes peeled and my ears wide open to make sure we didn't hit any more problems or snags. The vehicle did finally pop out and over the top and the granddaughter of the owner was able to drive off for her appointment.

As we were there for New Years eve the Italians always put on a splendid New Year's Eve festivities. It was something like a six or eight course meal. All washed down with plenty of Italian red and white wine. What a splendid evening and everyone was in such great spirits. It was at least three hours so by the time we finished we were not far off ringing in the New Year. We noticed folks were walking up from the village all in their warm ski suits and clothes and heading for the beginning of the ski slopes. We worked our way up onto our balcony that overlooked the end of the slope and at midnight noticed a line of red flares working their way down the mountain. This turned out to be all the ski instructors who at midnight lit their torches and, in a line, all skied down back to the bottom. As they were skiing, they were singing and shouting, and it was an amazing sight to watch. Even at the bottom they skied as far as they could before the snow ran out. What a lovely New Years Eve it turned out to be.

The final day was spent low key with a walk into the lower village a nice lunch at the local restaurant a few souvenirs purchased. and then back to the hotel to get packed and the land rover loaded for our final night. The next morning after saying our goodbyes. we left the village and took a slow drive back down off the mountain to the main road, up and to the train station. This time we were in luck and only had twenty minutes before the train arrived and we were heading back into the tunnel and back to Switzerland. The snow on the other side of the mountain seemed a lot thicker than on the side we had just left. We drove the ninety miles back to Montreux on Lake Geneva and took the motorway round the lake to Morges, a pretty village on the lake that we would stay for the night. The hotel we chose was right on the shore of the Lac Lamone and was a lovely hotel. We booked in took our overnight luggage to our room and then wandered off for a walk round the village. The walkway along the edge of the lake to the small harbour where little boats were bobbing up and down covered and protected waiting for the season to change when the owners can get out onto the water. One boat which we spotted had "Buster" written on the back. Now I know Phil Collins lives somewhere along the shoreline of the lake, and we really wanted to believe that this was his. What a lovely location to drive out onto the lake on a warm summer Sunday morning drop anchor and just spend time reading the papers and enjoying the tranquillity of the location which I have read is what he does. The village commercial street itself reminds me of one of those paintings "Rainy day in Paris" the cobbles and the buildings were all shiny from the rain. The shops were all pretty lit with their Christmas and new year lights and the whole area seemed so cosy and inviting.

Sadly, we could only stay for one night. The next morning, we were loaded back in the land rover and heading north for the Swiss French border. We travelled through countryside I am more than familiar with having spent many happy times in this area. Soon we were through Vallorbe the Swiss border town climbing up towards the border checks of both Swiss and French border guards. We were then through and heading up and over the thirteen miles pass through the Jura Mountains. It was very pretty all covered in snow and my fears of driving on treacherous roads were unfounded. I did find a complete ski resort at the top complete with ski lifts, button lifts, etc. which I didn't know was there. We came over the pass down to Pontarlier and then drove the motorway for the six-hour drive north to Calais. Arriving at Calais we boarded the shuttle train and came home back to England. This had been a short adventure but being in the land rover and driving across France and Switzerland in the snow made it all the more exciting.

CHAPTER 29

SECOND ADVENTURE TRIP TO MOROCCO

I had spent three years upgrading and re-designing the Land Rover to conform with what I thought were necessary improvements to cope with another trip to Morocco. I had sought out a fabricator who helped me with drawer units and various plates inside the vehicle. I had heavy duty springs and shocks fitted, a heavy-duty winch at the front with tree wires and a new roof rack to hold the roof tent. Inside, I had customised the cab with VHF radio, CD, radio and other necessaries such as compass and level indicator. I was more than ready now to go back and tackle the demands of this rather dramatic terrain.

It was after such a long time of preparation and anticipation as well as excitement that I was to receive my biggest blow. In the November it was confirmed I had bowel cancer. This put a whole new complexion on my life. Unknown to me at the time I was to undergo an 11-hour operation and spend months in rehabilitation. It would mean I would have to be fitted with a temporary colostomy bag which would eventually require reversing. Now nobody ever wants to hear the "C" word in their lives. However, the hospital was truly magnificent. The care and support I received was second to none. Not only did the hospital deal with the medical issues themselves but they also had an experienced team to deal with the emotional issues that go hand in hand with this dreadful disease. Depression and feelings of end of life are inevitable with the C word. What I experienced therefore was the coupling of not only physical medical help but also the psychology needed to make the sufferer believe that there is hope and to mentally fight as well as physically to get better. Someone once said to me once the mind gives up the body will follow. Not only did the medical team have to ensure that confidence of full surgical recovery was possible, but also the mental state could be helped. Now most folks have an event coming up they were going to look forward to for example a wedding, an anniversary a big birthday celebration or something the hospital medical staff can lock onto. The basis is let's get you medically fit and healthy in time for the event that is taking place and to keep focusing on that occasion to add strength and mental determination. In my case I had nothing that was coming up in the near future. There were no big birthdays, no weddings, no anniversaries. That is until I happened to mention how disappointed I was that after so much hard work and effort into getting my land rover upgraded, I was now no longer going to be able to return to Morocco for another adventure trip. This was of course the green light that the medical staff were looking for. From then on with each simple step forward it was mentioned :"Come on let's get you back to fit and healthy ready for your Morocco trip". Little did I know at the time that my path to recovery was going to be a long and arduous one. I would have to undergo visits to the hospital on a regular basis to check the state of wound. That I would be wearing a colostomy bag for nine months which in itself had its problems. Eventually though my visits became less and less, the colostomy bag was removed. I discussed with the surgeon whether he thought it would be a bit premature for me to go ahead and book the trip I had been hoping for or postpone it for the time being. I was assured that as long as I was careful with my diet and day to day living routine, I should be okay. Armed with this assurance I got back in touch with Peter who had been standing by to receive the good news that I could be included on his list for that coming October trip. I suggested that rather than go alone perhaps I should be accompanied by my young grandson who was then fifteen to be sixteen on our return in November.

Persuading my daughter that it was indeed safe to take her son off to a North African country, where there was so much trouble and disruption in adjoining and neighbouring countries was not easy. In the end, Peter agreed to come and meet my daughter to discuss the safety and security issues. He was able to put her mind at rest on the basis that he would not even be thinking of any trips where the welfare and safety of his guests were in any way put at risk. Finally, she agreed that we could take him. Now throughout his little life I have taken him off hiking, camping in the woods, lighting fires, cooking, eating and sleeping out in the wild. We have canoed to destinations where we have set up camp for the night and all in all enjoyed a fun boy scout time together. This trip would be the final part of the jigsaw. This would put him into situations where he would be far away from civilisation having to survive on what was carried and adapt, adopt and improvise on day-to-day events and requirements. Indeed, this would be the psychological test to go with his practical knowledge.

One accessory that had eluded me this past three years was how to carry a water tank. I had tried to think up various schemes but each was not very successful. Having then inspected the foot well underneath where the rear passenger seats were located, I noticed on removal of the seats to fit the plate above holding the Engel fridge that this area was quite large stretched from one side of the vehicle to the other. I therefore designed and cut out a cardboard box that would sit in this area and be strapped down. I then found a stainless steel fabricator in Northampton not far from where I lived, who armed with my design was comfortable that not only could he make the tank but he could do this within the ten days remaining before our departure. We collected and fitted the tank with only days to spare. The idea was that the stainless steel tank had a heavy duty pipe coming out the side and fitted through a caravan pressure pump, then another pipe from the other side of the pump went to the back of the land rover. Here an outside tap as fitted to caravans was fitted with a shower head plugged into that. When pressing the nozzle on the shower head this would release the pressure for the pump to kick in which then fed water from the tank through. The shower head could be used to fill the kettle, the washing up bowl or of course to be able to wash. The tank held twelve gallons of water and more than sufficient for up to four days of isolation. We were now fully ready.

We left home at a very civilised hour fully laden with all the necessary items for the adventure. We could take a leisurely drive down from home heading for Plymouth in Devon where our boat would be waiting. We in fact arrived several hours before departure and it was so different to the trauma that had been suffered the first trip. Other members of the group had also gathered and we got chatting before boarding the ship and making our way to our cabins. The ship left on time, and we were soon waving England off in the distance as we settled down for our thirty-six hour trip across the bay of Biscay to northern Spain. The crossing was really relaxed. The meals on the ship were really enjoyable and by the time we docked we both felt very relaxed and raring to commit to our two day drive to southern Spain. We set off, fuelled up just outside the port, found the motorway and headed south. We had over half a day of daylight to get some miles behind us before reaching our first night stop in Salamanca. Again, we were on holiday and not a military exercise so we kept our eyes open for a nice hotel for the night. We found a lovely large hotel just off the main road beautifully decorated and set out and very reasonable at £50 for the night to include breakfast. I was obviously being very careful what I ate at that point getting my system used to no longer having the colostomy bag attached but that evening meal was lovely. The breakfast next morning offered us tables of virtually everything we could have thought of. Toast, hams, cheeses, cereals etc., coffee tea and various fruit juices. This certainly got us set up for our second day.

On our second day we teamed up with a couple of lads from our group at a petrol station that we pulled into. They didn't have any radio so I lent them a walkie-talkie so that we could communicate between us. We travelled down the highway through the middle of Spain used mainly by lorries. It is hot, dusty and the terrain is stone and gravel. It is in fact considered the only desert in mainland Europe. It is extremely remote and empty apart from the odd service station every 50 odd miles. We stopped for comfort breaks fuel breaks etc and as the late afternoon approached agreed that Seville would be a good location for our next overnight stay. Now Seville being a very old city it was not as easy as Salamanca to find a hotel. In fact, we ended up driving in convoy like something out of the Italian job around the ancient narrow back streets of Seville during the rush hour period. We certainly attracted a lot of attention as we really looked so out of place. Here we were kitted up Off Road Vehicles fully loaded and looking menacing. It got to the point when we really had to give up.

There were no hotels to be found. We therefore headed back out of the city back towards the main highway. We decided if all else failed we would make a heading for Cadiz and if a hotel came up along the route, then that would be a bonus. As if by magic though as we reached the outer skirts of the city, and opposite a retail park with a McDonalds was again this splendid tall modern looking hotel. There was no hesitation. We both pulled in and booked in to our respective rooms. The hotel was again very comfortable and very reasonable as had been the previous hotel. This time though we all decided that perhaps we would treat ourselves to a McDonalds tea of hamburgers chips etc. I must admit give the bland food I had eaten for the past 9 months it was like visiting a succulent banquet.

The next day was our last day to reach our camp site at Tarifa. We headed for Cadiz on the coast and spotted a sports outlet Decathlon. Darren wanted a few more bits for his trip. From there we were now off the motorway finally and heading down the coast road towards Tarifa. I must hold my hands up and admit I navigated an incorrect turning. We slowly climbed up this rather steep winding hill covered on both sides with thick trees. Eventually our winding road brought us into a village full of whitewashed terraced houses squashed together with narrow side streets and paths. The road reached the top whereby the whitewashed houses went in a complete crescent that led back down the hill. Intermittently placed between the terraced houses were a selection of street cafes and restaurants. So, we did no more that drive round the crescent past all the folks sitting outside having their refreshments lunches etc to head back down hill. We certainly got the same attention as we had received in Seville. In fact, I don't think we could have got any more attention if we had driven a convoy of old steam trucks through the village. Back down the hill we found the correct road and headed south onto the coastal road and having a good giggle headed for Tarifa. We arrived at the camp site late afternoon with plenty of time to set up camp and indeed get a camp meal cooked, which of course included camp chips. My grandson was in his element with chips again this time covered in Tomato Sauce. Peter had chosen a different camp site this time to the previous visit, and we found the owners very friendly and helpful. It was literally on the shore line where the Atlantic came rolling in with waves big enough to satisfy most surfers.

249

As the afternoon evening progressed the remainder of the group all arrived, and that evening had a group bonding drink together. What a great bunch of people this lot would turn out to be and what some characters.

The next morning we were up fed watered and washed reasonably quickly. My grandson and I disappeared off to the supermarket to fill up with fresh meat and supplies to be stored in the fridge/freezer confident that this trip we wouldn't be dumping it all after a few days. We re-joined the group and headed for Algeciras the port and to find our boat over to north Africa. The day was beautiful and we were soon all on deck of the ship enjoying the trip. This time however we were joined by this large playful pod of dolphins that rode the bow waves well out into the Gibraltar Straits. We were all mesmerised by the antics and fun they were having.

We went through the same suffering at the Tangier port that we had experienced on our last trip. It took ages to get through but eventually everything stamped and passed with currency bought and we were on our way. This trip was going to be different from the first which had been the classic tour. This was the Grand Tour. The difference was the first trip took us more or less in a straight line over the riff and Atlas Mountains and down to the desert. This tour was going to take a large semi circle following the Algerian border and was an introduction to the desert a lot earlier and lasted a lot longer. Our first night though was to the of village of Chefchaouen in the Riff Mountains famous for its blue painted houses . Once we arrived at the village and heading for the camp site Peter unfortunately took a wrong turn. Instead of following the main road round to the right, which was steep enough, he took the village road which literally went straight up. Bearing in mind the weight and load of our vehicles and the fact we were in close proximity with each other the inevitable happened. The vehicle in front of me, that happened to be Darren and his son in law, stalled. This meant I had to brake and suddenly I am now stuck. Not being able to get the revs high enough to work the turbo to go forward and not being able to reverse with half the group behind me. Luckily with a little bit of knowledge gleaned from previous trips I immediately engaged the hand brake which of course locks the diff. This enabled me to disengage the gear box from high

250

ratio and quickly put it into low ratio. First gear would climb the outside of a building if asked. And so revving engaging the clutch we lurched forward and up and over this very, very, steep hill. Phew, we did it. The camp site was very basic indeed and the toilets were at the very best basic. I am glad we were only camping for one night.

Leaving this rather interesting blue and white village and coming down the right route off the mountain we were soon back on the main highway. We were now going to be heading away from the tourist areas deep into the remote eastern region of the country. First though we needed fuel. We stopped off at the first motorway petrol station we came to. Nothing too unusual as we pulled up the service road and into the forecourt next to the pumps. We were impressed that we were filling up at 19 pence a litre given the prices back home. Between the normal petrol and station and the motorway was this large triangular piece of grass gently mowed and part of the clean look of the service station. What did rather look out of place were the three cows happily grazing on the grass without tether restriction or care. They certainly didn't take any notice of us. This was another of the many peculiarities we would meet in Morocco. Once back on the motorway we then passed a guy walking up towards us completely unaware or not even caring he was on a motorway.

As we passed over the Riff mountains we dropped down and encircled the ancient city of Fez. We drove up to the fort sitting high on the ridge and walked to the railings on the edge looking down on this very ancient city. Sadly Fez was not part of the itinerary of this trip as I would loved my grandson into the ancient streets of this incredible ancient place. What we did do however was head to the camp site not far from the fort. This was a revamped site beautifully laid out with bungalow chalets that were lovely. Needless to say, we chose the chalets.

Next day we were back on the road and this time heading further East . The entire tour would be a huge horseshoe round the border with Algeria till we leave at the extreme western border and then head north. Soon the terrain turned from any signs of vegetation to just red sand with the intermittent desert fauna. It had rained the previous day and so the desert sand had turned into a thick red desert mud. We had pulled of the isolated road for a comfort break while Peter surveyed the terrain. He had been telling us about this French foreign legion abandoned fort that was some miles into the desert. However, the conditions of the terrain was making him a little hesitant. Asking if everyone could stay where they were he invited me to accompany him out and survey what the desert would be further in. We drove through what was very sticky red mud that spat and cascaded up the sides of our vehicles leaving the back of the land rover looking more like a mud hut than a vehicle. We had gone for probably a couple of miles when over the radio Peter suggested that I don't slow down but make a bit wide ark and we would try to return back to the group. The way forward was clearly not safe to continue and for all our vehicles getting stuck would prove to be a nightmare. I would like to think that Peter chose me as I was had been on more adventures and courses than the others and probably stood a better chance of not getting stuck and getting out of that horrible place. I was very grateful when we finally pulled in and round into the group. The state of the vehicle was just mind blowing. Just trying to open the doors found piles of mud trying to fall inside. Anyway we would have to re -schedule. the old abandoned French foreign legion fort would have to wait for another day. We headed off on more secure ground although the terrain now was devoid of any vegetation. We drove for a few hours off road till we approached an abandoned concrete building next to a single railway line. It transpires that the French when they occupied Morocco and Algeria decided to build a single line railway line that would pass from the northeast of Morocco along the border, cross into Algeria and beyond. Its purpose was to carry workers travelling to and from the rich minerals fields that were scattered throughout the south Eastern Morocco. The trains would also transport this precious cargo north back to the coast and then shipped back to Europe. However the plan failed once Algeria seized independence and closed the border and the train access. Later Morocco also gained independence and so the railway ceased to form any commercial use at all and fell into disrepair. The story goes however that a rather wealthy Swiss banker bought the line along with rolling stock. When he has time to go and play with his oversized train set which was a couple of times a year he would fly over to Morocco and run the train to its further destination along the southern border. Chris Tarrant on his recent television programme "Earths greatest train journeys" actually featured this very railway. He was met at the northern station by a very quiet insignificant gentleman who had come over to run the train. It was weird to watch Tarrant covering desert that we had driven not that many years ago. We finally reached the second and even more deserted railway station where the line terminated. This was such a remote, desolate, haunting location that was windswept with the very hot desert sands. Nothing grew there, there was no shade and was very spooky with a strange atmosphere. Talking to Peter he advised that unlike what I thought being a train load of nineteen fifties upper class tourists disembarking with their leather cases for a break in this exotic location it had a more macabre history. The trains came that was sure but this was during the war years and manned by Nazi soldiers with cattle trucks full of Jewish Prisoners sent here from all over Europe and to be guarded by the French Vichy supporters. To try to find any details of this terrible place with thousands dying in the boiling sun have all been more or less obliterated. Even Chris Tarrant failed to mention when he lighted from the train at the end of his journey. The only faint sign left was the odd lengths of now very rusty barbed wire. I personally felt very uncomfortable being in this area and thinking about the people especially the women and children shipped out to this hell to their uncertain deaths. We didn't overstay our welcome in this place and moved on. It was getting towards early evening, so we needed to find a camp site for the night. Peter knew of a wild camping area just outside a small town and headed there. We arrived just before dark and found ourselves in a small wood with trees modestly growing to give us all a nice place to park up for the night. We all opened up the roof tents got the chairs out and started to prepare our evening meals. Suddenly this old Moroccan chap turned up in his 4x4 vehicle and started chatting to Peter. Eventually he disappeared. It turned out he was the owner of this wood and had not given any permission for our wild camp. Peter thought his diplomacy had worked till sadly several cars turned up all with very heavily armed police inside each. A long conversation with Peter and he rather embarrassingly had to admit the old farmer was absolutely livid and insisted we must be moved. At this point I was getting a bit nervous. Iraq had reported several instances where people dressed up like the police turned up insisting westerners follow them never to be seen alive again. However, keeping an eye open for a quick escape we packed away our tents chairs etc., and followed the police cars out of the wood onto the main road and down towards the town. On the outset of the town and on this very large roundabout was a large house with tall walls surrounding and big iron gates. We were directed onto the roundabout while Peter disappeared. When he came back he explained that actually where we were parked was not particularly secure but where we were now was actually outside the gates of the police station. The Police assured us that we would be much safer camping here. With sighs of relief tents were re erected and we all got back to preparing evening meal and getting our heads down. Whilst we all seemed to sleep well I think we all had an ear open for any strange sounds and unwanted visitors.

The next day up fed washed packed we set off again. Into the desert and further into the remoteness. We were now several days from civilisation and heading even closer to the Algerian border. One of the group then complained that his vehicle seemed to lack any power and the fastest he could get was 35 miles per hour but that was with a struggle. Peter and his number 2 had a look under the bonnet and concluded that the turbo was playing up. We all limped into the border village of Figuig. This was once a very busy bustling border crossing where Muslims passed up from North western Africa on their pilgrimage to Mecca in Saudi Arabia. After the boarder was closed the Algerians let nobody through. The village became very run down and abandoned apart from the hard core. The camp site sat on a ridge of date palms that looked down into a huge valley through of fig trees that actually was in Algeria. The Moroccans had their own plantations this side of the boarder but sadly the two could not work together and harvest jointly the bountiful harvest. We set up camp again in what actually turned out to be a really nice camp site given its location and the fact we were well inside the desert now. While we got on with preparing our evening meal Peter and Karik helped our fellow traveller fix his turbo problem. They had been bent over the bonnet for some time arms now full of oil and grease when suddenly this voice came from behind us "Peter my friend, you have problems". When Peter looked up it was the owner of the garage in Zagora which we had visited on the first tour and where we would be in five to six days time. It turned out he had travelled over from Zagora to Figuig to visit his brother. Of course as soon as he knew

254

Peter had a problem up went his shirt sleeves and into the engine compartment where after a short while the problem was solved and we could happily continue our tour the next day. Needless to say we were all relieved especially the vehicle owner. Peter was just blown away what a small world it was for his friend to turn up at the hour of need. That night I got the last of the chicken pieces out, got my homemade barbecue going and cooked the chicken and accompanied by homemade camp chips. My grandson and I thought we were at a banquet. We had a piece of chicken left over so Karik was invited to join us given his own plate of barbecued chicken and chips and you could see from the expression on his face it was gratefully received.

We were now leaving the eastern side of Morocco and heading west. Passing through very hot desert my grandson was a bit agitated and asked when we were going to get to the desert. I pointed out we were in the desert. He said no the real desert. I showed him a dozen camels that were roaming wild and said this is the real desert. No he insisted that he meant the Sahara desert. I think he was expecting large shifting sand dunes that are seen in the Lawrence of Arabia films rather than this scrubby terrain that took more of an example of a building site with old ballast and cement. I assured him we were on our way and to bear with us. our lunch that day was parked facing east under the shade of an Acacia Tree. These trees are great for shade but not good to embrace. Their thorns are lethal and massive and will open up human flesh like a razor. Soon we were heading off again. This time after several days we came across the abandoned fort that we had hoped to reach several days before but prevented by poor conditions. We turned off the dirt track and headed up hill to the Fort. The old fort was located on its own hand made hill and had views in all directions for at least 15 miles including towards to Algerian border. What was going through my mind was that whilst the legionnaires could see anyone heading their way on the other hand how many eyes were looking at them day and night. The graffiti on the walls said it all. Apart from the "I was here " wording there were those that had "only 8 days left" etc., showing the sheer loneliness and isolation of this area and how insecure those soldiers must have felt. Anything of any value had been stripped years ago. All that was left were bare wind-swept, barren walls and empty buildings. It was a very sorry lonely, haunted place.

Instead of heading further Southwest keeping in line with the Algerian border we seemed to be heading further inland. It turned out that again Peter knew this family who owned a walled medina in the middle of nowhere which he decided we would head to and camp for the night. It was a dust bowl surrounded by a mud plastered high wall. The owners were very, very, hospitable and offered to cook us all a tagine for our evening meal. It was absolutely glorious sitting on old plastic chairs at this long table eating an original tagine under the myriad of stars above us. Of course, being a dry country we had to wash out meal down with coca cola and no alcohol was available.

By now the days became a familiar routine. It was hot the desert was barren and we followed each other in a dusty trail across the Sahara desert. Another adjustment I had made from experience was adding cowls to the front of the side windows. This meant that any wind sand etc., were deflected away from the vehicle rather than previously being sucked into the cab. This meant we could comfortable drive along with the windows open. My grandson was still far from pleased that we hadn't reached "the desert" and whatever I offered didn't seem to appease him. As the days travel turned into evening Peter suddenly turned at right angles and headed south with us all following. After about fourteen miles we saw what appeared in the darkness as a fort in the distance. As we got closer, we realised we had arrived at the Erg Chebbi and the desert Auberge D'Or. I had been here on the first tour and absolutely loved the place. We parked in the secure car park got ourselves booked in and given our room numbers. My grandson and I headed down the corridors with its metal Moroccan lanterns hanging above us the highly coloured bushes and plants and to our room. Letting ourselves in I pointed to the door at the far side of the room and told my grandson to open it and step outside. He was a bit reluctant as to what he would find but did open the door stepped out on the little patio the other side. Here he literally reeled back. In front of him and highlighted in the brilliantly lit moonlight were the Lawrence of Arabia sand dunes he had in his mind we would visit. I must confess in the moonlight even I was blown away as to how beautiful it was. he was just so stunned and taken aback. The Auberge D'Or is my favourite place to rest. It is little gem in the middle of the desert. The outer sand plastered walls hide an inner court equipped with swimming pool bar easy chairs and tables and all within palm trees Mediterranean plants and flowers and just to sit here and drink in the atmosphere just feeds to spirit. The first day Peter wanted to take everyone off to the co operative owned and run by the Moroccans offering handmade lamps and ceiling lamps, various handmade fabrics including long tunics shirts etc., and of course the famous Moroccan rugs. I decided that as I had visited this establishment in the previous trip I decided to stay behind. My grandson went along as it was a new experience for him. Also he had now started to establish a friendship with the members of the group in his own right. He was no longer just my grandson but a recognised member of the group and he was treated so well especially by the older members who seem to have taken him under their wing. It was lovely to see him blending in. my day was spent relaxing playing my guitar having a lunch with the Moroccan lads that served at the Auberge and we had some very interesting conversations. Travelling the opposite way round on this trip to the first visit to Morocco our washing was now building up and we were quite a few days from Zagora. I had therefore asked one of the lads at the Auberge if they did laundry which they confirmed. A black sack was duly handed over. On my day off I noticed all the washing now hanging on a very long washing line at the back of the Auberge drying in the sun. Later that evening I would receive back the washing all duly cleaned and ironed. When I asked the lad that agreed for the washing to be done how much I owed them he confirmed the equivalent of five pounds. Now I had seen who had done the washing and it had certainly was not him but a very hard working lady. I therefore decided that I was not going to hand over payment to this lad as he had not done anything, so I found the lady that had done the washing and gave her the payment, only I added some on and gave her eight pounds which she was thrilled with. The lad didn't look too happy though missing out on a bit of easy money. The group eventually returned and after the welcome bottles of coca cola we all went through to the dining area where we enjoyed a wonderful slap-up Moroccan salad and cooked meats.

The next day after breakfast and while it was still warm Peter took us out and up onto the sand dunes. Here we sat on the sand and he explained to us how the dunes formed by the wind blowing a long slope of sand up and then as the wind disappears over the top a short drop the other side. He showed us how we should approach each slope using the long steady drag stopping at the top (I remembered the struggle I had with using the clutch and not the brake from the previous trip) then having worked out the steepness and direction of the slope on the other side to slowly head down the other side. He explained how sand is soft on both sides and the weight of our vehicles unless managed properly and not lined centrally could cause the vehicles to tip over sideways. We then mounted our vehicles, and we were off up and into the lower dunes. Here we drove round and round up and down over and down the other sides and just had so much fun. I was able to put into action a technique that I had learned on a course in Peterborough when my vehicle stalled going up a slope. Putting the handbrake on turning the engine off putting it into neutral then back into reverse and handbrake off. We are now suspended only being held by the reverse gear. Feet off everything I started the engine and as if by magic the vehicle slowly rolled back down the hill. At the bottom I regained momentum and launched forward up and over. After a couple of hours Peter obviously thought we were ready for intermediate and steeper slopes. We followed him round and up deeper into these magnificence sand mountains till we were on a ridge with a very steep slope off to our left. We had a group meeting where again we were given tips on how to tackle this sand monster. Peter then elected me to go first probably as I had limited experience from the previous tour. So into low ratio first gear quickly into second and then straight into third down with the acceleration peddle to bring up the revs and the turbo and off I went. Keeping the revs high I slipped down the slope hit the bottom and went up the other side with no effort. Considering this is a 2-ton vehicle was fully loaded I am never ceased to be amazed at its capabilities if used correctly. Next to be nominated were our friends that accompanied us through Spain in their short wheel base land rover. Sadly whether he hadn't not taken in the instructions or felt he could take the slope at a leisurely pace he drifted down the slope but when he arrived at the base and tried to climb the other side the wheels just dug in and he was now stuck. He couldn't go forward to back but just sat there with his wheels spinning. Peter shouted at me across the gap if I could work my way round and come back to the top of the slope where everyone was waiting. This was going to be a baptism of fire as I am now on my own having to put into effect all that I had been shown.

It was with great relief not only to find my way up round and back to the group but making it without getting stuck. Once I rejoined the group the baptism of fire was to be extended. Peter asked me to set my winch up and get the hook and rope out as far as I it would open. Now I had only used the winch once before and certainly not in these extreme conditions. Peter positioned two vehicles behind me and anchored my vehicle to them. Walking my winch hook down the slope connecting another couple of tow ropes to it he finally go to the stranded vehicle. Now came the acid test towing a vehicle backwards up a steep slope in soft unforgiving sand in the main heat of the day in the Sahara. slowly, slowly, the vehicle was plucked out of its suspension and slowly, slowly, back up the hill where with its own power and still with the winch was able to gain freedom from its temporary prison. It was a brilliant exercise even though unintentional and we all learned so much from it. Needless to say Peter aborted the mission of taking each person down and up the slope and we took another easier route back to the Auberge where a welcome drink in the shade awaited along with enjoying the buzz of a really eventful day out in the desert.

Sadly the next day we were packed up saying our goodbyes to these lovely people

And set off into the desert once more. We were driving deeper and deeper into the desert now and further away from any form of civilisation. On the first tour we would come across remote villages where from seeing our dust from miles away the children would run down to greet us. here they would hold their hands out begging for whatever we could give them. On this trip there were no such villages and no such children trying to stop us with their begging. In the huge plateaus that we drive through we experienced mini tornados heading up the valley. In one instance there was a "Daddy" a "Mummy" and a "Baby" Tornado all in a line moving along slowly. It looked really surreal. As we travelled through we came across the Bedouin well in the middle of nowhere. There was literally nothing around us apart from this hole in the ground with a large pole suspended across with a rope leading to the water below and a leather bag to collect the water. We felt we were in a Lawrence of Arabia film and just needed Omar Sharif to appear. Another few miles on and Peter suddenly stopped and got out of his vehicle. He came over to me and asked if I had my hunting knife available. I handed over the knife a little perplexed as to what he wanted to do with it. Summoning us to follow him Peter wandered out about ten yards into the desert and to a wild plant growing along the ground with what looked like mini melons growing out of it. He picked one of the melons off the plant and held it in his hand. He advised us that if we were ever short of water or hungry not under any circumstances must we put any part into our mouths. Even Camels won't touch them. They are so toxic that Moroccans will if necessary extract the juice boil up a small drop of it and drink it as a laxative. Apparently, you then have only a limited amount of seconds to get to the toilet. Had the melon been eaten in its entirety then the dehydration would be very quick and very dangerous so avoid these little beauties like the plague.

We drove across the large dried-up lake that we had passed in the opposite direction the previous trip and past Kiwi Corner. This was an affectionate name Peter had given to the spot where our infamous couple from the previous trip had got stuck in the sand and the wife stormed off across the desert ashamed of her husband embarrassing her. This lake is a dustbowl in the summer and is about 20 miles plus long and over 8 miles wide. On the lake there are limited areas of scrub which Peter advised us not to drive over or nearby. The scrub indicated that there was water underneath and if driven near could cause the wheels to sink. When it rains the dust surface quickly becomes a very wet, very soggy mud surface that vehicles would quickly sink into. If it did rain while we were driving on it we would have less than six minutes to get off the lake before we would get caught. A strange thing to encounter though is full road signs pointing to various locations on the lake itself. Once we were out of the lake we headed into the 60 mile section that looked like sand dunes at the beach but the sand here was extremely light and came up like talcum powder when disturbed. I remember my last visit struggling to stay close enough to the guy in front without getting too close whereby the dust was so bad we couldn't see anything. On the other hand we couldn't hang back too far and loose the route the vehicle was taking and ended up lost in all this scrub. On the other hand we also had to remember to work the turbo in low ration so as not to get stuck in the sand. It was a very fine balancing act for the next 60 miles knowing the guy in front and the chap behind was struggling the same as you. Luckily this was my second visit, so I knew what to expect and adjusted my driving accordingly. We stopped halfway across this area to allow the engines to cool down a bit having been run with very high revs in such a desert heat. As we cleared the dust bowl area the sun was beginning to lower and we headed off to the far side where more sand dunes had appeared and where we would be spending the night together. We each chose our location and set up camp. Peter suggested that once we were all settled we could come together around the camp fire. My grandson volunteered to get the campfire going. Peter looked at me and I just nodded. My grandson had been laying fires since he was 5 or 6 and certainly had been lighting them for seven or eight years with the amount of camping, we had been done. By the time we all gathered round the camp fire a good roaring fire was well going and everyone praised him for a job well done. Later that night and shortly before we were heading for our beds suddenly a row of traffic lights appeared from the location we had come. The lights were getting closer and closer and heading our way. Now at that time of the night suspicions are aroused about smugglers kidnappers or even worse. To our relief as these vehicles came within recognition they turned out to be ex-American military Hummers and part of the Moroccan long distance desert control. They had seen our fire and decided to come investigate looking for smugglers or some other illegal activity themselves. Satisfied, we were legitimate adventurers they all shook our hands and disappeared into the night. Before they went their leader said they would be within watching distance of us to make sure we had a undisturbed night but if anything changed they could be with us very, very, quickly. We felt easier knowing they were out there to protect us. Our night was just heavenly. My grandson and I sat on the roof the land rover for ages before we climbed into bed. We were both completely blown away by the myriad of stars all shining on this perfectly clear sky. We both slept very well that night.

The next morning, I was up early trying to catch the sun rising up from the desert. Armed with camera I stood there alone as the remainder of the group like my grandson were still in bed asleep. Looking over my shoulder and towards the mountains in the distance was a line of some 90 camels all working their way across the desert heading for water while it was still cool and before the sun came up.

It was a sight I will always remember. Sadly, nobody else had seen this spectacle.

We were now heading towards several large plateaus before leaving the main desert and back to civilisation. The past several days we had been accompanied on and off with a group of motorcyclists who themselves were touring through the desert on their own adventure. After climbing over the southern mountain range and stopping for a comfort stop on the high plateau we looked down into the bowl of the valley below us. It was about 20 miles across and on the far side coming towards us was this large cloud of dust. As the cloud got closer to us it turned out to be the bikers. They had reached the far side and the main road leading to Zagora and decided they had reached their destination. So now they can turn round and head back the way they came which would take another 4 days for them to get back home.

After leaving the plateau dropping the twenty minutes down camel trails winding their way down hill we were on the valley floor and soon after 20 miles on the tarmac heading for Zagora. In a way it was quite sad to think that the best part of the adventure was fast coming to an end. We arrived in the city and headed for the familiar hotel I had stayed at those years previous. Most of the group chose the camp site. I thought we deserved a little bit of luxury. After dropping off our night luggage we headed outside into the beautiful gardens and the bar that was calling our names. As we stepped towards the bar a familiar figure appeared in the doorway of the dining room and recognising me pointing smiling and started singing out very loudly "I am sailing – I am sailing" the blighter remembered me and that awful song. I told him for his humour I would play it on my guitar just to pay him back. Now as you can imagine the internet connection as far away as Morocco is not particularly brilliant. In fact, it is quite Spartan and very much hit and miss. However there seemed to be one location that was particularly reliable. That location was the last stool along the bar in the garden. My grandson adopted this as his and low behold anyone that was sitting on it when he reappeared hoping to use his wi-fi. In fact years later I was at an Adventure show at Donnington when a guy came up to me who was the leader of another group of four by four adventures that came to the hotel.

He straight away asked me how my grandson was, and raised his eyebrows and laughed when he mentioned that nobody dared go and sit on that stool while my grandson was about to cause him loss of wi-fi. We both laughed but my grandson clearly left an impression. We were at Zagora for several days. First was a rest day but the second was the trip to the garage where Peter was reunited with his friend that like a knight in shining armour had appeared at the camp site in Figuig. Each vehicle was thoroughly tested and each got the green light for the remainder of the journey back to the coast and the boat back to Europe. I did indeed play my guitar at the hotel including "We are sailing" which actually went down better than I thought and left a happy bonding with the staff. We took a drive to the famous Michael Palin sign and each had our photos taken in front of it. We bought our oils and lotions ordered by our ladies back at home and set out once more into the wilderness.

Our journey now took us inland off road ending up on the south side of the Atlas but where the mountain side and all the buildings rocks and sand were all this bright red/pink colour. We stopped off at a village, parked up and walked down through the cobbled streets past the pink red houses with a snake charmer sitting trying to get folks to give him money for his demonstration with a sack full of live snakes. At the bottom we crossed over a virtually dry river bed with a trickle of water running through the middle. Sadly, for the villages this river was extremely salty and whilst one of the cottage industries was making salt it was no good for drinking. On the other side was the most remarkable view. Heading up hill was the ancient village of Ait Benhaddou dating back over a 1,000 years built entirely from mud sand and horse hair. It resembled a large red sand ant hill. There are still 5 families living in the historic village. The route takes us through very narrow passages and streets till eventually we reached the top. At the top was the ancient "treasury" where the grain was stored to be paid out to the work force in the same vein as a modern bank. The views from here were incredible. The village and the river bed below had been used many, many, times for all sorts of films including some of the star wars films, Gladiator etc., after we walked back to our vehicles we headed north just out of the new village to a small camp site with chalets for the night.

The next day we hit the pass that would take us over the Atlas mountains. The road was very twisty very windy and snaked up and over through this deep pink red landscape of rock and dust with nothing growing. It was very sobering watching young girls as young as seven and eight walking up the main road. They had been sent to collect water in vessels carried mostly on their heads from the water source some way behind us as had been the tradition over centuries. I still wonder to this day why it was only the girls that were sent and no boys. Passing what was now a basic road over the Atlas we then picked up the highway heading for Marrakesh and our penultimate night before reaching the coast. Apparently, the last time Peter had passed this way the route formed the familiar dirt track with loose rock and stone with hair pin bends sharp inclines and declines. Our camp site was on the edge of town surrounded by another high sandstone wall. The camp site was owned by a French couple who looked very hippy in their dress and status. In the camp site itself were many camper vans and motorhomes enjoying their tour of this magnificent country albeit they would not experience the places we had visited with our 4x4`s.

Finally, we were on our last day heading north back to Tangier. We were too late for the last crossing so one more night in a camp compound and down to the dock the next day. We had a far easier time booking in and getting onto the dock side than in the other direction. We still had to register our vehicles out of the country surrender any currency we had and still had to go through the vehicle X-Ray machine looking for weapons drugs or anything illegal. The crossing from Tangier was in glorious sunshine and we were accompanied by another large school of dolphins that I think most of the boat were watching. At the back of the boat was Peter and Karik in conversation but looking at the disappearing coast of north Africa. I had the feeling then that these two were both in love with this country and were sad to see it slowly getting smaller on the horizon. It would be another 9 months before they could get back again.

At the Spanish port we all said our goodbyes and said we would meet up again at the Santander port in three days time. We all set off in various directions. My grandson and I headed up the coast motorway enjoying the magnificent views of the Mediterranean passing through and over the white painted villages and towns. As we had been on the lunchtime crossing we were able to make great progress in driving up the country. I was unable to find the wonderful hotel that I had stayed on my first visit but nonetheless found another that was just as luxurious. We were both still dressed like Indiana Jones and his assistant and all we wanted to do was get out of our dusty clothes. A well deserved shower and something to eat was high on the list too. The novelty now, after being in the third world country for so long, was finding everything here at this hotel actually worked. The toilet flushed the taps delivering water out of both hot and cold taps and the shower worked just wonderfully. The beds were made up with beautiful white linen and the breeze through the windows was cooling. Dinner was gratefully received and consumed, and we both retired for an early but long and deserving deep sleep.

We took most of the day next driving up to Alicante. As we passed by I stopped for a quick nostalgic look in Roquetas and the little villa of my friend Bob where we had spent some lovely holidays. It was a strange feeling walking the pathways and standing in front of the villa with my grandson who was now older than his mother was when she had come with us. In Alicante we found another hotel overlooking the harbour. We had yet another well received comfortable night's sleep. After breakfast the next day we turned inland heading back to the north and the port awaiting us. As we were going to pass close to where my grandsons other grandfather and grandmother had a house I promised to drop in for his nostalgia as he had spent a few happy school holidays here. We found Blanca the town where the villa was located on the outside but we did struggle to find the villa itself. Eventually it sort of found us. We parked up my grandson went through the gate and into the garden and showed me various bits he had helped build. Now his other grandparents were not in the villa but were in fact at his home back in Towcester in England. He therefore rang his home and his grandfather answered. Apparently, it was pouring of rain back in England while we were stood in his garden in glorious sunshine. I could hear the light hearted jealousy coming down the phone. As we had a long way to go we had our last look round and departed. It really was a hard drive now to try to get to Bergos the last city before the coast. We arrived after dark due to rush hour traffic and queues on all the motorways leading in and out of Madrid. We were really struggling to find a hotel with a suitable garage for the land rover and getting stuck in the middle of this ancient city which was in fact now pedestrianised I had to turn to drastic means. I flagged down a local taxi. In broken Spanish and sign language I got the taxi driver to understand that I wanted to pay him to lead us, him in front we behind in the Land Rover, to a nice hotel but which had to have garage parking. The taxi driver was brilliant. He led us through the narrow medieval streets and out of the centre to reach a lovely hotel that had a garage large enough and deep enough to house several double-decker buses. Again, we booked in got ourselves settled and after dinner found our beds.

We were only a few hour's drive now back to Santander. At the port we booked ourselves in parked up on the jetty and slowly, slowly, the rest of the group all turned up. We boarded the ferry took our belongings needed for the return trip to our cabins and all met up at the bar and for our final meal. The banter jokes and memories were still flying when we retired for the night. Once we got back to Portsmouth, we said our goodbyes came out of the Hampshire port and within a few hours I had delivered my grandson back to his mother safe and sound but with a lifetime of memories to share both with his children and hopefully his grandchildren. My job was done. I had taken a young boy out camping lighting fires and living in the woods. I had taken the young man to a foreign country and introduced him to extreme adventure travel and living. Watched with pride him deal with the mental issues of isolation keeping clean and coping with the thought of being wholly independent. He had triumphed in all the scenarios with flying colours. It was now for him to teach his own children and maybe have the privilege the same as I to share his knowledge with his grandchildren.

CHAPTER 30
ADVENTURE TRIP TO CORSICA

Having now travelled on a couple of trips with Atlas Adventure Overland I really wanted to get another one under my belt. I was fast approaching my sixty fifth birthday, and what greater present to myself but another Adventure. I had read that Corsica was a lovely island to visit and so booked to go with Peter and his wife Jo travelling in late June. I booked my own ferry from Dover but relied upon Peter to organise the France to Corsica sailing.

I was still running my office when I booked the adventure holiday. However, in early March of that year I spoke to the Government's Pensions Department, who confirmed that I was in fact entitled to draw my pension as from next July. I thought I had another year to go. I also spoke to my practice indemnity insurance company who confirmed that my annual indemnity insurance was going to be due in July. I decided therefore that this trip would work out as my retirement present to myself. However, it did get a little bit complicated as it meant that when I returned from the trip I would only have a week left before closing the business. Under the circumstances I stopped taking on any new clients. Having spoken with those limited clients remaining, with their permission I passed their files to a very competent conveyancing lawyer locally. I kept about four clients towards the time of my departure for the continent to be completed the week I returned and the final week before my retirement. This enabled me to be a lot less stressed as I knew clients were not being let down by my absence.

This was going to be a solo trip and I duly left home with the land rover fully serviced and equipped for my adventure holiday. I had a leisurely drive down to Dover,, and booked into a Travel Lodge for the evening. I was joined by a previous traveller Darren that had been on the second Morocco trip with me. This time he was accompanied by his wife. We had a lovely meal, and I left to go off to bed for my early departure the next morning. Darren was not travelling on my ferry but was due on a later ferry in the day. I headed off on my own, heading down into Dover. I registered myself through the customs and joined my place in the queue for the ferry. Soon we were ushered onboard and set off heading across to France. Once in France I settled down, armed with my chewing gum and music. Another modification I had made was to swap my radio for a new radio that also played CDs and was Bluetooth to take phone calls. The Bluetooth also allowed me to play through the radio speakers my entire collection of music now stored on my iphone. Travelling abroad I had previously set myself the discipline of driving for three hours then stop for comfort break and fuel. Another three hours another comfort break and something to eat but if I needed a further three hours this would mean looking for accommodation for the night. Obviously, this was another holiday not a survival test and so decided a little bit of luxury on my first night abroad was justified. I had found on the internet back at home and pre booked a nice-looking hotel somewhere in Dijon. Not being particularly confident of sat-navs that have let me down several times even adding unnecessary miles to journeys. I tend to only use the sat-nav when I am a few miles from my destination to simply guide me to the final location. I prefer the good old fashioned paper road map. I had written previously written down the directions to the hotel from the motorway. However unfortunately my previously researched directions were hopelessly wrong. My preferred method of navigation had failed miserably. I therefore had to swallow my pride turn the sat-nav on and key in the co-ordinates not expecting it to be successful at all being abroad and presuming the post codes etc would be a lot different. To my delight the sat nav immediately worked out where I was where I should be and took over directing me first back to the motorway junction I had left earlier. Heading back north from where I had come for about thirteen miles I was directed off the third exit. I was then taken through a whole rake of back roads through industrial areas and arrived smack bang in the car park of the hotel suitably impressed. I was not disappointed with my choice and had a lovely meal of steak, chips and salad and a good night's sleep.

The next morning I was back to the motorway and heading south this time for the camp site recommended by Atlas Overland at Avignon the rendezvous point for some of our other adventure members. This night, I set up the roof tent which only takes a few minutes and then headed up to the camp site restaurant for find something to eat. Opposite where I had parked the land rover up for the night was Kieron and Linda who had already set up camp. They also had a roof tent on top of their land rover defender. By the time I had returned after something to eat another member booked on our trip joined us and had set up his camp. With all the roof tents we gained quite a lot of interest from other campers who were curious as to who we were and what we were doing.

The next morning having had breakfast washed etc., we all closed our roof tents and headed south. The Convoy would now head for Marseille and the port from where we would leave for Corsica. On the dock side we were joined by yet a few other vehicles that made up our group. Peter and Jo were already in Corsica as they had led another group the previous two weeks. Sadly the loading of vehicles from Marseille to Corsica was not going to prove as fast as the Channel crossing had been. We sat there for hours, waiting our turn to be brought abroad. The ship only had one loading area which was at the front, unlike the channel ferries that had front and rear openings to enable speedy loading and unloading. Each vehicle had to be carefully loaded to ensure correct weight and balance. We would be accompanied by large lorries, coaches, caravans, motorhomes, cars and even two wheeled vehicles. Each vehicle had to be separately loaded and reversed up the long steep ramp onto the ship. This proved a bit challenging for the large articulated lorries and the six-wheeler coaches and motorhomes. Eventually our group were ushered forward one at a time and reversed up to our positions which gave us first to exit once reaching our destination. After being loaded we were then sent off upstairs to find our allocated cabins as this was going to be an overnight trip. Having disposed of our personal items in our cabins,

I always take my own pillow etc, we all met up to see the ship leave the port. We then all headed for the onboard restaurant for a bit of team bonding, and a nice meal and drink before settling down for the night.

Our arrival in Corsica was quite early morning. Unloading, I am glad to say was very speedy as we were all located at the front and cleared quickly. Being all together we could head for the port exit. Waiting, for us in the lay-by outside were Peter and Jo in their off road vehicle . They had driven to the port to ensure their previous group were successfully loaded for their return to France and their long journey home. After initial greetings we followed Peter and Jo along the coastal road into the town. Here we went to a little café to have our first pep talk on what was going to happen and the schedule for the day. After our pep talk, we all went back to our vehicles and set off again in convoy making sure all our VHF radios were tuned into the same channel so we could talk to each other and headed out of town. My first impressions was that I had arrived in an Italian influenced Island and everything looked very Italian including road signs and café signs etc., How wrong I could be as Corsica is a very heavily subsidised Island by France. However the Italian signage was in fact the Corsican dialect which very much looked like Italian. We took a slow drive out of the area and wound our way slowly up through high tree covered hills. The main road in Corsica takes a circular route round the coastline and can prove very crowded in the height of the tourist season especially with motorhomes and caravans. The mountain and hill roads can prove quite difficult, narrow and steep. Unless driving a four-by-four vehicle like we all were most avoided these routes. After a really lovely relaxed drive we stopped off at a mountain village for coffee and refreshments and last minute supplies. It was obvious this village was a popular meeting place and passing place as it was on the junction of about four or five roads heading off in different directions. It turned out that our camp site was only a couple of miles away and we were soon driving through the gates into a very warm, dry and dusty site located in a pine tree wood. At first, I thought oh dear what a very basic looking campsite with toilet facilities resembling the poor state and condition of those in Morocco. However, I was to be pleasantly surprised. The camp site was terraced with places between the trees to pitch up camp. We each were left to find our own spot to suit. I had decided prior to my departure that I am now getting a little old to be climbing in and out of roof tents. My main problem is that at night, I am of an age where nature calls, sometimes several times during the night. It can be a bit cumbersome climbing out and off the roof and then back again once relieved in the middle of the night as proved by my overnight stay at Avignon. For this reason, I decided I would try a new system, and bought myself a second-hand blow-up tent. If the idea didn't work, then fine, I can go back to using the roof tent. Having set out and pegged down the four corners of the tent I then blew up the three tubes which erected the tent in what seemed minutes. The tent was complete with sewn in ground sheet an inner tent for the bedroom which all fell into place once erected. All I had to do was lift the frame bed and make it up lay the sleeping bag on top and set up the folding table and chairs and a my camp toilet and I was done. This tent proved absolutely brilliant. Of course, having the tent separate to the vehicle meant that as we were on each site for three nights, I could leave the tent erect each morning zipping in my belongings clear for the day and come back in the evening and not have to set up camp like my fellow travellers. Everything was safe and free from creepy crawlies inside.

Our first few days we simply drove off and into the mountains on mountain tracks and trails rather than tarmac. We drove between the trees and saw such a lot of wildlife. Corsica is famous for wild boar and in several locations a complete family of wild pigs/boars would appear out of the forest complete with little piglets and coming round our vehicles while they search for food etc. Whilst they looked very cute nobody actually was unwise enough to get out of their vehicles as the parents especially the males had very large and sharp teeth some with tusks and would happily attack to protect their young.

On our next day we took a rather steep narrow track down hill for a good hour's drive. We had to drive over huge boulders and gulley's till we eventually reached the bottom. Parking up we then walked to a deserted beach only a few yards away. No other vehicles could have gained access to this beach unless with 4x4 abilities. We all had a well-deserved swim in the welcoming Mediterranean sea. On the beach there were the most amazing huge butterflies. Having just come out of the sea I was obviously covered in salt water and holding my hand out one of these amazing, coloured creatures came and landed on my thumb and sat there for ages presumably taking in the salt from my hand. After our days excursion and having taken another hour to get back to the road we made our way back to the small village above the camp site where we had stopped on our first day. Here we sat at a roadside café and people/vehicle watched. Now I should explain that Corsica is the playground of the rich. They brought their huge yachts and motor launches over from the mainland or their rather expensive cars and sports cars to drive the coastal road around the island. While we sat at the café we had several of these tour groups pass us. Peter got really excited when he spotted a nineteen thirties style Rolls Royce convertible pass by. Only as Peter pointed out the logo at the front was red which means it wasn't a Rolls Royce but an original Rolls that was worth thousands and thousands of pounds and was here driving round the hills and mountains roads of Corsica.

While we were at the first camp site, Hugh one of our companion travellers suffered a puncture in his short wheel series three land rover. Now this doesn't really seem particularly strange apart from the fact that Hugh had driven this land rover for thousands of miles and for years on the same old tyres that now were all cracked and literally long overdue for change. Having taken the tyre off and the spare put on Peter tried to take the actual offending tyre off on the camp site. Most of us carried a tyre lever as well as a spare tyre. However, one of us had an inner tube so the thought was to take the outer tyre off, insert the inner tube, replace the outer tyre and this would at least get Hugh out of trouble if he should suffer another puncture. However, every effort to remove this old, cracked tyre from its rim proved impossible. It was so old it had literally fused itself to the rim. Peter, who has so much invaluable knowledge, came up with a brilliant idea. Placing the tyre flat on the floor the land rover was then driven with one wheel over the edge of the flat tyre. Slowly driving the land rover up and onto the rim it dislodged the tyre from the wheel. It took several goes, turning the wheel and taking the land rover up and onto the wheel again before the tyre finally gave up its connection with the tyre. Sadly, however once the tyre was removed it really was in so bad a condition and so perished it really was not worth putting an inner tube inside as this would last no time especially given the off road conditions we were asking our vehicles to go through. The next day Hugh and Peter drove down to the nearest large town and a tyre fitter and pride was swallowed and new tyre fitted. What an ingenious simple idea to remember if ever a vehicle is off road miles from anywhere and a tyre needs to be removed.

During our stay on this first camp site Peter was very gentle in where we went and the off-roading we were to do. We did follow a few mountain roads up to remote villages that were way up high on the mountains. These places are amazing and everything so clean and fresh. What on earth they all do for a living beats me as they can't work the land which mostly are sheer drop forests and there doesn't seem to be any other industry. But the driving and the views were just amazing. We stopped at a few of these villages for coffee and comfort stops and found the people so amazingly friendly. There is the odd "popular front" members that occasionally demonstrate against their political controllers. In fact, at one village some bright spark decided to show his revolutionary spirit by shooting at a telephone box with a shotgun at night. Another had thrown a brick through a library window. In all the villagers just dismiss this group as total morons with no cause to fight for, given the extreme support France gives Corsica in annual grants etc.

Having now exhausted the mountain roads and tracks in the area of the first camp it was time to move on to our second camp site. Having had my forebodings when first arriving I was quite saddened to leave this little site which was so perfect for our needs. After another day's drive down various tracks and routes off road we finally came out on the mountain side at Michael's farm. Now this was a pretty location overlooking mountains and valleys high up in the middle of Corsica. Having arrived in what I thought was Italy passing through what then felt like parts of France we now arrived in countryside that felt like Switzerland. What an amazingly beautiful location. I set up camp and put my tent on the edge of this camp site overlooking a valley with high hills and snow-capped mountains behind. Back in the UK my previous work partner had told me how they had visited Corsica and how wonderful they found the island. In particular how they took this outstanding mountain railway from the seaside town in the west up and through the mountains to the east. I mentioned this to Peter and he pointed way up high to part of the side of the mountain that had a spanned bridge erected across it. As I looked and found the bridge, approaching from the left was indeed the very scenic train crawling up the slopes that my ex work partner had travelled those years before. Now one of the specialities that Michael always prepared for each group that Peter brought to his farm was an evening banquet. This banquet comprised of a whole boar cooked over an open fire. Sure enough, he had been out that morning caught the boar, brought it back, gutted and dressed it and had been slowly cooking it ready for us that evening. With the local Corsican wine and with all the salad accompanying it, that boar tasted absolutely exquisite.

Now the routes taken from Michael's farm were a little more extreme that the first camp site. Peter always likes to turn up the heat with his customers and whilst we had all started off feeling we were all fully qualified to tackle whatever situation was brought to us, it became obvious quite quickly that there was still a lot to learn. I had been lucky to have been on a few previous trips with Peter and was now getting familiar with what he had on his itinerary. Having a bit more experience than the others and Peter not having his second driver with him I had volunteered to sit at the back of the group, this way I could radio ahead should there be a breakdown or a go slow or indeed a problem. One of the things I had noticed from the offset was the amount of red lights that would come on with most descents down trails etc. Nobody at that stage had been experienced enough to use the four-by-four asset of engine braking and low ratio rather preferring to use the brakes. However, on one track through the forest Peter asked if we could all stop get out of their vehicles and pop down to him for a group meeting. When we were all gathered together, he then announced to all the group that there were two methods to proceed further. One was to follow the track round to the left and then round to the right up and onto the plateau above. The other was to literally hit this cliff face and head straight up. He looked at me and I just thought 'Oh here we go'. The trip has now moved up a gear. The first driver was a great guy but "All the gear but no idea". He got into his vehicle, a long wheel based land rover defender and revving his engine launched himself forward to find the slope soon killed his speed the loose terrain would also help him slip slide and stall and roll backwards. It was quite an unnerving route with potential rolling sideways and down the slope which would be awful. Having failed his attempt, the remainder of the group then shuffled and side stepped trying to avoid eye contact or volunteer to go next. However, having been shown by Peter and on some the courses I had attended, I said I would go next much to the relief of the remainder of the group. So back to my vehicle, starting the engine and dropping it first of all into low ratio four wheel drive, I launched myself forward first in second then straight into third and pressing my foot on the accelerator pedal to get the turbo fully working and screaming I hit the slope and the vehicle launched itself forwards and upwards. I am told at one point my front wheels came off the ground as I bounced over tree roots but I kept going. My friend with all the gear and no ideas' girlfriend was standing near the top and in my path armed with camera. Whilst she got some amazing shots of me steaming towards her it became obvious very quickly that the gap between her and me was closing rapidly so screaming, she turned and started running with me closing down fast. Luckily at the last minute she stepped sideways as I cleared the top and pulled up on the track. The next couple to be persuaded was this young couple who had not been off-roading at all and looked terrified. I just quietly told him what to do, the change into low ratio how to ride the turbo and coached him on to the slope and upwards. He cleared it absolutely brilliantly. His example was then followed by each of the group who each reached the top unscathed and without trauma. From then on I noticed that brake lights on all the vehicles in front of me from here on became less and less predominant and engine braking and gear change became the norm.

Having come out of the forest we were now in the north of the island and back onto normal tarmac and roads. Peter had pre warned us that this particular part of Corsica was used frequently by the rich boys out to play in their expensive Porches, Lamborghinis and other expensive toys that they had brought over from the French mainland. We were advised to look out for them and give way wherever possible. And so, we started climbing along a very scenic winding coastal road when all of a sudden in my mirror appeared to be a very expensive sports car, top-down, lights on and looking mean and lean. At a safe point to overtake I announced to the group that a very expensive sports car was behind us and indicated for the driver to overtake. All I heard was this deep rumble and roar of an engine as it passed me then slowly worked its way along the group. The radio was melting as this was apparently the top of the range Porche. Next came this red car that I was educated to be a Ferrari followed by several other Porches, Lamborghinis until they all disappeared in a cloud of tyre dust. Most of my group were having fits of excitement at this amazing collection of super cars. Unfortunately, I am so unimpressed that I couldn't have distinguished one vehicle from the other apart from the badge on the back. Some twenty miles further on there was a little roadside café that Peter decided to lead us into for some refreshments. Low and behold all lined up on parade were all these fancy flash fast cars that had passed us some miles back. What I found hilarious was that when we pulled up in our dusty dirty four by fours they all came over with their cameras asking us for permission to take photos of our vehicles which they found truly amazing. Just goes to show really.

The next day we had another trip that again took us through the mountain tracks down to the coastal road but this time we dropped down to a fishing village on the coast. The only difference was that this fishing village had undergone a huge face lift with French grants and support. What an amazing place this was. Money no object. All the roadways and pathways were now block paved with marble curbs and side stones erected. There was a new shopping precinct for the tourists with cafes, hotels and even a brand new harbour with very expensive Gin palaces that had sailed over from the main land presumably for the weekend. We found parking for our now rather dusty and dirty four by fours amongst the expensive and the rich and all looking like Indiana Jones had arrived. We walked down and found a suitable restaurant to sit and eat. Now having still suffered from problems resulting from my bowel cancer operation a few years before and the ensuing stoma bag I was still being very careful on what I ate and drank. However, on the next table I spotted this guy having a lump of wood delivered to him with what was the largest steak I had ever seen. The smell left me with no choice but to order the same but a little smaller. For the first time in four years, I sat and just revelled in my steak which I really didn't want to come to the end. The drive back to the camp site was very fulfilling and content.

We headed into town on our final day at Michael's farm to replace provisions. Now being on my own and my diet still being reasonably restricted, I asked the young couple who I had helped up the sheer face inside the woods that if I bought a chicken would they like to join me. They jumped at the chance said they would bring all sorts of side dishes. I pointed out that I was restricted so apart from basic salad the only thing I could offer was chips. Now they both looked at me in total surprise and each other and looked at my land rover as it I had an oven or microwave on board. They then asked how on earth I was going to produce chips in such a remote camp site. I again looked at them and thought they can't be serious. I suggested that I would peel the potatoes cut them into chips and cook them in a chip pan. Well I might as well have been talking to them in a foreign language as they didn't have a clue what I was talking about. Anyway we returned to the camp site. I pulled out my collapsible BBQ box that I had made and got it lit with the chicken now slowly cooking. While I was waiting for the meat to cook I produced several potatoes peeled them and cut them into chips. The young couple were watching me like hawks. When I started chipping the potatoes, they actually came over to watch what I was doing. I was still convinced they were winding me up. Anyway, the cooking oil added to the pan was hot enough on the cooker on the back door of the land rover for me to drop the chips into and so to start cooking. By this time, it seems the word had got out that I was making camp chips. I started to get visits by other members of the group to see first of all was it true and secondly how I was going to cook this magical dish. I was still not convinced they were winding me up. By the time arrived that food was to be served I literally had a queue of curious fellow campers lined up to try one of these magical chips. I was just blown away that none of them had ever prepared camp chips, as this is something my parents had done since I was 11 years old and on our first camping trip. Recently, I have been asked if I would be accompanying the group of a trip to Portugal as they want me along to make the chips. I have had to confirm that due to ill health I would not be able to make this trip so they will have to wait a little longer.

With great sadness we had to leave Michael's farm and head to our next destination and camp site on one of the shores of Corsica. This was a different type of camp site again. This time we were on a large commercial campsite. The site was full of other tourists and campers from Europe that could reach the site via the coast roads in ordinary vehicles. We pitched up on the sandy plots between bushes and trees with the very sandy beach and open sea only yards away. This site was far more commercialised than where we had been previously. The site owners also had what could be described as a little precinct of tourist shops, café and restaurant. The restaurant was quite large with individual huts erected on stilts over the sea itself. We certainly headed for this area for food. Our views were out over the Mediterranean Sea and in the far distance a pair of islands. One of the islands was Elba famous for its connections with Napoleon. This camp site was so lovely and relaxing and gave us a two-night rest from our travelling and adventures. I had brought my guitar with me, so thought it good time to perhaps get some playing time in. Now, I always try not to annoy or spoil other campers' space with playing so after a few songs I caught the chaps eye who was camped on the next plot and apologised if I was playing too loud and asked him to let me know if I was annoying them at all. He assured me that he was enjoying my playing and please carry on. With that another chap appeared from a plot behind us who I had seen walking past earlier looking at me playing and who I thought was heading for the office to complain. The second visitor said the only complaint he had was I was playing too softly. Also, he confirmed they were going to move on but when they heard me play decided they would spend another night there and in fact he was on the way to the office to pay for another night rather than complain about me. I really was elevated in my playing confidence.

Our short stay on our third camp site came swiftly to an end and we were all packed up and ready to head off for our next and final camp site. After a full day touring we ended up on the north east side of the island to another commercial camp site which was quite a large site. This camp site was even more fully laid out this time with grass pitches. Now from past experience grass near water in the Mediterranean means that things that bite are lurking within. I decided to go for the less densely covered plot and proved right. My fellow companions were duly bitten in numerous places by very hungry and very annoying insects. From this camp site Peter led the group down a very steep rocky and narrow route through the bushes and overgrowth growing along the small cliffs along that part of the coast. I am glad to say by this time the red lights were few and far between with most drivers now using engine braking and lower gears. The whole journey down to the bottom took nearly two hours and seemed to go on forever. It was very nice at the bottom, again finding a secluded beach, but it was very hot. After our return I said to Peter that I wouldn't accompany them on the next day's similar excursion to an even longer track but opted to stay on the camp site. This was our last day and so thought I would simply take it easy take my guitar and chair over to the waterfront just in front of the camp gates. Here under the silver birch trees I could watch the Gin palaces float in and out and play a few songs far from anyone that may find it offensive. The feeling of relaxation was just wonderful. I played my favourite songs and just chilled out for the afternoon. Eventually this couple came over and the lady asked if she could take my photograph. I said no problem, why I had no idea. She said afterwards that they had been listening to my playing and was so enjoyable they stayed much longer than expected to listen to me and take in the harmony of the views and area. Again, I was very, very, flattered.

When everyone was back on-site Peter arranged for us to meet at the camp site restaurant for a last meal together because tomorrow we would be heading back to the port and our journey home. We had a lovely evening swapping tales and fears of the adventure we had all shared together. The slope in the wood I think took the most conversation. Before we knew where we were the morning had arrived, we were packed and ready to leave. Following Peter out of the gates again it was very sad to leave. The holiday was not fully over as we had to still get back to the port which was a full days touring through the narrow mountain roads. It was just lovely heading up and through villages so high up you wondered how they got there and how they built these homes etc., in one location was this most amazing church. It was completely alone and not near any town or other houses. It had been built to look like a Lego church. Each square block seemed to be a different colour and stacked just like a Lego building. Inside though was absolutely beautiful and highly decorated. Not being religious I nonetheless felt compelled to light a candle for my Nan who turned out to be a Catholic and would I know appreciate the gesture.

Having reached the port we all dutifully queued up for what seemed to be hours before we were ushered on board. Once again, we were ushered on board one at a time backwards. We manoeuvred our positions and headed for our cabins. Leaving Corsica was a very sombre moment and certainly very sad for me. Out of all my adventures and travels this certainly took one of the top spots. I had loved it. We again all met up for our final meal and then to bed ready for our early start and our long and winding, road journey back to Calais and home.

I found myself off the ship and onto the docks at about seven thirty in the morning. I was armed with my bottle of water, my chewing gum and my selection of music playing through the speakers via my iphone and bluetooth. The signage pointed to the motorway and then the long-haul northwards. I stuck to my regime stopping every three hours, comfort break and fuel, comfort break food and fuel, comfort break and fuel and to start looking for a place to stay for the night as it was now mid afternoon. However, I had done so well, the land rover was running so sweetly and I was so far up the country I thought why not, go for it. We were all booked on the ferry on Friday the next day from Dunkirk. This was Thursday afternoon, and I was only three to four hours from Calais. Should I risk it and try to bluff it? I arrived at Calais at six forty-five in the evening and explaining to the ticket office that I was booked on one of their boats but the next day and from Dunkirk. However, due to "problems at home" it was necessary for me to try to get home early. My bluff worked, I was waved through and told I would be on the eight thirty evening boat back to Dover. By the time I got to Dover it was of course an hour's difference in my favour. I headed north for London, the M25 and the last bit of road home. I went round the M25 at just before ten that night and finally came off the motorway exit at home at just after eleven. I had driven from Marseille in southern France all the way to home nonstop apart from comfort and fuel brakes in nineteen hours. I felt so pleased with myself but slept very well that night. I have to say the next day when I rang one of the two clients left to move on Monday, she was very relieved I was back although there was in fact no problems and her move went very smoothly.

CHAPTER 31
DRIVING THE NC 500

I had finally retired. A present to myself to enjoy as part of my retirement was the purchase of a wonderful six-wheel Autotrail motorhome. I had looked at quite a few styles and layouts but this to me was just perfect. It had an island bed at the back of the vehicle with wardrobes and side cupboards and could be closed off with its own door for privacy. There was a walk-in shower one side of the corridor between the bedroom and the kitchen. Opposite was the toilet and sink. Again, a door could be closed off so after a shower stepping into the bedroom in privacy. The kitchen had a full-size fridge freezer, full size gas cooker and microwave. The sink had full running hot and cold water. The lounge area contained two large sofas that themselves could be turned into another bed. There was a separate double bed located above the cab which was used more for storage. This vehicle would hopefully help me to explore places not previously visited and enjoy the freedom of the road. Leaving home was literally drive off the driveway. Driving along was powered by a large three litre engine and arriving on a camp site was a case of reversing into a space, hooking up the electricity cable turning the gas on and power on inside the motorhome. The water tank was already filled with fresh water. Within five minutes of arriving we were able to use the motorhome to its full capacity. As an addition to the luxury I also purchased a Renault Clio as a tow car complete with all the tow facilities. The idea was to drive the little car to the tow bar at the back of the motor home, hitch on, lift the jockey wheel and plug in the electrics to work the brake lights and indicators on the little car. There was a camera that pointed down from the rear of the motorhome to keep an eye on the tow vehicle with a monitor in the way of the reverse mirror on the windscreen of the motorhome. It was all just perfect. I had taken the motor home to the eastern counties of Lincolnshire, Norfolk, Suffolk and other local locations but felt the need to broaden my horizons and head further afield.

I was now a member of the social media app and in particular the motorhome members group. I had noticed a lot of traffic between members discussing this route that I had never heard of called the NC500 which stood for North Coast 500 miles. This was a tourist road tour that started at Inverness and in a large loop went up to John O`Groats along the north-western shore to Ullapool and then round to Gairloch before heading back to Inverness. Now not a lot of people realise the distance it is just to reach the start of the route. From where I live in the Home Counties if I chose the take two routes, first of all to the motorway and turned right and drove to Switzerland or alternatively to the motorway and turn left and headed for Inverness the distance to Switzerland would actually be closer. At this time my mother had deteriorated in her health. I was therefore not really able to be away too long from home, in case of an emergency if a decision was needed, as I was acting as Power of Attorney. As it was Social Services decided my mother should be taken into care for a respite so she could be assessed how far she had deteriorated. She would be in very good hands and looked after for about a month. This gave me a window of opportunity to disappear for a couple of weeks and explore. It also coincided with a wonderful local folk festival held every year at the pretty Yorkshire Dales village of Settle.

My partner Isabel and I therefore loaded up with provisions for at least a week, loaded ourselves on board with Cassie the cocker spaniel and hit the road. Straight up the M1 over the M62 and turned right up over the Moors and down into Settle. We stayed on a lovely camping caravanning site just outside the village that was very well laid out very quiet and very convenient. This would be perfect for a couple of days over the weekend not only to enjoy the festival but also to explore the Dales. It is a festival organised by Mike Harding a lovely man who is very supportive of folk music and folk players. The festival is free and attracts players of many genres. There are folk dancers and a myriad of very interesting colourful visitors and characters.

Our first trip down was on the Saturday, and being able to use the little tow car meant we were saved the mile and a half walk down. Parking was not a problem and soon we were in the heart of the village. Mr Harding was perched in the entrance of his old VW camper van selling programmes. We went and said hello and then drifted round the village. We watched several groups of Morris dancers including ladies clog dancing teams. The pubs each had open mike music being played by guitarists, violin players, mandolins etc. we found shelter in a tearoom contained in one of the oldest buildings in Settle that dated back to Elizabethan times. After spending a wonderful few hour In the village we then reluctantly departed heading back to the motorhome for something to eat and a deserved relax.

At the top of the camp site was an entire field dedicated for any dogs to roam. I noticed in this field a footpath that led over the famous Settle to Carlisle railway where the steam train takes regular passengers through the Dales. The next day we took a stroll up a rather steep footpath over the railway line and up into what was a lovely village above Settle. It is here that Mike Harding lives and now having visited can understand his choice. What a pretty stone village that overlooks the valley where Settle is located. The village was a real gem of ancient stone houses with its village green and ancient church and just delightful. We both felt we had been rewarded for our rather long arduous walk up the side of the Pennine Hill to reach the top.

On the Sunday rather than spend another day repeating what we had done on the Saturday and knowing that there were going to be even more crowds in the previously heaving pubs etc we decided to tour the Dales. Climbing into the little car we came out of the camp site and turned left up a narrow winding road and into the Dales proper. Every turning, every brow of the hill revealed yet more of this beautiful countryside. We meandered through the Dales countryside past a medley of cyclists and walkers. Eventually we came to Hawes the home of the Wensleydale Cheese factory. We stopped and took it in turns to go round the little shop sampling the free selection of cheeses before buying several for our trip. As we came out the Wensleydale Morris dancers had turned up. Fully kitted out in their colourful uniforms they performed for the visitors to the factory. After they had finished I went over to have my photo taken with the lads and one of them placed his hat on my head complete with beads, feathers, flowers etc., I was well impressed. When we left the factory in Hawes, I noticed a very narrow single track road that would lead us high up onto the Dales and eventually drop us back down into Settle. This route was just so pretty. It was a glorious sunny day anyway but we drove up and over hills and Dales passing brooks and slow running streams. The villages that were scattered were very remote but, in the summer, very inviting. I should imagine in the winter they were rather difficult to get in and out of. At a pub stop at one of these remote villages we managed to scrounge food out of time for the lunchtime period. The landlady must have felt sorry for us and came out with this baguette full of freshly cooked roast beef. All washed down with the local ale. What a wonderful afternoon we had and it was sad to reach the top of the final hill before heading back down into Settle and back to the camp site. We had certainly covered a lot of miles.

On Monday it was time to leave and head further north. I thought It would work out cheaper to try to get refuelled here rather than pay motorway prices. Driving down to the only petrol station in the village I was a little dismayed to find it closed for refurbishment. I was advised there was a petrol station some eleven miles out. Reluctantly a drive there was necessary to get fully filled before returning to the camp site. Hitching the tow car on the back and putting on board any final bits we set off. We retraced our steps back past the petrol station that was open and on to the M6 short of Carlisle and then North. This is such a long drive now I tried to make myself as comfortable as possible. For this reason I now wear my plain Irish cloth kilt. I cannot believe how comfortable it is. It took us a few hours and a couple of stops before we found ourselves into Scotland. Passing Perth, we were then heading on the A9 towards Inverness. There was no race so we pulled over at next town being Dunkeld. This is a another pretty stone town sitting on the River Tay. It is here my folk music hero Dougie McClean lives. The camp site is on the other side of the A9 and sits next to a little trickling tributary river of the Tay. They had room and we were able to back the motorhome into a camp plot with the gentle flowing tributary right below us. We drove into Dunkeld for a cheeky beer at the local hotel where apparently Dougie McClean plays when he is in town. Would have been a shame being so close not to drive up to Butterstone a small village some eight miles out to find the schoolhouse where Dougie lives. With a lovely drive down twisty roads through the forest we came to Butterstone, a very small village and there on our right was the old schoolhouse with Dougie's new camper van sat in the driveway with his land rover which meant him and Jenny were home. I wished I had raised the courage to knock and say hello having met them both at various folk festivals but bottled out and returned to the motorhome.

Tuesday morning we were off again heading out on the A9 with a ninety mile journey ahead of us before reaching Inverness. This road passes through so much history and is pretty spectacular. In winter very often the route is impassable due to bad weather with snow gates at both ends of the mountain area. The thick heather covered moors are mostly above the tree line with the rugged menacing looking Grampian mountains in the distance. There are several Scottish whisky distilleries scattered out in the middle of nowhere. If there is time then this route is really enjoyable and the scenery well worth enjoying. Either side are the mountains some towering above us looking very majestic.

Whilst Inverness is the start of the NC500 that we had come to drive we nonetheless turned right and headed out along the Moray Firth. We had planned a couple of days break so that we could re-fuel, re-stock and re-charge for the trip. I had been here before and went as far as the town of Forres. Turning off the main road and driving down a spur road we followed the river Findhorn. The river eventually meets the sea at the Moray Firth. Here is the old village of Findhorn where it would be home for a few days. Now, the old village of Findhorn is a stone built rustic village with a suitable harbour giving access out into the Moray Firth. A fishing history is fundamental here with its own ancient ice house. Fishing boats, sailing boats and dinghies all bob out in the river while the old village boasts several pubs and shops. A mile short of the old village is the Findhorn Foundation. Now this foundation takes on the face of a modern eco village that would not look out of place amongst the styles of houses found in Sweden or Denmark. Brightly coloured and individual homes where the priority is to be eco friendly. However, it did not start off like this. Three university dropouts headed north back in the 1960`s dragging an old caravan behind them. They were looking for the alternative life of self independence. They found a field they could buy and set up home much to the opposition of the locals. Over the years, and despite a lot of protests they were joined by others and so a commune formed. They grew most of their own food. Homes were formed out of strange materials. There are still the original old whiskey barrel houses some being two stories with residents living inside. Now however with its own shop, café, theatre, meeting place and avenues of housing etc. It looks like a very modern day concept that would not look out of place in one of the many new towns built up in England. The folks that live at the foundation are so warm and friendly. A lot are now middle aged and live very simply. The all seem the ideal folky intellectual people. The whole place has an aura about it that although it does not follow any religious persuasions still has a spiritual feel to it. One of the original founders who has only recently died at the age of hundred, had a saying "Expect a Miracle." That comes across time after time during visits which draws me back time and time again. The foundation has its own camp site to include glamping huts and residential mobile homes for hire. The camp site has all the modern facilities including electricity and water etc whilst still maintaining its eco friendly theme. The end of the camp site and through the static mobile homes bring us straight onto the main street with its main store. My favourite place is the "secret garden" hidden in the back of the eco village where amongst the vegetables and flowers grown, I can sit and play my guitar and feel the magical atmosphere of this place.

One of my ambitions was to be able to play one of my favourite songs "Caledonia" written by one of my folk heroes Dougie McClean on my guitar up at the pub in the Findhorn village itself. I have never really had the courage before. The pub itself has a small front terrace with a few picnic benches overlooking the river. After having some lunch on the terrace and helped with a couple of beers I picked up my guitar asked those guests still sitting on the benches if they would indulge in me for a few minutes while I played this song explaining the reasons why. After I had finished they were all very polite. The lady next to me thanked me and then told me it was one of her favourite songs. No pressure there then.

Having been on the road now for nearly a week it was time to restock supplies and get the motorhome clean etc. The foundation has a laundry room open to everyone and this proved very useful to get all our smalls and bedding washed and even tumble dried ready for re use. We found a Tesco supermarket in Forres just three miles down the road. The little tow car was very useful to load up with replacement food and drink that we had consumed during the past week. We then headed back to the motorhome. On the roundabout just on the edge of Forres we spotted in a large glass case this huge granite wedge that seemed to look very important. A closer inspection revealed that this large piece of granite that must have stood some six metres high was engraved in ancient Pictish carvings and drawings and had been discovered buried on its back. It had been carefully restored and stood upright and is one of the oldest Pictish stones in Scotland. Very impressive. Its proper name is Sueno's Stone.

The evening walks were made across the camp site down the farm track and across the main road leading to Findhorn. Here we found a scrub area that leads down onto the banks of the tidal part of the Findhorn River. As the sun sets over to the right and down under the forest it is possible to step onto the riverbed when the tide is out. You can stroll out 100 yards onto this wide broad river along with the hundreds of waders and other birds all making their late evening songs. It was just so serene and relaxing. Cassie was in her seventh heaven being able to run and splash in the shallow puddles. We also took time out to explore the beach of the Moray Firth which leads down to the mouth of the Findhorn. Here we could spot the seals playing just off the shoreline. We could beach comb for bits of flotsam and jetsam including some discarded feathers and washed-up pieces of wood. A very stunning piece of sculpture now sits in my hall created by Isabel from these bits collected. Sadly, the chicken taken from the fridge had not fully thawed so we had to rely yet again on the foundations facilities. Next to the small shop was a pizza facility offering vegetarian pizzas cooked in an original wood oven. I have to say it was a very good way to end our temporary stay here at the foundation.

It was now time to leave Findhorn and head out on the main part of our Adventure. We had towed the little car the seven hundred plus miles from home and it had proved very useful during our trip so far. However, the next part was going to be a lot more testing. The motorhome itself was over eight metres long. To add the tow vehicle would mean a total length of over forty feet. Given the single narrow roads with the intermittent passing places we thought it would be a bit difficult. The decision was made therefore to leave the tow car behind. We would be returning to the site at the end of the trip and could collect the tow vehicle then. We confirmed with the camp office we could park the little car outside and off we went. Back to Inverness back onto the A9 and across the mighty suspension bridge that crossed over the Moray Forth and into the north of the country. The weather was not its best with high winds that shook the motorhome so violently Cassie shot up and onto Isabel's lap and buried her head till we had got over the other side. We headed up to Wick on the far north-eastern coast of the route. It was all quite nice but didn't impress me any more than say the Lake District. The views out to sea were again nothing more than we had seen. At Wick there was a suitable camp site which we would stay on for the night. The route into the camp site that most visitors would take was not available to us as it passed under a very low railway bridge. As an alternative there was another route back through the centre of town. We had to drive up a steep slope towards the railway station and then a very sharp turning off to the right which then dropped dramatically down to a single-track road that ran long side the river and through a large park. Luckily the camp owner had advised the best times to arrive. This avoided meeting anyone else coming the other way which would have been a nightmare. The camp site itself was clean level well groomed and ideal just for the one night that we were staying. Wick itself was not very impressive as a tourist town. It was very old was a very bland stone built town where folks worked and lived normal lives but being as high into Scotland as it was suffered from very severe weather and had paid the penalty but looking very drab.

With a new day arriving we filled up the onboard water tank on the motorhome emptied the toilet cassette and waste tank and headed for the gate. Now came the rat run to get down the single track road back to the main road. We covered the three quarters of a mile without incident but had a bit of a wheel spin trying to get back up the slope and keep the revs enough to make sure the road was clear and pull left and back down the hill into Wick town itself. The petrol station in the centre was well located for us to refuel. One of the secrets of the NC500 was to try to keep the fuel tank topped up as petrol stations were going to prove few and far between. The day itself was overcast and windy. The weather became even more intense as we approached John O`Groats and the extreme north coast. The visitor area was very well organised and very well laid out. The car park was large enough for the cars, camper vans, motorhomes and coaches and all the visitors that would arrive during a normal day. We were there at the end of an organised cycle race that had started at Lands End. We saw the first cyclists arrive looking extremely fatigued, wet and cold at the reception table set up in the car park. In the meantime, the rest of the visitors braved the inclement conditions to have their photos taken at the famous road sign pointing out how far Lands End stood. The little ferry boat ready to take any brave visitors to the Orkneys, bobbed up and down in very heavy seas and was not going to be able to set sail for the short journey across that day. We stayed long enough for a cup of coffee and some sausage and chips in the café. Cassie was thoroughly spoilt by the owners with her own little dish of cut up sausage. We left as we had a bit of a drive to make for our next nights camp site. The road that we had travelled up from Wick was quite narrow but having turned onto the coast road that we would spend quite a few days driving now turned into a single-track road. It became more and more interesting with every mile driven. For many miles we were passing the worn out remnants of the cycle race up from Lands End. How on earth they managed to find the strength to not only tackle the extremely steep hills that awaited them but also the cold strong wet winds that seemed to want to push them back. The route now was to say the least as being spectacular. As each crest of each hill was crossed so we were left aghast at the sheer rugged beauty that opened up before us. We were to twist and turn climb and drop along this most spectacular road. We passed lonely lochs, empty beaches, farms and houses out in the middle of nowhere. Occasionally there were homesteads that had converted part of their property to a tearoom or café offering the traveller a break for a cup of coffee and a piece of homemade cake. It was time for lunch. We came over a steep hill and below us a wide loch with a long winding road bridge. As we approached there was a turning off into a car park overlooking the loch. Now one of the benefits of motor homing is that pulling up for say, lunch, it was just a case of turning the gas on (should not travel with the gas tank turned on) fill up the kettle with use of the twelve vault electricity system and make the sandwiches and lunch while the kettle is boiling. Then it is a case of sitting down on the sofas with the little table pulled out watching two fishermen trying to retrieve their spinning equipment from the rocks that were hidden just under the surface. Washing up was no effort either. The hot water tank from the morning's wash and breakfast still had sufficient hot water to get all the plates cups and cutlery clean and back into the cupboard before setting off again. We were heading for Durness. However, our journey took us down even more remote rugged countryside, round deserted lochs, past even more tiny villages with tall mountains around us and numerous waterfalls. The road took a long sweeping bend round the large loch to bring us back on the other side up the steep hill where Durness appeared in front of us. This village apparently is where John Lennon went for his summer holidays with his mother when he was young and now holds a statue to his memory. The camp site is on the far side of the village on the top of the cliffs overlooking the bay. We were early enough to be able to choose a suitable plot for the night. We were literally on the edge of one of the terraces overlooking the sea and the bay called Sango Sands. Sadly, because we had left the little car behind us we were unable to visit the famous Smoo Caves as the car parking there was not sufficient for our large vehicle. So we will return one day and complete our tour. What we were able to do was walk to take the coast path down and onto the beach. With the soft yellow sand that we sank into as we walked, and the crashing waves it was so beautiful. Cassie just ran and ran and ran chasing her ball running in and out of the water and wearing herself out for the evening. By the time we had climbed back to the motorhome the camp site had filled up with everything from motorhomes camper vans and tents of every size and description. The evening and night proved very interesting with high winds rocking the motorhome on the top of the cliffs.

As we left the next day, we realised how lucky we were with our location as the wind had brought the rain in the night and much of the camp site was very muddy. Motorhomes are not very successful in mud even with six wheels. Luckily we had a scattering of concrete base behind us and managed to ease our way out. The couple who decided to park next to us and further downhill were not so lucky. The camp owner must have worked out that I was positioning myself and my motorhome to attempt to tow the stuck couple out and shot down with his four by four and handy tow rope and in a few minutes had done the job for me. We were able to leave with a clear conscience that we had not left someone behind stuck. We carried on with this spectacular road with even more spectacular scenery as we went along. We just had to keep stopping to soak in the breathtaking views. For our lunchtime break this day we pulled off the road onto a small car park again in front of another loch. To our right was a deserted medieval castle ruin. Closer inspection revealed this was Ardvreck Castle where the laird had kept the enemy at bay until they finally over came the castle, killed the owner and sacked the castle. What a location to have lived in during its heyday. The day itself was miserable. It was raining slightly, very windy and not very warm. However, this did not put off a very hearty soul who without any wet suit walked bravely into what must have been freezing water for a splash round and swim as a wild swimmer. I have to say she certainly got my vote. I was shivering just looking at her. We left her to her magical swim and after lunch and a welcome hot cup of tea pulled out of the car park and headed off. We now approached Ullapool. Given we were driving five hundred miles and had eight days to achieve it we needn't drive any faster than forty miles an hour and still reach each destination easily and in reasonable time. We arrived on the camp site overlooking Loch Broom. As we were way ahead of the rest of the touring campers, we had choice of loch side pitch. Now this location was pretty special. Coming down the loch shortly after our arrival was the CalMac ferry making its way along the coast and outer islands and passed within a hundred yards of where we were now parked. There is something romantic about these ferries as they make their way round the coastline and Western Isles. We walked the short distance out of the camp gate and onto the quayside to watch the boat back in and unload its cargo of foot passengers as well as touring vehicles, lorries and vans etc. Ullapool is a small fishing village and port and as such it has a tradition for fresh fish sold in its restaurants and pubs. I really liked this little place, it

291

seemed to have an atmosphere all of its own. In the back street is the famous Fish Shack. Literally a wooden shack that cooked and sold all sorts of fish dishes and was so popular there was a queue waiting to be served. The queuing and wait for the fresh dishes to be prepared was all worth it. We sat on the bench in the car park area and ate our meal amongst other tourists. Most visitors to Ullapool seemed to mention this famous shack in their conversations. We decided that as we were in no rush, were in such a fabulous location in front of the loch that we would stay an extra day. We were not particularly anxious to do very much apart from a walk round the village and in front of the loch as far down as we could go along the front of the camp site. We spotted an elderly gentleman, who had a caravan behind us, beach combing the shoreline and with a stick moving the stranded kelp that had been washed up. I was so fascinated (nosy) that I wandered over to him to ask what he was looking for as he had with him a plastic bucket with a lid. He was in fact looking for mussels and had a real success, with his bucket over half full. This was going to be his tea after first boiling them in whisky infused water. He offered us a handful but both Isabel and I are both a little cautious of cooking mussels, especially caught in the wild, so we declined. However, the offer and the friendliness of this gentleman was lovely. I spent an hour playing my guitar and staring out of the front window while Isabel got out her paints and paper and produced three lovely little paintings of the scenery in front of us. We spotted cormorants diving for their food and even a seal at one point.

We were now well into our routine and fuelling up at the edge of the village were soon back on the road heading now for Gairloch. Every turn in the road revealed another vista. Every day the scenery just seemed to get better and more spectacular than the day before. I will say it becomes more and more remote as we travelled along. However, having travelled the alps of France, Switzerland, Italy and even Austria, driven over the Rif and Atlas Mountains of Morocco, this route became one of my favourites and just as spectacular as anything I have ever seen. Lunch along the way this time was a break in a small car park opposite a little bay with a very sandy and very deserted beach. Cassie was able to run and run again chasing her ball in and out of the water to her heart's content. Just truly remarkable. Arriving at Gairloch mid afternoon the sun had finally come out and was just glorious. The camp site is at the far end of Gairloch on a spur overlooking this huge bay with the coastline wrapping itself round the other side. Some days before, my daughter had texted me to say that whales had been spotted rising and falling in the bay. Alas they were well gone by the time we had arrived but our imaginations still recreated them out there as if they were still with us. On the far side of the loch and beyond, the landscape lifted upwards to one of the most stunning mountain ranges with all the colours and shades from the sunshine now beating down and was just incredible. We walked back down towards the village to a pub/restaurant that seemed to have established a good name for itself. We thought we would book a meal that night. It clearly had a very good reputation as it was fully booked even though opening time had not yet arrived. So disappointed, we walked back to the camp site and visited the more village style pub next to the camp site for a welcome pint and a bag of crisps. We managed to scratch a lovely meal from the contents of the fridge. As if by magic the early evening and setting of the sun attracted a huge flock of geese calling and passing in front of our eyes. Waking the next morning and opening the curtains the view was just staggering. The bay was shimmering in the sun light and the mountains in the background seemed to be smiling down on us. This has clearly been a secret that has been kept for decades and we were only sharing it with a handful of fellow campers.

The last day of any adventure is always sad. This trip had been of such high-octane adrenaline with amazing views and experiences that it was hard to accept we were now on our way back. Having said that it was a beautiful morning with varying shades of blue. Gairloch shimmered in glorious sunshine as we pulled away from the scenery of high mountains deep wide loch and little boats all bobbing on the tidal waters. The drive back through valleys and over mountains was as breathtaking as indeed the whole journey had been. We were still gasping at the amazing scenery twenty five miles from Inverness. We found one spot for one final stop and break. We had climbed up onto a plateau overlooking a vast loch below surrounded by forests of pine trees. It was and had all been so very beautiful. Mother Nature had shared her very best but only on her terms. It was as if we were allowed on her terms to witness her raw rugged beauty which at any time could change from clement weather to the other extreme. We were grateful for having been allowed to witness such natural beauty.

We arrived back at Findhorn having completed our five hundred mile epic journey. Having set up the motorhome I retrieved the little car. We walked over to the Foundation café for a coffee and a couple of blackcurrant flap jacks that were homemade and delicious. That evening we walked Cassie over to the shoreline where the tidal waters had receded leaving the wading birds to squabble over the evening meals. What also had appeared since our departure were a great number of pink footed geese. There were literally thousands. It turns out this is an area preferred as a stop-over during migration, for relaxation and to regain their energy. The area was rich on food for the geese. However, the noise they were making was amazing. The cackling was to continue throughout the evening and the night. Whilst we were behind reasonably solid walls those in the tents on the edge of the camp site tucked behind the hedge leading to the protected area must have had a very sleepless night. The next day we revisited Tesco's in Forres to restock and then had a walk along the beach for a bit more beach combing. We ended up at the estuary to listen to the early evening calling from the large colony of seals that had now gathered on the protected, deserted sands on the opposite side of the estuary. An obligatory final visit to the village pubs first of all to the Crown and Anchor where a very dour landlord was making it clear he was not serving food or indeed welcoming anyone to stay. We obliged drank up and went to the pub a few doors down where I had played my guitar in the front. Here the atmosphere was so much more friendlier and a lot fuller. Final photos were taken of the sinking sun over the estuary and then back to the motorhome to get ready for our return journey the next day.

We were up quite early the next morning to pack away the bits and pieces ready for our journey. I took Cassie for a last walk over to the river bank and was just blown away with the sight awaiting. I quietly retraced my steps called Isabel and we slowly walked back over the edge of the riverbank. Here we witnessed thousands upon thousands of pink footed geese that had gathered in the night. They hadn't seen us and were therefore all squabbling and cackling amongst themselves. However, it only takes one as a spotter to spook the rest. As if by magic there was an exodus of wild geese launching themselves into the air. We later learned that there were in excess of over fifty thousand birds. What a sight and what a sound!

We arrived back at Dunkeld that late afternoon for an overnight camp next to the little tranquil stream for a night's stop before venturing on and back into England. We had booked another couple of nights at the caravan and motorhome club site in the Lake District. Now the book advised the best route to the site was from the West. We soon realised why as the road got very narrow and twisty along the way. We were now towing another twelve feet behind us so attention to the road and oncoming traffic especially lorries and buses was paramount. We found the site in the pouring rain, and pitched up on a large plot under the trees. It was a lovely camp site, very quiet apart from the owls calling each other from early dark through the night. We had not really been to this area before so the next day we set off to tour the area in the small car. On our day out we went to Beatrix Potter's cottage and had a welcome coffee in the pub next door. We caught the little car ferry across the Lake Windermere having visited the castle on the hill that the Potter family rented each summer back when she was a young girl. Driving round the various small picturesque villages we were grateful we had taken the western approach to the camp site as the eastern approach was extremely narrow and twisty and would have proved very difficult with the motorhome on its own let alone towing a car as well.

After a couple of days in the Lake District it was time to go home. This was going to be a long drive back and we did the usual three hours stop for a comfort break 3 hours and stop for food and fuel. We finally found ourselves entering the toll part of the M6 that circles round Birmingham. What a surprise we had when there on the verge of the motorway was a complete family of red deer quietly grazing on the grass completely oblivious to the danger of the traffic passing them at great speed. We had just driven round the most deserted and remote parts of Scotland where wild deer are advertised and yet we had not seen a single one. Here we are on a busy motorway when we pass a whole family of them. So surreal but by default a fantastic, unexpected end to a memorable adventure.

CHAPTER 32
COPING WITH COVID AND LOCKDOWN

Nobody was expecting that we would ever be restricted in such a way that every day life would be affected. We would be restricted from the places we worked, from the places we would seek leisure time, and even from travelling abroad for our annual holidays. Flights were cancelled, countries were blocking us from visiting. Even travelling in this country was proving difficult. We would have to adhere strictly within the requirements of wearing masks, avoiding crowds, avoiding restaurants pubs etc. For short windows of time, we would be allowed to sit outside certain pubs certain restaurants but the constraints were very restricting. One industry that was to boom because of the natural barriers involved, was the industry of camping, caravanning and motorhoming. Never in many, many, years were the sales of the various forms going to prove so lucrative. The dealers were making a fortune with the sales of anything that could house people overnight. However, this all had a knock on effect. Folks not being able to travel abroad were purchasing a mass of new camping equipment and were trying to find campsites or leisure sites on which to enjoy this limited freedom. For a lot of people this was proving difficult if not impossible as bookings for any break were being snapped up. As such the chances of anywhere in the West Country, the counties of Cornwall, Devon, Somerset and Dorset were proving impossible. The south coast was fully booked. From my own personal circumstances, I had very reluctantly sold the motorhome. I had to raise funds for my mother's pending confinement into care with her failing health. In its place I purchased a very nice caravan of similar set up to the one I had before the ownership of the motorhome. I had to run the gauntlet through the restrictions to purchase the caravan from near Birmingham, venture out separately to purchase the awning from near Nottingham and to acquire the bits of kit that are required by a caravan owner. As such we then tried to find a location that was not fully booked and that we could hopefully get away to if only for a week. We were stunned to find that every camp site we investigated was fully booked as far away as the Scottish border right down to southern Yorkshire. The only window of opportunity we had left was to head east to the counties of Suffolk and Norfolk where we had visited many times over the years. I am pleased to say that these areas are not as popular as the other parts of the UK mentioned. We hoped this would help us not only to find a camp site but also with the driving and enjoying minimum disruption required by the pandemic. Phone enquiries with two of the sites previously visited revealed that they too were fully booked through the summer. The only times we could reserve were after the time when the children had returned to school in September. We were able however to book two consecutive weeks. First in Suffolk at a site east of Woodbridge for our first week. Second at Wells-Next-the-Sea for our second week. At least we had found something to get away to and enjoy a holiday break. Compared to previous adventures and locations this was all going to be somewhat tame but it was a holiday.

Our first destination was to be a village called Shottisham five miles south of Sutton Hoo on the edge of Woodbridge. The drive was very simple, and quite quick compared to previous holidays. Within two and a half hours we were navigating the small country lanes past Woodbridge and Sutton Hoo and heading into Shottisham. The village itself is quite small but very quaint. We had to take our time and be careful to navigate through the narrow windy lanes as this was harvest time. Huge farm vehicles were racing up and down the lanes towing their trailers collecting and delivering their harvests. As far as the farming world was concerned time was of the essence and therefore, they were not taking prisoners. The camp site itself is just ideal, it is tucked away just behind the village pub. A short walk through the church yard attached to the campsite dropped us down to the pub. The couple that now own and run the site had inherited the business from their father who had been passed it from his parents. It originally contained the grandparent's bungalow and it had a driveway along the right-hand side leading up into the orchard. Here there was enough space for twenty-five caravans to be parked. The couple that had now inherited the site had expanded the site retaining the small apple orchard with a few caravans to now include another couple of fields. One of the fields which now holds the main entrance had been converted to a pitched camping area with electric hook up and new toilet block and water taps etc. the other field was now converted to a smallholding containing pens for pigs, sheep, chickens, goats and even Alpacas. The site is also very eco friendly with the produce gathered and being sold on site. Each evening the young site owners would wander over to collect the eggs and all the children on the site were invited to join them. Not only were the children able to collect the eggs but could stroke the sheep, water the pigs, and fuss the Alpacas and it was an hour that you could see was so enjoyed by the young ones. This camp site was ideal during these difficult times and we had a fully serviced caravan. With the onboard water tank, waste tank, toilet and washing and shower facilities it wasn't necessary to subject ourselves to any threat of contamination from the communal facilities. As such we were able to maintain a distance from other campers thus maintaining the governments advisory standards to fight the Covid epidemic. We were able to visit the local pub albeit that we were only allowed to enter the pub one at a time then only to order drink which was delivered to the tables outside. Many pubs and restaurants had closed to serving food.

We particularly love this camp site with its dog walk. We could come out of the caravan cross over the field and into the animal small holding field. Walking down between the pens and the animals to a public footpath running parallel to the site. This itself led into the most beautiful wood of oak trees and forest vegetation. Walking through the wood we joined up with other footpaths crossing through. One in particular, leads down a country track past the northern top of the camp site, past a huge play field dedicated to the children of the village and down to the tarmac road. The road then took us back to the main road by the pub. By the side of the pub was a steep footpath up into the church yard and through a track back into the orchard of the camp site. Cassie absolutely loved this walk as once we were off the camp site, she was let off the lead and could sniff, run and investigate to her hearts delight.

All in all the camp site offered a really peaceful location that had remained protected and undisturbed. There became a routine of certain places that had to be visited each time we came to the area. The first trip was to drive the country lanes in what basically would be a huge fifteen mile triangle. The tip of one end was Bawdsey an eccentric village located right smack bang on the shore of the river Deben. This is close to the estuary with the sea. The village boasts a little secret that is only obvious as you drive through. Quietly sitting behind a wood and a rather high wall is an even higher set of aerials. This was an early warning system set up during the second world war to detect German airplanes making their way to the English coast. The Germans never did find out about this little secret. As the roadway reaches the Deben there is a car park for those wishing to enjoy the view of the boats piloting in and out from the sea to the inland ports. Around the car park on one side are the lovely Suffolk Edwardian cottages with the tall chimneys and black and white woodwork. They over look the river and on the other side a ramshackle collection of huts and sheds that lead on to Old Felixstowe with the tall cranes of the port beyond. Standing here it is easy to imagine the long ships of the Ancient Britons and the Vikings entering the estuary and rowing up the river towards the inland port of Woodbridge and of course the settlement at Sutton Hoo. Those that wish to cross the river have the opportunity of using the little river taxi. On the jetty that allows access to the water stands a round disc attached to a metal pole. It looks like a giant lollipop. The idea is for folks to lift out the pole and wave it in the air towards the shacks on the other side of the water. Hopefully the river waterman will see the pole being waved and will then launch his ships lifeboat sized clinker built boat and come over to Bawdsey shore to pick you up. Years ago, the propulsion was by a pair of oars and very strong muscles working against the tide. These days they have updated the waterman up to include an outboard motor. The system works extremely well and saves a round trip via Woodbridge of over forty miles. Because of the size of the river taxi only foot passengers with the odd bicycle can be carried. Leaving Bawdsey the second part of the triangle takes us through beautiful narrow country lanes through fields of wheat and barley and down to another shoreline of the Deben at Ramsholt. At the water's edge is the Ramsholt Arms for a while a derelict hotel but now re-built. It offers wonderful terraced lunches of fresh fish etc, as well as local beers. It was here that the recent film "Yesterday" had certain scenes filmed. To the side there is a concrete jetty with an old derelict fishing boat sitting slowly rotting on its side. It still serves the purpose of the harbour masters hut. It has to be seen to be appreciated just how eccentric but how befitting this vessel is and fits into the area along with the equally eccentric harbour master. He is a real sea salt who would keep you chatting with his river yarns for hours. He told us that he once lived in the village of Ramsholt itself. This made us curious as there was no village around the Ramsholt Arms. As we pulled back out onto the road leading us back to Shottisham the next turning was marked "church". Curious we drove up to it again only a few hundred yards from the river but completely isolated from any building or homestead. We parked up and went over to this curious building with its round turret and in the entrance were an array of photos including one of our harbour master from Ramsholt Arms. It was then that we realised that surrounding the church was the small hamlet of Ramsholt itself that had been alive and well up to only a couple of decades ago. The powers that be then decided that the village should be knocked down rather than renovated. The evidence is that there is now no sign that a hamlet ever existed only fields of produce and this lovely church still used for services. The inhabitants have all scattered within the villages surrounding the area. Back in Shottisham we pulled up outside the bright pink pub of the Sorrel Horse where a drink was necessary to finish a lovely afternoon and where we could watch the world, or at least very little of it, pass us by.

Another part of the triangle tourist route that requires its own visit is Shingle Street. A strange name but again part of this area of Suffolk that oozes eccentricity. To reach it we leave the camp site drive down a single lane with trees branching over into the adjoining village of Hollesley. We pass typical pink and white washed painted houses and turn off again onto a narrow lane. This twists and turns through countryside where time has been forgotten for three miles out to the coast. As we near the coast line the road has to make its way around and over numerous mud ditches. These ditches are all tidal and are often explored by canoeists when the tide is actually in. I would suggest that a good knowledge of the area is essential as the view from the canoe is that of tall grass banks and nothing else. The chances of getting lost amongst this maze of watery ditches must be very high. Once the coast is reached there is a solitary row of white washed coastguard houses that all face out to sea. Their back gardens are a short fenced in area that leads through wooden gates straight onto a very pebbly "shingle beach". This is a site of scientific interest. Here the tides have moved the shingle and the shoreline has been redefined and reshaped over the centuries. Set to one side away from the coastguard houses is a solitary bungalow cottage. I don't think anyone lives in the bungalow as we often see film sets here shooting various scenes. One film that has recently been released it the film "Yesterday". Here towards the end of the film the hero of the plot visits the cottage and finds John Lennon living within. A walk onto the beach itself reveals a sea that is not ideal for swimming. It has very strong tides and tidal pull. However the sea has carved out a couple of large pools which are in fact large enough to safely swim in and practice canoeing, water rafting and even kite surfing. Cassie absolutely loves getting in here and has not yet worked out that what she is chasing are the stones thrown in for her to chase. Along the shore line further down from the Coastguard houses and located every three quarters of a mile are huge round turrets. These turrets were built by Henry Eighth as part of his sea defences. He was always fearful of the French invading England and, this area being so close, for a march on London itself. Now several of these turrets have been turned into holiday homes let for weekends and week breaks. However, there is another sinister tale that brings in a far more modern war that of the Second World War. As an experiment the military (apparently) constructed a series of pipes in the water and out onto the land. These pipes were connected to a gas supply. The story that is of course strongly denied by the M.O.D. and only remembered by the dying few remaining locals. There was a German unit that (apparently) did in fact land on the beach as part of a probing exercise. The pipe line was ignited and most of the Germans killed by being burnt to death. If this was true then a war crime had been committed thus it was also kept quiet and not admitted. A nicer story lies further down the beach off the edge of the last Coastguards cottages. There is a long line of white whelk shells that have been laid from the cottages in a snaking line all the way to the sea's edge. They look very strange and completely out of place. The story goes that two ladies both suffering from cancer came to the area and started laying a line of shells. As time progressed and their disease was put into respite so they returned numerous times and continued their task until eventually the line of shells reached the sea's edge. To their surprise years later they were completely taken aback when they returned and found not only had the line of shells remained but people's imaginations had been taken over and they too had added heart shapes of shells within the line and other additions. We walked as far as the first large round fortification which is magnificent close up. It is still completely intact and in fact it too has been converted into holiday lets for up to five different family units.

Travelling back inland past Sutton Hoo, famous for its Viking hoard and buried long boat made more famous by the recent film "The Dig" is the market town of Woodbridge. This stands at the very end of the tidal river the Deben. It is very quaint with its old historic buildings and many pubs. The town itself was once a very busy bustling inland port town because of its tidal river. On the river front is one of the last remaining and working tidal mills complete with its tidal pond. The main pond was converted years ago to a marina housing some very nice expensive boats. However there still remains a pond sufficiently large enough to capture water from the incoming tide to give visitors a demonstration on how this pond was put to good use to turning the giant paddle of the mill to grind the grain. It is still possible to buy the flour from the grain milled in such a manner inside the mill. Next to the mill but now long past their former glory are the ramshackle sheds, huts and warehouses where trade materials were stored while waiting to be loaded on the ships in the river. Now they simply house small businesses such as rope making, sail making and water orientated trades. Along the muddy river were scattered old barges now converted to permanent live aboard residences of all colours, shapes and ages. In the centre of Woodbridge is the most pretty square around the church. In the square are the old Victorian houses, several pubs that would have once served the water trade and also a Dickensian shop which is in fact a violin maker and repairer. It looked so at home with all the instruments and tools hanging up in the windows. Of course what also makes Woodbridge such a popular town is the very busy railway station that gives access to daily commutes to London.

From Shottisham it is possible to follow the coast road up to Orford with its famous twelfth century Henry II castle keep. The castle once gave immediate access to the sea which now has receded to over three miles away as the sea has withdrawn. The village has several pretty pubs and a lovely walk down past the alms houses to the waterfront. A small boat will take you out and round the Orford Ness, now a bird reserve but once a top secret military base, housing all sorts of early warning systems both through the Second World War and after the Cold war. Access to the island is still restricted. For those that want to go further afield it is also not that many miles to Suffolk's flag ship town of Southwold. We of course were very much aware of mixing with crowds with most public facilities closed so Orford for a short visit was as far as we would wander.

The rest of our time at Shottisham was spent reading, barbecuing and of course in my case playing my guitar. Just to be here was such a lovely break and a well deserved recharge of the batteries. One of the books I was reading was about the Thames barges that had fascinated me since my early visits to London and also out to Essex. It turns out that Isabel's great uncle was a Thames barge captain and was based for many years at a place called Pin Mill. This is a small hamlet on the tidal river Orwell on the southern shore south of Ipswich itself. Isabel was fascinated to learn more about her mother's uncle as all she had was a photo of her mother when she was younger visiting Pin Mill. It was a short drive back along the A12 over the famous Orwell bridge and along the southern shore. Pin Mill is located down this very narrow tree lined lane and drops straight down onto the jetty once busy with the river trade. Now it is more of a tourist spot with its pub on the shore line and the ship building yard on the other side of the jetty. It turned out that Isabel's Great Uncle was part of the family that owned the boat yard. The Great Uncle helped run the sea faring side of the business while his brothers ran the boat yard. Some generations later the boat yard is still run by the same family. In its heyday any skippers of Brown Sailed Barges were held in great esteem. The boats were only manned by two persons being the skipper and his assistant. Given the tonnage that these boats carried and the

303

routes sailed from the Thames as far as North Yorkshire the skippers were considered very skilled. Of course the currents and dangerous waters along the coast to London themselves demanded great skill. Unfortunately, Great Uncle was forced presumably by economic needs to leave Pin Mill and move back to London where the use of Brown Sailed Barges were more in demand and more lucrative. It must have been a wrench leaving such a pretty part of Suffolk.

After a great week of lovely weather, peace and tranquillity it was time for us to leave and head north into Norfolk. I was so pleasantly surprised that once we cleared Ipswich along the A12 then A14 it was not long before we were pulling off this major route and heading north west. The roads here have greatly improved in recent years and although the traffic was busy it still enabled us to pass without difficulty into Norfolk and then to Wells-Next-The-Sea being our destination for our second week. Wells again is another port mostly used now for fishing but still boasting its old warehouses where grain and corn were stored ready to be shipped out of this tidal town. Our camp site was away from the town itself along a spit leading out towards the sand dunes and sea. We drove into Pinewoods and booked in. The camp site falls into two sections, first the section that is full of permanent mobile static caravans and the other side of the site is the large camping field for caravans and motorhomes. Each pitch has its own concrete hard standing. Each hard standing has a water connection, waste drain and electricity connection. We were now entering another level of camping we could not have even imagined would ever exist. We backed the caravan into its spot and wound down the stabilising and levelling legs. The electricity cable was wound out and connected to the electricity pole on the plot. The water pipe was connected to the mains supply again next to the power supply. This worked by way of a pressure pipe direct into the mains tap. As the water was turned on and off inside the caravan so it drew water in from the external supply. This meant we no longer had to wheel the five gallon water drum over to the main tap but had it all connected. Another pipe led from the waste pipe to the drain by the service post. This means the only visit we now had to make was to empty the toilet cassette to the facility fifty yards away from us along with the rubbish bins. What a world away this was from the old two gallon water container we would have to carry over to the communal tap and from the different world where waste water had to be wheeled over to the communal drain and emptied. The camp site forms part of the Holkham Estate parts of which these days has been set aside in many, many, acres to conserve nature. As such much of the grasses in between the rows of where we were parked were left uncut. This attracted all sorts of wild life and birds. From the back of the camp site a gateway leads onto a dirt track adjoining large fields. Again these fields were set aside with only cattle and sheep grazing. As such many twitchers are constantly in the lane armed with heavy binoculars, spotting the various birds visiting the area. Being so close to the sea and the Wash itself this area was very popular for migrating birds to stop and rest and re-charge before their onward flights. One of the main visitors was the pink footed geese we had encountered up on the shores of the River Findhorn. Not quite the same numbers but still thousands turning up each evening greeting each other with the row they are able to cause. In addition we saw red deer, foxes, rabbits and other wild life that were so used to the peace they just simply looked at us secure that we were not going to harm them.

From the campsite through the gate and along the dirt track led us after about half a mile to a pine forest planted by the Holkham estate to protect the land from the savage north sea winds. A footpath then led us round and up some steep steps and down onto the most wonderful sandy beach I have seen. The tidal river that feeds Wells-Next-to-the-Sea to the open sea flows from the right of us. The sea itself was some three quarters a mile ahead of us. As far as we could see both forwards and to our left were vast areas of soft yellow sand with the odd grassed sand dunes and ponds left by the receding sea. This was Cassie's heaven. Once at the bottom of the steps and off the lead she would run and run yip and yap and chase her ball for anyone who wanted to throw it. It was like having a three year old toddler on the beach for the first time. It was just wonderful to see her have the freedom to run and play and even though she is getting an old dog she certainly gave no indication of that for the time she was there. The walk can extend as far and beyond the actual Holkham Estate some five miles away, but we never pushed our luck while we were visiting. Instead we walked out parallel to the river to one of the big puddles large enough for Cassie to run in and retrieve her ball. It was deep enough for her to need to swim out and back. She just didn't want to stop and every time she dropped her ball so she yipped and yapped till someone picked the ball up to throw it back into the water and off she went again. Eventually we were able to persuade her that we could leave the water and head back although we were still having to throw the ball. There was no point in returning back to the caravan as we had a very wet dog with a very soaked coat. I am not so worried about the land rover for the few times we drove to the beach, but in the car park was a lovely café that not only offered coffees and teas, but also freshly baked cakes. This was going to be a daily routine where we sat and shared filter coffees along with blackcurrant flapjacks encased in a yoghurt coating. Cassie would also have a chance to dry out and was also not going to allow us to leave her out of the feast.

We would take the land rover to the beach if we were going to head out afterwards to another location. There were a couple of pubs we had found further along the coast towards Sheringham. One of these pubs was still serving food albeit outside. The pub is located in another bird and wildlife nature reserve and therefore is frequented by the twitchers and nature lovers. The pub itself offered all sorts of wonderful sea dishes but I was not brave enough to try lobster (I need someone who can show me what to do, which bits to eat, which bits to leave and even to finish it off if I didn't like the taste as was the case with crab) but shellfish was very popular being obtained from local sources. I stuck with my cod and chips washed down with a nice pint of cider. Isabel sampled various offerings of freshly cooked fish. Not a great distance from the coast road are the little quaint villages including the one where Nelson himself was born and lived. Being sat in a Land Rover I felt a little more confident and safe driving through these long winding lanes and round these pretty villages. I still have to drive through the ford that crosses one of the rivers that pass through one of the villages but hopefully in the next couple of years I can return and fulfil another wish.

Wells itself is a pretty old town full of old pubs, chandlers and tourist shops with its narrow streets that have served the local trade and tourists for many years. Parking is challenging but is worth a walk round just to see what the town is like. Of course it is now expected that the local fish and chips have to be sampled along with a couple of pints in the pretty pubs subject of course to complying with the regulations governing Covid. Our week in Wells had now formed a pattern. Obviously we were greatly restricted by what we could do and where we could go. The main thing is we were away, we were having a lovely break. The weather had been very kind up to this point so reading, playing guitar and walking Cassie were the core activities most days either in the mornings or afternoons. The wi-fi here is very intermittent but that was not a bad thing. Peace and recharging had been the order of this holiday and we were enjoying it in spade loads. What was amazing was that we were still caravanning in early October. Back in the camping days there was a window mostly in July and August when the weather was warm. To camp outside those months was very much hit and miss and earlier than June and later than August definitely was not heard of. Of course, the evenings were dark by the time the end of September arrived. We are of course spoilt first of all with warm heating and secondly with the on board television. So once the day was shut out, the awning zipped down and the caravan door closed, the low lights were turned on the heating up and the TV switched on. The glasses of pink gin and tonic helped us mellow for the evening and our night's sleep. I even now after several years cannot get over the novelty of having a television on a camp site.

We were due to leave on the sunday, however, the weather had now taken a turn for the worse. Threats of high winds and gales were forecast to hit our area. The thought of taking down an awning and driving towing a caravan in force five winds did not fill me with much excitement. We therefore made the decision that perhaps we should take the awning down on the Thursday and if we could leave the site on the Friday and head home. Certainly, the awning was easy to take down on an evening that you could never suspect was about to receive such extreme conditions. However, that night I was very glad I was in a caravan and not a canvas tent. The caravan rocked so hard that the rolled-up canopy that sits on the back of the caravan was lifting and falling and making the noise of a heavy duty door knocker. It was so violent that I was worried at one stage that the canopy would damage the side of the caravan. I therefore donned my bad weather gear headed outside with torch and rope and made secure the canopy by tying it down as best as I could and retired back to the warmth. I am glad we had carried out our bad weather measures as the next day there was devastation. Several caravans and motorhomes that hadn't bothered to bring theirs in had suffered the consequences. Many were ripped, support poles bent and damaged and some awnings even being ripped off the caravans and vehicles themselves and lay flapping along the grass like fish out of water. I felt so sorry for the owners. As for us we made the decision that given the narrowness of the lanes that would take us from Wells to Kings Lynn and beyond it was not going to be wise to try to tow a caravan in the conditions that was now with us. Whilst the land rover defender is very heavy, being two tons, nonetheless the caravan is quite light and able to be blown about. We therefore decided to sit it out one more day and see if we can leave on the Saturday. We would have stayed longer but the pitch was needed as it was fully booked on the entire site till the end of October when the site would close for winter.

Saturday morning was a different tale again. There was a breeze, but the sun was out. We had made the decision to leave early to try to avoid as much of the local traffic as we could which was very successful. We passed by Kings Lynn within an hour. Another hour and a half and we were back on home territory. The journey had passed very well apart from a couple of roads leading into Kings Lynn that was very heavy with holiday traffic and vehicles heading home. Having got home we soon had the caravan via its motor mover back into its location, fridge emptied dirty washing removed and heating turned on in the house with a welcome shower to celebrate getting home after our "Covid Dictated Holiday" which turned out in the end to be extremely successful and another "Story for the Grandchildren".

CHAPTER 33
EPILOGUE

Forty years ago, I met the most remarkable elderly lady. She was a widow and had been married to her beloved husband for many, many, years before he had passed. He had been a farm manager. Between them they had produced sixteen children. As farming people they never actually took a holiday. Instead, he would get disillusioned with his job and change to move to another farm. In their married life, they had moved twenty six times. To up sticks home and sixteen children and move to another must have been a logistic nightmare. However, I was highly fascinated by the life they had led in the countryside. As far as she was concerned life was ordinary and not really worth talking about. I disagreed and would hassle her to share some of her memories. We have sat till the early hours of the morning me mesmerised by her tales. She would explain the simple ways of life in the country. She would explain how they would grow their own vegetables how husband would go out and set his snares to catch rabbits. All in all I could just talk to her for hours and hours. She had such a nature that nothing phased her. You could go to her with the most awful problems or tale of woe, and she would just listen and give a quiet mature and experienced solution. She was so masterful at moving home, that one weekend we arranged to move her to Milton Keynes from Hampshire. I had used a seven ton truck to bring back from Lancashire the contents of a house that I had inherited. It was quite obvious by mid afternoon that I was not going to return in time to return the lorry to the compound. A quick phone call to Hampshire confirmed we would come down a week early to collect belongings. We would then return to Milton Keynes unload and get the lorry back to the compound Monday morning. We arrived in Hampshire early Saturday evening. By this time the three-bedroom house was virtually all packed into cardboard boxes etc. Every box was labelled and most bound with farmers hay bale twine. Sunday everything was loaded into the lorry in record time. All procedures were directed by this wonderful lady. She told us what to put on the lorry first, where to put each box etc. when we reach Milton Keynes and in particular at the one bedroomed flat the operation was reversed. She supervised the emptying of the lorry, where to put all the boxes and contents. I returned the lorry to the compound that night and was back in the office Monday morning. Monday evening, I called round to the flat and couldn't believe my eyes. The whole place was finished. Curtains were hung, ornaments unloaded and stored in the china cabinets. The kitchen completely fitted out. It looked like several weeks had been spent getting everything sorted rather than twenty four hours. She really was a old hand at the art of moving home. Eventually the lady passed. Once she had gone, I then began to think about her lifestyle. I mulled over all the stories she had shared. I then realised that all these stories had now gone and passed with her. Nobody had written them down or recorded them and they had disappeared. I then realised we all have our own stories to tell. Whether we are bank managers, airline pilots, road sweepers or shop assistants, we all have a tale to tell. I then thought of my own working life. I daily related my own stories to clients mostly as an example of why something should or should not be done. It was at that point I decided that when I finally passed, I would leave my own record of who I was and what I did. I set to and wrote down all the stories as they came up. By chronologically listing the stories and after five years I was ready to start writing. It took me another nine months to put all my notes into writing. Sadly, I was then diagnosed with my bowel cancer. This meant a rapid conclusion to my project. I had a weekend to find and take photos and get the draft to the publisher. I was not sure if I was going to survive the operation but at least the job was done. The first copy was delivered to me in hospital the day after my operation. I was so grateful that I was alive and there was hope I was going to survive the operation that I donated the first copy to my surgeon. Having written about my working life I then started thinking about all my Adventures. I decided that perhaps I should repeat the exercise of writing down notes of what I had done and where I had been. This time it would be all about my experiences of camping and travelling and the exciting stories of what I had experienced. Again, it has taken me five years to put it all together. However, I am pleased I have achieved this record and hope those reading it will get some enjoyment from this book. I am still hoping to travel, still have lots of places to visit and things to achieve. It's in the blood I suspect. However, I would like to dedicate this book to the memory of Peggy without whose inspiration this book would never have been written. Having written about my working life I then started thinking about all my Adventures. I decided that perhaps I should repeat the exercise of writing down notes of what I had done and where I had been. This time it would be all about my experiences of camping travelling and the exciting stories I had experienced. Again, it has taken me 5 years to put it all together. However, I am pleased I have achieved this record and hope those reading will get some enjoyment reading this book. I am still hoping to travel, still have lots of places to visit and things to achieve. Its in the blood I suspect. However, I would like to dedicate this book to the memory of Peggy who without her inspiration would never have been written.

Lightning Source UK Ltd.
Milton Keynes UK
UKHW021352271122
412909UK00012B/206